Metropolitan College of NY
Library - 7th Floor
60 West Street
New York, NY 10006

CHINA IN THE 21ST CENTURY

CHINESE CIVILIZATION IN THE 21ST CENTURY

Metropolitan College of NY
Library - 7th Floor
60 West Street
New York, NY 10006

CHINA IN THE 21ST CENTURY

Additional books in this series can be found on Nova's website under the Series tab.

Additional e-books in this series can be found on Nova's website under the e-book tab.

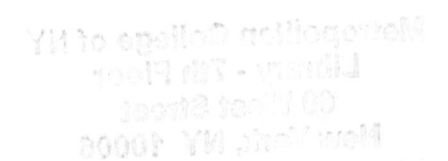

CHINA IN THE 21ST CENTURY

CHINESE CIVILIZATION IN THE 21ST CENTURY

ANDREW TARGOWSKI
AND
BERNARD HAN
EDITORS

publishers
New York

Metropolitan College of NY
Library - 7th Floor
60 West Street
New York, NY 10006

Copyright © 2014 by Nova Science Publishers, Inc.

All rights reserved. No part of this book may be reproduced, stored in a retrieval system or transmitted in any form or by any means: electronic, electrostatic, magnetic, tape, mechanical photocopying, recording or otherwise without the written permission of the Publisher.

For permission to use material from this book please contact us:
Telephone 631-231-7269; Fax 631-231-8175
Web Site: http://www.novapublishers.com

NOTICE TO THE READER

The Publisher has taken reasonable care in the preparation of this book, but makes no expressed or implied warranty of any kind and assumes no responsibility for any errors or omissions. No liability is assumed for incidental or consequential damages in connection with or arising out of information contained in this book. The Publisher shall not be liable for any special, consequential, or exemplary damages resulting, in whole or in part, from the readers' use of, or reliance upon, this material. Any parts of this book based on government reports are so indicated and copyright is claimed for those parts to the extent applicable to compilations of such works.

Independent verification should be sought for any data, advice or recommendations contained in this book. In addition, no responsibility is assumed by the publisher for any injury and/or damage to persons or property arising from any methods, products, instructions, ideas or otherwise contained in this publication.

This publication is designed to provide accurate and authoritative information with regard to the subject matter covered herein. It is sold with the clear understanding that the Publisher is not engaged in rendering legal or any other professional services. If legal or any other expert assistance is required, the services of a competent person should be sought. FROM A DECLARATION OF PARTICIPANTS JOINTLY ADOPTED BY A COMMITTEE OF THE AMERICAN BAR ASSOCIATION AND A COMMITTEE OF PUBLISHERS.

Additional color graphics may be available in the e-book version of this book.

Library of Congress Cataloging-in-Publication Data

ISBN: 978-1-63321-960-1

Published by Nova Science Publishers, Inc. † New York

Published with assistance from the Timothy Light Center for Chinese Studies at Western Michigan University, Kalamazoo, Michigan, USA

CONTENTS

Foreword		vii
	Andrew Targowski and Bernard Han	
Part I. Civilizing Society		1
Chapter 1	The Civilization Index and Chinese Civilization *Andrew Targowski*	3
Chapter 2	Spatio-Temporal Boundaries of Chinese Civilization *Harry Rhodes and Lynn Rhodes*	17
Part II. Civilizing Culture		43
Chapter 3	Old Faith for the New Millennium: Religions and the Chinese Civilization in the 21st Century *Patrick Fuliang Shan*	45
Chapter 4	Chinese Civilization and Contemporary Pop Culture in the 21st Century *Shan Li*	65
Part III. Civilizing Infrastructure		83
Chapter 5	Chinese Civilization and the State of Infrastructure in the 21st Century *Guo Yang*	85
Chapter 6	Is China on the Wrong Path of the U.S. Agricultural Development in the 21st Century? *Agnieszka Couderq*	105
Part IV. Globalizing Chinese Civilization		135
Chapter 7	The Myths and Realities of the Clash of Western and Chinese Civilizations in the 21st Century *Andrew Targowski*	137
Chapter 8	The Chinese Civilization: Driving Forces, Implications and Challenges in the 21st Century *Bernard Han*	159

Chapter 9	Chinese Civilization versus Global Civilization in the 21st Century *Andrew Targowski*	**175**
Chapter 10	Where Is China Heading? *Andrew Targowski*	**191**
Index		**213**

FOREWORD

Andrew Targowski[1] and Bernard Han[2]
[1]Western Michigan University, US
President Emeritus of the International Society
for the Comparative Study of Civilizations (2007-2013)
[2]Western Michigan University, US

Chinese Civilization is the oldest civilization in the world. It has existed for 5,000 years,[3] i.e., 83 percent of the history World Civilization, established about 6,000 years ago in Mesopotamia. Records indicate the Egyptian Civilization came into existence about 5,100 years ago. Now, however, ancient Egyptian Civilization has been replaced by the Islamic Civilization.. In contrast, China today is still structured by the Chinese Civilization, although it has recently been threatened by the deceptive opportunities of Global Civilization (Targowski 2014).

Will the globalized Chinese Civilization (Figure F.1) provide a way for the world to sustain human civilization in the 21st century or will it expedite its downfall due to the depletion of strategic natural resources?

Needless to say, the Sinosphere is essentially a derivative form of the Chinese Civilization that influences nearby countries, including Japan, Korea, Vietnam, Singapore, Taiwan, and Cambodia. The Sinosphere developed when Chinese Buddhism spread over East Asia between the 2nd and 5th centuries AD, mixed with Confucianism. These countries developed strong central governments that had been long-institutionalized in China. In Vietnam and Korea, and for a short time in Japan, scholarly-officials were selected through a

---

[1] Andrew.targowski@wmich.edu.
[2] Bernard.han@wmich.edu.
[3] We assume that Chinese culture began in Neolithic Times (5000 BC) with the Yangshao Culture (仰韶文化), which was established around the Yellow River valley and lasted until 3000 BC. Later, the Yangsaho culture was superseded by the Longshan culture, which was centered on the Yellow River from about 3000 to 2000 BC. This culture was developed under the administration of Jinan city, during which time it was considered as the upsurge of the Chinese Civilization. One of the characteristic features of the Longshan Culture (龙山文化), i.e., the early Chinese Civilization, was exemplified by the intricate wheel-made pottery pieces produced in this city. Today, about 7 million people live in this city. The early history of China was disguised due to the lack of written documents about this period; however, later accounts have attempted to describe events that had occurred several centuries previously. There are some written ancient documents that describe the Xia (夏) Dynasty (2100 – 1600 BC) as the first one in Chinese history.

series of examinations on topics related to Confucius' teachings, which were developed by the Chinese for civil-service examinations (Fogel 1997). Shared familiarity with the Chinese classics and Confucian values provided a common framework for intellectuals and ruling elites across the whole region (Reischauer 1974).

Figure F.1. The Chinese on a hot day are resting at the beach nowadays. What is their strength: a 5000 years old civilization, large population, or both? (Photo: public domain: piximus.net)

Among contemporary civilizations, the Chinese Civilization is about 500 years older than the African Civilization which is considered as the hub of all civilizations. For example, the Chinese Civilization is about 3.6 times older than Japanese (650 AD), Buddhist (600 AD), and Islamic Civilizations (632 AD), about 3 times older than Eastern Civilization (325 AD), and about 4 times older than Western Civilization (800 AD). Such a long lasting civilization indicates that this is a special civilization that may last for many more centuries, possibly millennia. The question is what will be its role in the development of the world civilizations today and in the future?

Nowadays, Chinese Civilization is experiencing a "second coming" as the world leader. At one point in the first half of the Second Millennium (AD), China was roughly at the same level with Europe in scientific knowledge and far ahead in the technologies of printing, naval navigation, and ammunition (dynamite). However, the worst political mistake in the history of world civilization was certainly a decision made by the fourth Emperor, Hongxi (洪熙) in the Ming (明) Dynasty, and the last voyage was ended in 1433. The exploration of new territories overseas was terminated along with the abolishment of a capable fleet of ships that is able to make long voyages. Documents of those trips were also destroyed to avoid any good memories about these successful adventures and political achievements. It was a suicidal move that put China in a disadvantageous position among the strongest countries of the world.

Since the destruction of its own fleet and securing its borders with the construction of the Great Wall (Figure F.2), several centuries passed, China has not only been isolated from the rest of the developing world, but rather transformed into a passive subordinate of foreign rulers and invaders (e.g., the Mongolians, Manchurians, British, and Japanese[4]). Since the Long March in the 1930s, the Chinese have been awaken and begun to think again about themselves as the original settlers of China and have tried to throw off their submission to foreigners over the last several centuries.

Figure F.2. The Great Wall of China isolated China from the rest of the world for several centuries. (Photo: Wikipedia).

As a consequence of the ending of exploration voyage in 1433, China fell behind Europe (i.e., Western Civilizations) in science and technology; however, they have started to catch up in the beginning of the 21st century after 600 years of isolation from the rest of the world, and the defeat and colonization by the invaders and western powers. To date, Western Civilization is considered the most developed and productive one among all civilizations, and it has been sustained at the expense of the Chinese Civilization. The United States is the most fortunate since the U.S. has about 6 percent of the world's population while it consumes about 30 percent of the world's resources. From now on, China will become active and will consume a very large portion of the world's resources.

The question is whether the U.S. will give up its current status and let China use more resources, or will it fight to maintain its unsustainable life style? On the other hand, will China give up its dream and let the American Dream (Figure F.3) continue to prevail? This is an age old question - "to be or not to be" (raised by William Shakespeare in his play Hamlet, 1603 AD) since our Earth is already overpopulated.

---

[4] The Sino-Japanese War (1937-1945) is considered as the beginning of WWII, in which about 14 million Chinese were killed (12 million civilians and 2 million military) (Westad 2012). This loss is a very large number if compared with the loss of the Soviets during WWII, which was about 15.7 million people (World War II by Wikipedia). Furthermore, the civilian loss of Chinese war is 6 times larger than that of the German (2 million) (Cavendish 2005).

Figure F.3. The American Dream as superconsumerism in the 21st century. Is it the model to be followed by the Chinese Dream? (Photo: Public domain: popularresistence.org)

Today, China is one of the key players in all sorts of talking points in politics, economics, science and technology, society, and so forth. This is happening because China plays a critical role in the Global Economy in the 21st century. First, China is the World Factory, and second, it is the main debt collector of Western Civilization. Needless to say, the Chinese have the largest population in the world, including people living in China and its diaspora. In fact, Chinese is present almost in every country in the world. The Chinese people are considered most active not only in business but also in tourism (Figure F.4). The Chinese are all over the globe and now they also reach to the Moon - the second nation in human history. China built the fastest computer (Figure F.5) in the world and their adventures are beyond the Great Wall.

Figure F.4. The Chinese globally traveling toiurists in the 21st century. (Photo: Public domain)

Foreword

Figure F.5. The Chinese super computer Milky Way-2 - the world's fastest in 2013 (33 quadrillion calculations per second, about twice faster than the American TITAN - Cray)
(Photo: Public domain: npr.org)

In fact, it is Western Civilization that has woken the Chinese Giant through manufacturing outsourcing that provides technology and training to China. Nevertheless, the Chinese have outsmarted their trainers and now can develop and make whatever products they want to. The Chinese are innovative, hard-working, and good learners and have capitalized on these opportunities which have come to them unexpectedly after 600 years of waiting.

Today, from a global viewpoint, China is the World Factory (Figure F.5), Hong Kong, the World Banker (at least the Asian Banker Figure F.6), Taiwan, the World IT Lab, and Singapore, the World Wise Society Lab. Altogether, China and its diaspora have created an impressive chain of wise civilization (which used to be Western Civilization) and are becoming the dominant global civilization.

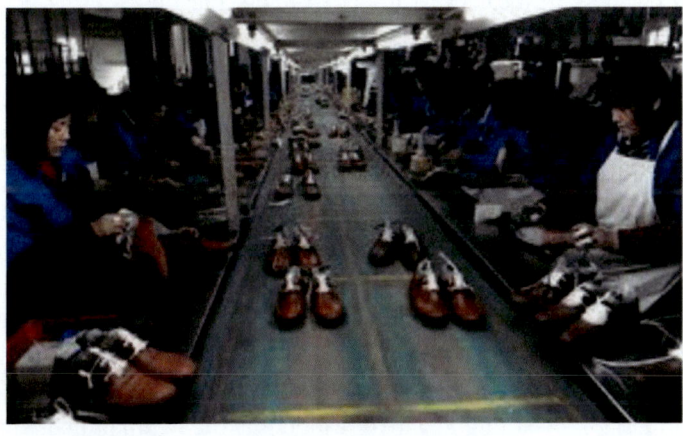

Figure F.5. China as the World Factory in the 21st century.
(Photo: Public domain, The Guardian)

Figure F.6. China as the Banker of Asia, The People's Bank of China (PBOC) in Beijing in 2013 (Photo: Public Domain: Reuters/Jason Lee)

In the past 80 years, the Chinese have undergone many social revolutions (i.e., Long March-1934-36, Cultural-1966-1976, and Eight Elders (Economic) -1978-1992), which were about 246 years after the English Revolution in 1688 and 145 years after the French Revolution in 1789 in Europe. Now, China outperforms the European Industrial Revolution (i.e., from 1820 to 1900) that occurred 194 years ago. And yet, even Chinese are still behind the West, who underwent these revolutions many years prior to the 19 and 20th centuries, today the West are deindustrializing. After the downfall of the Soviet Empire in 1991, the West called for "the end of history" (Fukuyama 1992) because democracy and liberal Capitalism had won and supposedly the West would rule forever. Indeed, Capitalism was so liberal such that it caused further transformation from Capitalism with human face into turbo-Capitalism, which has subsequently lost its democratic characteristic.

This transformation makes the world more favorable for those who are strong and can compete in the realm where the sky is the limit. As a result, it creates enormous economic inequality and put the entire well-to-do Western Civilization at risk. In effect, this turbo-Capitalism has already been mixed into Global Civilization, whose religion is super-consumerism and business. It means that today's society must do what is good for business, while all other matters are secondary. This political paradigm shift has created much political and social confusion in Western Civilization since it has fallen off its peak of social solutions, which took about 1200 years to establish.

Today, China is faced with multiple options: Should it follow the ideals of Western Civilization which used to be successful, or learn "what has been wrong" with Western Civilization in order to avoid future mistakes? China is at the cross-roads. According to *Forbes-2014*, there are 152 billionaires in China, and they are followed by thousands of millionaires who are followed by millions well-to-do Chinese civilians. The remaining one billion plus Chinese people are on their way with one full meal each day, if lucky.

There are other options. China may ally with Russia in sharing a common anti-American ideology or take her own way. Particularly, after the annexation of Crimea by Russia in spring 2014, regardless of the strong negative reaction by the international community, China chose to abstain during the resolution vote that condemned Russian's action in the Ukraine at the Security Council of the United Nations in March 2014. Perhaps China may reverse the Silk Road and take another way toward the outer world.

But, if China follows the path of western consumerism and modernization to satisfy her own needs, then China and the whole world will be at risk of committing a civilizational suicide due to insufficient strategic resources to sustain such super consumerism. Regardless of China's decision, the world's strategic resources can support only about 2 billion people, while today there are about 7.4 billion people on earth, each with an "American Dream" in his or her life. Now China promotes the "Chinese Dream," (Figure F.7), another version of the American Dream to be implemented in the 21st century. This dream may turn into the Chinese Nightmare (Figure F.8) since too much economic activity could deplete all fresh water in China, without which no one could live.

Figure F7. The Chinese Dream as a small Fiat 500 for every Chinese whichused to play the same role in Italy in the 1950-60th for every Italian? Perhaps depleting the world's oil resources soon? (Photo: Public domain, phys.org).

Figure F.8. The Chinese Nightmare – too much industrialization and luck of fresh and clean water may lead to a disaster of the biblical scale (Photo: Public domain: csrpioneers.org).

China has a special opportunity to have its own way by applying market socialism with Chinese character (Figure F.9) that requires a clear understanding by all Chinese about the critical situation caused by Global Civilization, i.e., the limits of resources to sustain Chinese Civilization for years to come.

Figure F.9. Market socialism with Chinese character (top-down strategic directions), as the ideological response to Western turbo-capitalism (also known as crony-capitalism and liberal democracy in the 21st century. (Photo: www.npr.org).

Spectacularly, the rising China at the dawn of the 21st century is mostly impressing foreign politicians and businessmen in terms of its economic potential and market size. On the other hand all these positive opinions are immediately extended by some negative opinions about its administration and political quality. Supposedly this is not compatible with those which are practiced by the Western Civilization, such as liberal democracy and capitalism.

It is a classic cliché which could be right in the past but not nowadays. First of all Western liberal democracy and capitalism was so liberal for so long that it allowed it to transform into crony-capitalism. It is practiced by billionaires who are "rent-seekers" by making money through political connections and deregulations of natural resources, financial-banking services, casinos, oil, gas and chemicals, defense, infrastructures and pipelines, ports, airports, real estate and construction, mining, utilities, and telecom services as well as in transferring of public assets to firm at bargain prices. The commodity boom has inflated the value of oil fields and mines, which are invariably intertwined with the state. The index of crony-capitalism's power across countries (developed *by the Economist*) illustrates how huge fortunes dominate the states.

Figure F.10. The crony-capitalism index (*The Economist*).

As shown in Figure F.10, among the world's big economies, Russia scores worst. The transition from communism saw political insiders grab natural resources in the 1990s, and its oligarchs became richer still as commodity prices soared. The unstable Ukraine looks similar. Mexico scores badly. It is mainly because of Carlos Slim, who controls its biggest firms in both fixed-line and mobile telecommunications. French and German billionaires, by contrast, rely rather little on the state, making their money largely from retail and luxury brands (The Economist, March 15th 2014, p. 57).

This index shows that the Sinosphere (Singapore-23, Hong Kong-22, Taiwan-17, and China-13) has among the strongest institutions in the world. The strength of U.S. of institutions is at the level 15, only 15 percent[5] better than China's. China's institutional quality is almost equal to France's – 14. Hong Kong and Singapore were colonies of Britain (21) hence they had positive impacts on their institutions' *modus operandi*. One can assume that middle land China may learn easily from its compatriots in Singapore and Hong Kong how to improve its institutions. If its compatriots can do it, so can China.

Furthermore, perhaps the Chinese do not have to follow their Western advisors in these matters. The truth is that China for millennia practiced top-down government which had been well structured into specialized jobs and an efficient bureaucracy, which in Western Civilization came into being more "recently" with the development of the Industrial Revolution in the 19th century. Later, after World War II, the Western bureaucracy transformed into a technocracy, which is now being replaced by a plutocracy, while China is quickly learning this knowledge and skills.

Figure F.11. Singapore and Hong Kong have the highest quality institutions in the world. (*The Economist*, March 15, 2014, p. 58). (Photo: Wikipedia)

---

[5] [(15-13):13]=0.15

Unfortunately, efficient government is no guarantee of a good score: Hong Kong and Singapore are packed with billionaires in crony industries. This reflects scarce land, which boosts property values and their role as entrepots for shiftier neighbors. Hong Kong has also long been lax on antitrust laws: it only passed an economy-wide competition law two years ago.

China's billionaires, in whatever industry, are often intimate with politicians and get subsidized credit from state banks, which is understandable given that one third of China's billionaires are party members and are very influential in regional and local businesses. So criticized, China is dealing with corruption quite decisively. On March 5th China's president, Xi Jinping, vowed to act "without mercy" against corruption in an effort to placate public anger. In the year 2013, 182,000 officials were punished for disciplinary violations, an increase of 40,000 from 2011 (The Economist, March 15th, 2014, p.13).

Chinese market socialism broke with the centrally planned market as it used to be in the former Soviet Bloc. China has gradually improved its policies, which try to take good care of consumers. On March 15th 2014, a new consumer law was introduced to commercial practice, the biggest reform in this area in last 20 years. At face value, it appears to give a big boost to consumer protection. Retailers must take back goods within seven days; in the case of online purchases, consumers do not even have to offer a reason. Consumer data will be protected from misuse, and permission will have to be sought for any commercial use of them. Classic-action lawsuits, hitherto rare in China, will become easier to file.

The motivations for the law seem sincere. The government is keen to shift the economy towards consumption-driven growth. Also, China is catching up with the European Union's exacting standards of consumer rights in much the same way as it has begun imposing EU-style curbs on cars' emissions. In both cases, pressure from ordinary Chinese prompted the government to tighten standards. Besides benefiting the public, the pollution measures give an edge to firms with the most advanced technology, which in this case happen to be foreign multinationals.

Market socialism with Chinese character is the new challenge to the "current version" of Western capitalism, which lost its human face and became so efficient that it might deplete strategic resources soon, perhaps in the second half of this century. It is not "the end of history" but a new phase when capitalism is challenged again, and this time, not by Soviet socialism (1917-1991) but by Chinese socialism. It will be interesting which model, "Western" or "Chinese," will fit well when the wars for limited resources take place on our Planet.

In the meantime the world is curious whether China will expand its might far beyond its borders. Some perceive Chinese maneuvers in the East and South China Sea as a sign of that kind of expansion (Figure F.12). But China is just copying the Monroe Doctrine (1823) which allowed the U.S. to take over the control of the Western Hemisphere from the European powers in the 19th century. China is just seeking the Asian version of that Doctrine. Does China deserve to practice a similar doctrine? Whether the West likes it or not, China deserves it and perhaps will be staying within its Sinosphere only.

Figure F.12. The East and South China Sea and the Sinosphere are the subjects of the Asian Doctrine in the 21st century

Certainly the Sinosphere is a much smaller sphere than the Japanese "Greater East Asia Co-Prosperity Sphere[6]" planned in 1940-1945 (Figure F.13), which mimicked the IIIrd Reich.

---

[6] Although the projected extension of the Co-Prosperity Sphere was extremely ambitious, the Japanese goal during the "Greater East Asia War" was not to acquire all the territory designated in the plan at once, but to prepare for a future decisive war some 20 years later by conquering the Asian colonies of the defeated European powers, as well as the Philippines from the United States (Storry 1973). When the Japanese Prime Minister Hideki Tōjō spoke on the plan to the House of Peers he was vague about the long-term prospects, but insinuated that the Philippines and Burma might be allowed independence, although vital territories such as Hong Kong would remain under Japanese rule.

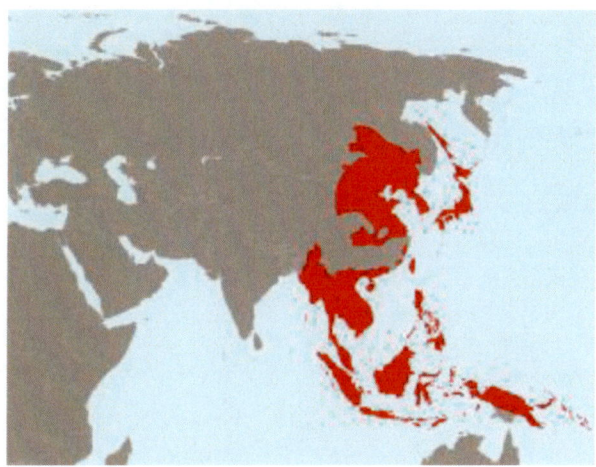

Figure F.13. The Japanese Imperial "Greater East Asia Co-Prosperity Sphere" in the 1940-1945, much bigger than the Sinosphere (Photo: Wikipedia).

China likes to win wars without battles. It has already won an economic "war" with other civilizations in the 21st century. Whether China will be wise enough to continue its "second coming" in the coming decades, time will tell. Its 5,000 years of being civilized should help in this endeavor.

China, like the Soviet Union, will not seek overseas physical presence, since China knows her weaknesses. However China certainly would like to win local wars, perhaps under the conditions of cyberwars, which are cheaper to conduct these days. Moreover, one can assume that China will not attack first, but if attacked, it will strike back. However, it is left to be determined what China considers as an attack. An attack does not have to be a kinetic strike, but rather China could consider other states' activities in waters claimed by China as an attack on its national sovereignty.

These kinds of issues will be debated in this book to increase knowledge and wisdom not only of the Chinese people, but all of us, mostly in Western and other Civilizations.

REFERENCES

Cavendish, M. (2005). *History of World War II*. vol. 3. Tarrytown, NY: Marshal Cavendish Corporation.
Fogel, J.(1997). *The Sinic world*. New York: ME. Sharpe. p. 686.
Fukuyama, F. (1992). *The end of history and the last man*. New York: Penguin Group.
Reischauer, E. (1974). The Sinic world in perspective. *Foreign Affairs* 52(2):342.
Storry, R. (1973). *The double patriots: a study of Japanese nationalism*. Westport, CT: Greenwood Press. pp. 317–319.
Targowski, A. (2014). *Global civilization in the 21st century*. New York: Nova Science Publishers.
Westad, O.A. (2012). *Restless empire, China and the world since 1750*. London: The Bodley Head.

Part I. Civilizing Society

Chapter 1

THE CIVILIZATION INDEX AND CHINESE CIVILIZATION

Andrew Targowski[*]
Western Michigan University, US

ABSTRACT

The *purpose* of this investigation is to define the roots of the Chinese Civilization and its role with respect to the rising Global Civilization in the 21St century. The *methodology* is based on an interdisciplinary big-picture view of the Chinese and Global Civilizations' developments and interdependency. Among the *findings* are: Chinese (Sino) Civilization is about 3700 years old and is the oldest civilization with a consistent religion, society, culture and infrastructure among contemporary civilizations. *Practical implication:* The Chinese Civilization Index of development is 45% which means that there is a lot of "room" for further development. *Social implication:* It is probable that Chinese Civilization is more able to cope with globalization in liquid times than other Civilizations, since it has a long history and successfully passed many adversarial encounters. *Originality:* This investigation defined the Civilization Index of Chinese Civilization which allows predictions of its behavior today and in the future.

INTRODUCTION

The purpose of this chapter is to investigate the roots of *Chinese Civilization* and compare its performance to other civilizations. The Chinese Civilization is reflected by China, which is a country with a very early civilization, and a long and rich history. The compass, gunpowder, the art of paper-making and block printing invented by the ancient Chinese have contributed immensely to the progress of mankind. The Great Wall (Figure 1.1), Grand Canal (Figure 1.2) and other projects built by the Chinese people are regarded as engineering feats in the world.

---

[*] Corresponding author: Email: andrew.targowski@wmich.edu.

Figure 1.1. Great Wall of China (Xinhua Photo).

Figure 1.2. Jing-Hang Grand Canal (Photo: lib.whu.edu.cn).

Man has lived for a very long time in what is now China, according to archaeological finds. In many parts of the country, for instance, fossil remains of primitive ape men have been unearthed. Among them are the fossil remains of the Yuanmou Ape Man who lived in Yunnan Province some 1.7 million years ago. Research findings show that the Peking Man, who lived about 500,000 years ago, was able to make and use simple implements and knew the use of fire.

One can assume that Chinese culture began in the Neolithic Times when the people of the Yellow River valley established the Yangshao culture (5000-3000 BCE). Later, the Yangsaho culture was superseded by the Longshan culture, which was centered on the Yellow River from about 3000 to 2000 BCE. This culture was developing under the administration of Jinan city, hence it is considered as the rise of Chinese Civilization. One of the characteristic features of the Longshan Culture, or early Chinese Civilization, was the intricate wheel-made pottery pieces produced in this city. Today, about 7 million people live in this city. The early history of China is obscured by the lack of written documents from this period, coupled with the existence of later accounts that attempted to describe events that had occurred several centuries previously. However, there are some written ancient historical documents which describe the Xia Dynasty as the first one of China, which ruled in 2100to 1600 BCE.

People in China take pride in calling themselves the offspring of Huang Di or Yellow Emperor, a tribal chief who dwelled in the Yellow River Valley more than four millennia ago. Pre-historical legends about the Yellow Emperor and other outstanding personages of his time abound in ancient Chinese books. Legend has it that the Yellow Emperor made weapons out of jade to conquer other tribes, while his wife, Lei Zu, introduced the rearing of silkworms. The Yellow Emperor taught tribesmen to domesticate wild animals and to grow grains, and as a result his tribes grew in strength and defeated the tribes under Yan Di (Emperor Yan). Later, the Yellow Emperor and Emperor Yan formed an alliance that conquered all the other tribes in the Yellow River Valley. Today the Yellow Emperor is regarded as the ancestor of the Chinese people, who call themselves the descendants of Yan Di and Huang Di (Emperor Yan and Yellow Emperor).[1]

Figure 1.3 illustrates four famous Chinese inventions: papermaking, gunpowder, printing and the compass.

This chapter will look at the earliest beginning of what is formally considered Chinese Civilization and its place among other civilizations. Prior to this, a concept of civilization will be debated.

The Civilization Index and its value for the Chinese Civilization will be defined in order to find out the potential for the further development of Chinese Civilization in the third Millennium. This will allow for some conclusive comments concerning the current status of Chinese Civilization and its further development. It is necessary to notice that nowadays when Global Civilization is rising, the Chinese Civilization is the biggest beneficiary of this new civilization, which to a certain degree is shifting the *modus operandi* of the world Civilization.

Figure 1.3. A set of special stamps issued by Hong Kong, under the theme of "Four Great Inventions of Ancient China" (papermaking, gunpowder, printing and the compass), (Photo: Xinhua File Photo).

---

[1] http://english.gov.cn/2005-08/06/content_20912.htm.

A COMPOSITE DEFINITION OF CIVILIZATION

Perhaps it is the time to combine *early* and *contemporary definitions of civilizations* (Targowski 2009b) by emphasizing these following important attributes:

1) Large society
   a. Specializing in labor
   b. Self-differentiating
   c. Sharing the same knowledge system
2) Space and Time
   a. Autonomous fuzzy reification
   b. Distinguished and extended area or period of time
   c. Reification not a part of a larger entity
3) Cultural system, values and symbols driven
   a. Communication driven (e.g.: literate and electronic media)
   b. Religion, wealth and power driven
4) Infrastructural system, technology-driven by, first, at least one of the following:
   a. Urban infrastructure
   b. Agricultural Infrastructure
   c. Other infrastructures (Industrial, Information and so forth)
5) Cycle-driven
   d. Rising, growing, declining, and falling over time

Based on these attributes, the composite definition of civilization is as follows:

Civilization is a large society living in an autonomous, fuzzy reification (invisible-visible) which is not a part of larger one and exists over an extended period of time. It specializes in labor and differentiates from other civilizations by developing its own advanced cultural system driven by communication, religion, wealth, power, and sharing the same knowledge/wisdom system within complex urban, agricultural infrastructures, and others such as industrial, information ones. It also progresses in a cycle or cycles of rising, growing, declining and falling.

A graphic model of civilization is illustrated in Figure 1.4.

THE CHINESE CIVILIZATION AMONG OTHER CIVILIZATIONS

In this study of civilization we begin with the construction of the empirical model of civilization development. Figure 1.5 illustrates this model and indicates that the world civilization has a continuous character, and it can be also perceived as a mosaic of autonomous civilizations.

The world civilization as a continuum never dies—it only evolves from one stage to another. This evolution takes place through the life cycle of autonomous civilizations. At the very beginning of human civilization, there were several successful formations of living processes that could be considered initial autonomous civilizations. The first autonomous civilization was the Mesopotamian Civilization (including Sumerian), which emerged in the valley of Euphrates-Tigris rivers in the Middle East, about 4,000 B.C. In the Far-East, the first autonomous civilizations rose inland: Sinic (Chinese) about 3,000 and Indus (Harrappan) about 2,500 B.C. In Africa the initial civilization was about 2500 B.C. and later the Berberic-Carthagean Civilization 600 B.C. and, in South America early autonomous civilizations included the Andean Civilization that emerged about 1500 B.C. In Central America the first autonomous civilization was the Meso-American Civilization which rose about 1000 BC. Both Central American civilizations fell about 1600 AD.

Autonomous civilizations rose in a response to physical challenges of nature (ecosystem). Humans began to organize themselves into a society, which provided exchangeable and specialized services, such as food from hunting, food production, house building, road construction, transportation, health care, entertainment, and so forth. These services and growing human communication led towards the formation of cities. These types of autonomous civilizations we will call societal civilizations.

In addition to the environmental challenges, societal civilization as a whole has been threatened by its own internal structure involving power, wealth creation, beliefs enforcement, family formation, leadership, and so forth. As societal civilizations evolved into more complex entities, they were managed by cultural manipulation. This type of autonomous civilization we will name cultural civilization. By culture, we understand a value-driven patterned behavior of a human entity.

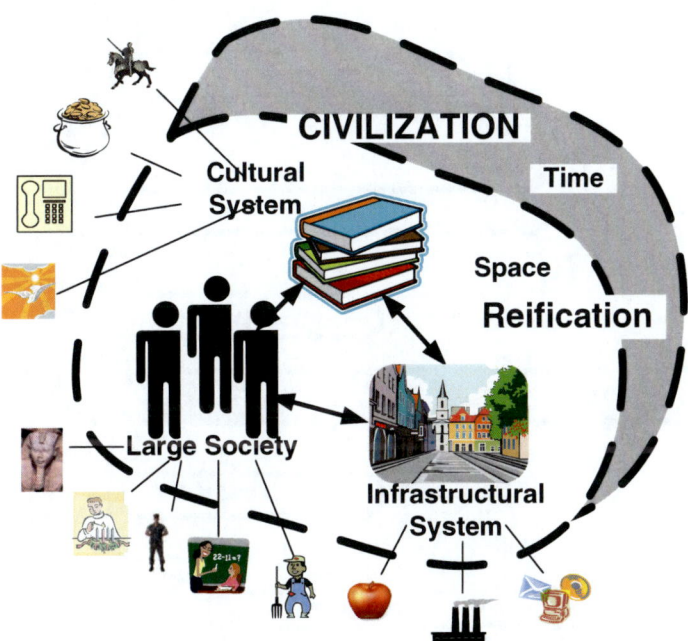

Figure 1.4. A model of civilization.

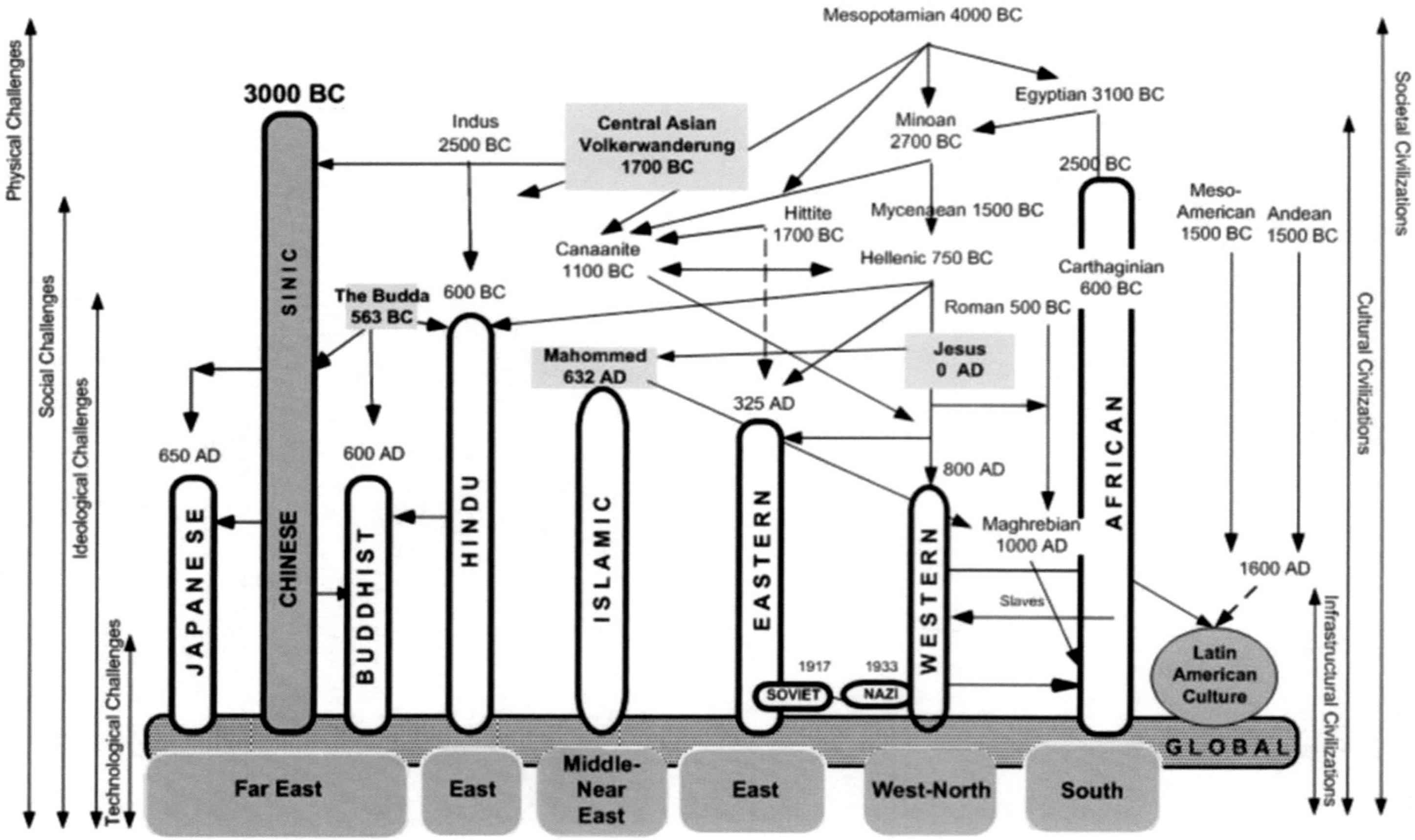

Figure 1.5. The Development of Chinese Civilization among other civilizations.

Ever since religion was transformed from beliefs in magic to beliefs in poly-gods and to then to a mono-god, the cultural civilization has applied religion as the main tool of cultural control. Religious and military forces were the foundations of the power apparatus that maintained society as a governed entity. These forces civilized society and moved it into higher levels of organization. Among cultural civilizations one can recognize about 16 cases, such as the Egyptian Civilization 3100 B.C., the Minoan 2700 B.C., the Mycean Civilization 1500 B.C., the Sinic (Chinese) Civilization 3000 B.C., the Canaanite Civilization 1100 B.C., the Hellenic Civilization 750 B.C., the Hindu Civilization 600 B.C., the Hellenistic Civilization 323 B.C., the Roman Civilization 31 B.C., the Eastern Civilization 325 A.D., the Ethiopian Civilization 400 A.D., the Buddhist Civilization 600 A.D., the Islamic Civilization 632 A.D., the Sub-Saharan Civilization 800 A.D., the Western Civilization 800 A.D., and the Maghrebian Civilization 1000 A.D. Cultural civilization evolves into a civilization with challenges generated by intra and inter-civilizational issues of war and peace. These types of issues have been managed by technological means of domination. Such a civilization we will call infrastructural civilization.

Infrastructural civilization's purpose is to expand spheres of influence with the means of technology. Technology drives the development of infrastructural civilizations. The prime target of technology applications has been a war machine which supports the main values of a given civilization. By-products of military applications of technology affect the civilian part of its infrastructure. Among eight infrastructural civilizations one can recognize the oldest and still acting Sinic-Chinese Civilization 3000 B.C., the Hindu Civilization 600 B.C., the Japanese Civilization 650 A.D., the Western Civilization 800 A.D., the Eastern Civilization 350 A.D., the Buddhist Civilization 600 A.D., the Islamic Civilization 632 A.D., and the African Civilization 1847 A.D. after the international treaty which established borders of states during the conference in Berlin in 1884-1985[1].

EXAMPLES OF CONTEMPORARY CIVILIZATIONS

According to Samuel Huntington (1996) the following civilizations exist in the post-1990 world: Western, Latin American, African, Islamic, Sinic, Hindu, Orthodox, Buddhist, and Japanese. A slightly updated set provided by Targowski (2008) contains the following civilizations in the post-2000 world: Western (Western-West, Western-Latin, Western-

---

[1] On November 15, 1884 at the request of Portugal, German chancellor Otto von Bismark called together the major western powers of the world to negotiate questions and end confusion over the control of Africa. At the time of the conference, 80% of Africa remained under traditional and local control. What ultimately resulted was a hodgepodge of geometric boundaries that divided Africa into fifty irregular countries. This new map of the continent was superimposed over the one thousand indigenous cultures and regions of Africa. The new countries lacked rhyme or reason and divided coherent groups of people and merged together disparate groups who really did not get along. At the time of the conference, only the coastal areas of Africa were colonized by the European powers. At the Berlin Conference the European colonial powers scrambled to gain control over the interior of the continent. The conference lasted until February 26, 1885 - a three month period where colonial powers haggled over geometric boundaries in the interior of the continent, disregarding the cultural and linguistic boundaries already established by the indigenous African population. By the time independence returned to Africa in 1950, the realm had acquired a legacy of political fragmentation that could neither be eliminated nor made to operate satisfactorily.

Central, and Jewish sub-Civilizations), Eastern (Russia, Ukraine, Belarus, Bulgaria, Moldavia), Chinese, Japanese, Islamic, Buddhist (Cambodia, Laos, Thailand, Sri Lanka, Tibet, Mongolia, Bhutan, Nepal, and Afghanistan), and African.

In the 21st century infrastructural civilizations have become civilizations responsible for world hemisphere influence and domination. Hence, Western Civilization dominates the Western Hemisphere, Eastern and Hindu rule the Eastern Hemisphere, the Islamic Civilization rules the Near and Middle East Hemisphere and some parts of the Far East Hemisphere, the Japanese Civilization governs some parts of the Far East Hemisphere, the Chinese Civilization influences the majority of the Far East Hemisphere, and the Buddhist civilization influences a small part of the Far East Hemisphere.

Furthermore, nowadays, the Chinese and Western Civilizations are the main organizers of Global Civilization, which has a horizontal character and invades other civilizations as its new layer of civilizational *modus operandi*.

THE CIVILIZATION INDEX AND CHINESE CIVILIZATION

Each civilization has its own dynamics, which determines its behavior. The civilizational dynamics are formulated by the scope of interactions among civilizational systems. Let's analyze them looking at the General Model of Chinese Civilization shown in Figure 1.6.

A civilization is autonomous because it has a guiding system, which through a structure of feedbacks keeps a civilization in a functional balance. Thus, an autonomous civilization protects itself by counteractions against factors that could destroy it. The clashes with terrorism in the 21st century is in fact the confrontation of values between Western, Eastern and Islamic Civilizations. An autonomous civilization tends to protect its existence through prophylactic measures against challenges coming from other civilizations and through control if challenges are coming from within it. The guiding system touches all system components of civilization (Figure 1.6).

The first level of civilizational operations generates awareness of events and challenges by the knowledge system. The more mature and experienced a knowledge system is, the more advanced the generated awareness of the challenges faced by the civilization is. Once awareness is passed to the guiding system, it triggers a reflection which is communicated as a response to stimuli. Civilizations with a weak guiding system do not generate strong enough reflections, and interactions between the communication, knowledge, and power systems reflect a reactional way of being.

The second level of the guiding system involvement deals with threats coming from the society system and all signals from other civilization systems sent to this guiding system. These signals are guided by the reflectional responses of the guiding system. The quality of the society system depends upon the level of available resources. Every autonomous civilization begins with some level of resources; however, along with its existence this level may decline or rise. If a civilization does not have enough resources, then it begins to search for them in the boundaries of other civilizations. This was the case of the Japanese Civilization in the first part of the 20th century, and it is the case of Chinese Civilization in the 21st century (with the rapid growth of the Chinese economy, China is contracting almost the whole Africa to secure the supply of needed resources such as oil).

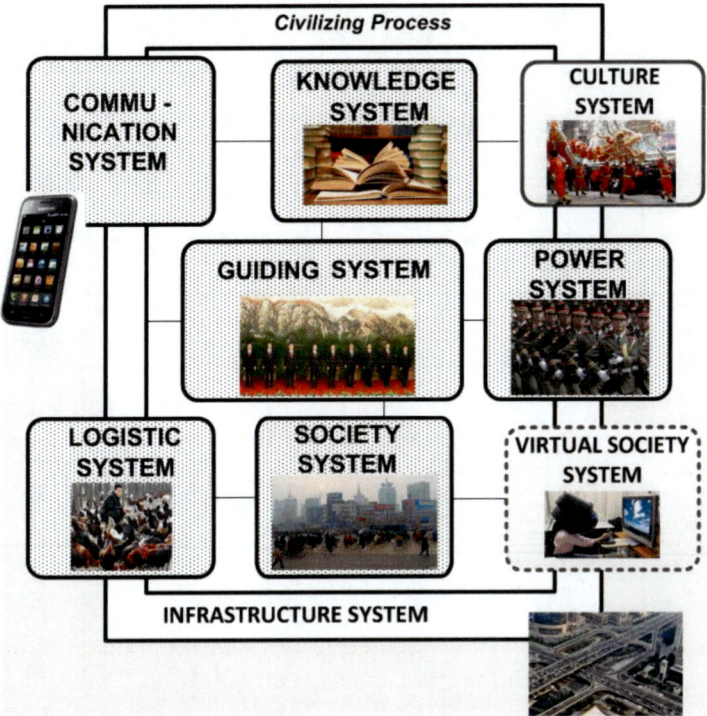

Figure 1.6. The generic system model of Chinese Civilization in the 21st century.

As the history of civilization indicates, the application of the power system (in the war mode) was the main solution in this quest for resources. The stronger power system was usually victorious in determining the outcome of the war and the well-being of the civilizations involved. This was the case of Germany in WWII(1939-1945) which was motivated by the assumed right for a bigger space (*Lebensraum*) for "higher culture." Germany therefore pushed towards the East (*Drang nach Osten*), taking the land of weaker states.

To assess the state of African Civilization one must compare it with other contemporary civilizations which are active in the 21st century, by applying the Civilization Index which evaluates each major system of a civilization (Figure 1.6)

The Civilization Index (CI), applies the following criteria (Targowski 2004b) weighted on the scale 1 to 7:

- Society system
- Communication system
- Knowledge system
- Guiding system
- Power system
- Logistic system
- Infrastructure system

The results are provided in Table 1.1.

Table 1.1. The Civilization Index (CI)

CIVILIZATION	Society System	Communication System	Knowledge System	Guiding System	Power System	Logistic System	Infrastructure System	Total	CI as % of Potential (77)	Ranking
Western- West	29	7	7	7	7	6	7	70	0.91	1
Western-Jewish	27	7	7	7	6	6	7	67	0.87	2
Japanese	21	6	6	7	5	6	7	58	0.75	3
Western- Central	20	5	4	6	5	3	4	47	0.61	4
Eastern	23	5	5	1	7	3	3	47	0.61	5
Western- Latin	15	4	4	6	3	2	4	40	0.52	6
Chinese	17	4	2	2	6	1	3	35	0.45	7
Islamic	13	3	2	4	4	3	4	33	0.43	8
Hindu	13	2	3	7	3	1	3	32	0.41	9
Buddhist	9	3	3	5	2	1	2	25	0.32	10
African	8	1	1	1	1	1	1	14	0.18	11

A comparison of civilizations at the end of the twentieth century permits us to draw the following conclusions:

1. The Western-West civilization is at the stage of "saturation," indicating that it is either ready to expand into other civilizations or to enter into social unrest. This civilization has an almost perfect Index: CI = 91%. Therefore this civilization pushes for the development of Global Civilization.
2. The Western-Jewish (CI=87%) and Japanese civilizations (CI = 75%) are very well developed and will approach the "saturation" point in the near future. Needless to say that these civilizations are strong participants of Global Civilization.
3. The African civilization is either at the beginning of the developmental process or at the stage of disastrous development. Taking into account its very short and tumultuous history, both statements may be correct (CI = 18%).
4. The remaining civilizations have a good prospect for further development or redevelopment. This is presently taking place in the case of the Western-Central civilization after the collapse of the Soviet civilization. Civilization Indexes of these civilizations vary from CI = 32% to 61%.

The Chinese Civilization has CI = 45% - this means that there is plenty of "room" for intensive civilizational development, and therefore this civilization is the biggest beneficiary of Global Civilization. The latter uses this civilization's cheap labor to make huge profits, but at the same time Chinese Civilization is getting stronger and stronger.

The Chinese civilization enters inter-civilization encounters in time rather than in space. This civilization challenges the Islamic and Japanese civilizations through its extensions in South Korea, Taiwan, Hong-Kong, Singapore, Malaysia, and, to a certain degree, Indonesia and even in the United States (where it was ready to "buy" political influence during the presidential elections). During the 1960s and particularly in the 21st century, the Chinese Civilization established its presence in Africa as the main player in economic encounters.

The Chinese civilization expansion is counter-measured by the Japanese civilization in Eastern-southern Asia, where Japan is aiming at an economic and eventually political dominance. This space-time oriented sphere will be witness to eventual "clashes of civilizations" as predicted by Huntington (1996).

Today, China is the second largest economy in the world and the United States' second-largest export destination. Many commodity-based economies have risen in recent years with China's growth. Moreover, China's opportunities and challenges are similar to what other emerging countries are facing, so it's a bellwether for a larger group of countries.

China's long-term growth story is fairly simple. In the late 1970s, Zhou Enlai (Chou En Lai) enacted reforms to allow farmers to cultivate family plots rather than communal farms. He tolerated small entrepreneurs. A migration from poor rural areas to cities with opportunities was ignored though it was illegal. These reforms substantially raised the productivity of poor people in the country. Foreign investment followed, further increasing productivity. Trade with other countries increased, again tolerated by the government. In short, economic reforms allowed poor people to become more productive, and they earned rising incomes.

In 1978 paramount leader Deng Xiaoping launched *gaige kaifang*, or "reform and opening." At that time, China was a much more agricultural country, with less than a fifth of its people living in cities. Since then hundreds of millions of rural residents have left the countryside, many seeking jobs in the export-oriented factories and construction sites that Deng's policy promoted.

In 1978 there were no Chinese cities with more than 10 million people and only two with 5 million to 10 million; by 2010, six cities had more than 10 million and 10 had from 5 million to 10 million. By the following year, a majority of Chinese were living in urban areas for the first time in the country's history.

Figure 1.6. Shenzhen's modern cityscape is the result of the vibrant economy made possible by rapid foreign investment since the institution of the policy of "reform and opening" which created the Special Economic Zone in late 1979; before it was only a small village. In 2011 it had 10.5 million habitants. (Photo: Wikipedia).

Now urbanization has been designated a national priority and is expected to occur even more rapidly. On March 16, 2014 Premier Li Keqiang's State Council and the Central Committee of the Communist Party released the "National New-type Urbanization Plan (2014-2020)," which sets clear targets: By 2020 the country will have 60 percent of its people living in cities, up from 53.7 percent now.

What's the ultimate aim of creating a much more urban country? Simply put, all those new, more free-spending urbanites are expected to help drive a more vibrant economy, helping wean China off its present reliance on unsustainable investment-heavy growth. "Domestic demand is the fundamental impetus for China's development, and the greatest potential for expanding domestic demand lies in urbanization," the 2014-2020 plan says (Dexter 2014).

This story won't go on forever, but there's substantial room for further gains. China ranks 93rd in the world on GDP per capita, indicating substantial room for improvement. China's per capita output would have to grow by 32 percent just to match the current world average. It would have to more than triple to equal the European average. There's no reason China won't eventually get close to the output level of the developed world. That will drive above-average growth rates for many years.

The Economist has noted a decline in the number of Chinese who are of working age, caused by the one child policy. The policy began in 1979, so the first generation of this policy is now 39 years old, about halfway through their working years. The Economist calls the phenomenon "peak toil," but it is less relevant to China than to a developed country such as Japan. In China, increased productivity of existing workers is a huge force, while growth of the total labor force is a relatively small factor.

As the result of its large potential reflected in a huge labor force, its talented workers, professionals, and scientists, a huge marketplace, hardworking habits and national pride – the Chinese Civilization should by pass several civilizations which are more developed and take a place in world rankings just after the Japanese Civilization, or it could also overtake it, since the latter has been stagnant for many years.

CONCLUSION

One can draw the following conclusion on the role of Chinese Civilization development among other civilizations since its birth till the present:

1. Chinese Civilization is the oldest civilization among contemporary civilizations with a consistent structure of religion, society, culture and infrastructure. This factor gives this Civilization strong feeling about its legacy and strength in overcoming many adversarial encounters.
2. Chinese Civilization's relatively low CI = 45% allows for the strong motivation of civilizational development at the level of industrial and informational modernization *a la* Western Civilization without Westernization since the latter is considered by the Chinese as a negative factor in social life.
3. As long as Chinese Civilization is an effective provider of cheap labor for outsourcing by Western Civilization manufacturing of goods, it may enjoy a

relatively successful process of modernization. What will happen when the Chinese enrich themselves and demand higher wages depends on the wisdom of Chinese government and the society.

REFERENCES

Bosworth, A. (2003). "The genetics of civilization: an empirical classification of civilizations based on writing systems," *Comparative Civilizations Review*, *49*(9).

Coulborn, R. (1966). "Structure and process in the rise and fall of civilized societies," *Comparative Studies in Society and History*, VIII-4(404).

Dexter, R. (2014). China wants its people in the cities. *BloombergBusinessWeak*, March 20.

Fernandez-Armesto, F. (2001). *Civilizations, culture, ambition, and the transformation of nature*. New York: A Touchstone Book.

Foster, J. B. & Holleman, H. (2010). The financial power elite. *MONTLY REVIEW*. *62*(1).

Hord, J. (1992). Civilization: a definition part ii. the nature of formal knowledge systems. *The Comparative Civilization Review*, (26), 111-135.

Huntington, S. P. (1996). *The clash of civilizations and the remaking of world order*. New York: Simon & Schuster.

Targowski, A. (2004a). From global to universal civilization. *Dialogue and Universalism*, XIV(3-4), 121-142.

Targowski, A. (2004b). The civilization index. *Dialogue and Universalism*, XIV(10-12), 71-86.

Targowski, A. (2004c). "A grand model of civilization." *Comparative Civilizations Review*. (*51*), 81-106.

Targowski, A. (2009a). *Information technology and social development*. Hershey, PA: IGI Publishers.

Targowski, A. (2009b). Towards a composite definition and classification of civilization. *Comparative Civilization Review*. (*60*), 79-98.

Toynbee, A. (1935). *A Study of History*, 2d ed. Oxford: Oxford University Press.

Chapter 2

SPATIO-TEMPORAL BOUNDARIES OF CHINESE CIVILIZATION

*Harry Rhodes and Lynn Rhodes**
International Society for
The Comparative Study of Civilizations (ISCSC)

ABSTRACT

The *purpose* of this investigation is to define the central contents and issues of the rise and development of Chinese civilization. The *methodology* is based on an interdisciplinary, long-view of the Chinese Civilization's stages of development and their interdependency. Among the *findings* are: long (5,000 years) and continuous evolution of culture, agriculture, civilization, technological innovations and applications; systems of order, law and government; evolution of trade practices; environmental protection, governance. *Practical implication:* In order to understand the world today, one must have a working knowledge of China, her history, her remarkable innovations, and current state in order to make meaningful real-world decisions on an interrelated, large or small scale. *Originality:* By providing an interdisciplinary and civilizational approach to this subject, we provide a foundation for continued research and future civilizational analysis on the culture and geopolitics we call China.

INTRODUCTION

Confucius said "Study the past if you would divine the future." It is sometimes disputed but often said that China has the longest continuous civilization in the world, going back 4-5,000 years and generally agreed that early Chinese civilization developed along the Yellow and Yangtze River valleys. The area we now know as China was inhabited by Homo erectus more than a million years ago. From early man, the rise of small settlements based on agriculture, small villages, ancient historical texts, the first and subsequent dynasties and world-changing inventions, China was and is extraordinary. Many things from which the

---

[*] Corresponding author: Email: Harrydet@hotmail.com.

modern world evolved, originated in China, including paper, gunpowder, credit banking, the compass and paper money.[1] A readable and brief digest of China's history is worth an exploration especially because of the lack of written records from pre-history and the early cultures from which complex civilization subsequently evolved.

CHINESE IN THE PRE-CIVILIZATION STAGE

Human history in China extends back at least 1.7 million years. Fossil discoveries, including those comprising Peking Man, one of the most famous examples of Homo erectus from Paleolithic times, were found during a series of archaeological excavations at a site near Beijing in 1926-27. At the very least, the famous discovery tells us that man inhabited the area nearly a million years ago.

The Neolithic age in China can be traced back to circa 10,000 BC and concluded with the introduction of metallurgy about 8,000 years later, and was characterized by the development of settled communities that relied primarily on farming and domesticated animals rather than hunting and gathering.[2]

Archaeologists continue to make new discoveries about Chinese prehistoric civilization. According to scholars (Zhou Jixu 2006), from the Neolithic period to the beginning of the Xia dynasties (about 7000-2000 BC) there were many prehistoric cultural sites in the middle Yellow River valley and the middle and lower Yangtze River valley, such as the Yangshao Culture sites (4600-3000 BC), the Longshan Cultural sites (3000-2200 BC) in the Yellow River valley, the Hemudu Culture sites (5000-4000 BC), and the Liangzhu Culture sites (2800-1800 BC) in the lower reaches of the Yangtze River. These sites showed that the Yellow River and Yangtze River valleys are among the earliest areas in the world to yield agricultural civilization. It is surprising that many of these sites possessing very developed agriculture occurred long before the emergence of agriculture (about 2100 BC) as it was mentioned repeatedly in a number of Chinese classical books. There is a large disparity in the times (and in the areas) between the archeological discoveries and the ancient documentary records.

The rise of settlements that were based on agricultural economy emerged circa 8000-2000 BC in eastern coastal regions and along the rich river deltas of the Yellow River and Yangzi River. These evolving civilizations relied mostly on hunting, fishing, and gathering. Cultivation of millet and rice in these river deltas evolved. A mature agricultural civilization existed in the Yellow River valley in the period 5000-6000 BC. Early evidence for proto-Chinese millet agriculture is radiocarbon-dated to about 7000 BC.[3]

According to the Peiligang Site referenced by China's Ministry of Culture, excavation of a Peiligang culture site in Xinzheng County, Henan, found a community that flourished in 5,500-4,900 BC, with evidence of agriculture, constructed buildings, pottery, and burial of the

---

[1] China country profile: BBC News Oct 18.2010 http://www.bbc.com/news/world-asia-pacific-13017882 Retrieved on 2014.03.18

[2] Department of Asian Art. Neolithic Period in China. In Heilbrunn Timeline of Art History. New York http://www.metmuseum.org/toah/hd/cneo/hd_cneo.htm Metropolitan Museum of Art 2000. Retrieved on 2014.03.19

[3] Chinese History Timeline. http://www.china-mike.com/chinese-history-timeline/part-1-early-dynasties/ Retrieved 2014.04.14

dead. With agriculture came increased population, the ability to store and redistribute crops, and the potential to support specialist craftsmen and administrators (Pringle 1998).

The Metropolitan Museum of Art, Helibrunn Timeline of Art History describes a distinctly Chinese artistic tradition that can be traced to the middle of the Neolithic period, about 4,000 BC. Two groups of artifacts provide the earliest surviving evidence of this tradition. It is now thought that these cultures developed their own traditions for the most part independently, creating distinctive kinds of architecture and types of burial customs, but with some communication and cultural exchange between them.

One group of artifacts consists of painted pottery found at numerous sites along the Yellow river basin, extending from Gansu Province in northwestern China to Henan Province in central China. The culture that emerged in the central plain was known as Yangshao. A related culture that emerged in the northwest is classified into three categories, the Banshan, Majiayao, and Machang, each categorized by the types of pottery produced. Yangshao painted pottery was formed by stacking coils of clay into the desired shape and then smoothing the surfaces with paddles and scrapers. Pottery containers found in graves, as opposed to those excavated from the remains of dwellings, are often painted with red and black pigments.

Another group of Neolithic artifacts consists of pottery and jade carvings from the eastern seaboard and lower reaches of the Yangzi River in the south, representing the Hemudu, the Dawenkou and later the Longshan and the Liangzhu. The gray and black pottery of eastern China is notable for its distinctive shapes, which differed from those made in the central regions and included the tripod, which was to remain a prominent vessel form in the subsequent Bronze Age. Some pottery items made in the east were painted (possibly in response to examples imported from central China). Potters along the coast also used the techniques of burnishing and incising. These same craftsmen are credited with development of the pottery wheel in China.

Of all aspects of the Neolithic cultures in eastern China, the use of jade made the most lasting contribution to Chinese civilization. Polished stone implements were common to all Neolithic settlements. Stones to be fashioned into tools and ornaments were chosen for their hardness and strength to withstand impact and for their appearance. Nephrite, or true jade, is a tough and attractive stone. Few of the jades in archaeological excavations show signs of wear. They are generally found in burials of privileged persons carefully arranged around the body. Jade axes and other tools transcended their original function and became objects of great social and esthetic significance.[4]

THE FORMATION OF THE CHINESE (SINO) CIVILIZATION

As evidenced by evolving cultural sophistication, particularly with the creation of art, the early seeds of Chinese civilization developed and existed extensively along Yellow River. The Yangshao culture was one. The Yangshao culture was a Neolithic culture dated from around 5000 BC to 3000 BC. It was named after the discovery of a representative village of the culture, discovered by Swedish archaeologist Johan Gunnar Andersson in 1921. The

---

[4] Department of Art. Neolithic Period in China. In Heilbrunn Timeline of Art History. New York: http://www.metmuseum.org/toah/hd/cneo/hd_cneo.htm Metropolitan Museum of Art 2000. Retrieved on 2014.03.19

culture flourished mainly in the provinces of Henan, Shaanxi and Shanxi. Early studies suggested the Yangshao and Longshan cultures were the same entity. However, it is now accepted that the Longshan culture is a later development of the Yangshao culture.

The Yangshao people cultivated millet extensively. Some villages also cultivated wheat or rice. They kept animals such as pigs, dogs, sheep, goats, and cattle. They fished and hunted for meat which was eaten on special occasions. They practiced an early form of silkworm cultivation and wove hemp. Women used cloth to wrap around themselves and were found to have tied their hair in a bun. The Yangshao built houses with rammed walls, dug in rounded rectangular pits. A lattice of wattle was then woven over it and plastered with mud.

The Yangshao culture is well known for its fine pottery; white, red and black, with human, animal and geometric designs. Unlike the later Longshan culture, the Yangshao culture did not use pottery wheels in pottery-making. Excavations found that children were routinely buried in painted pottery jars.[5]

Late Neolithic culture, the Longshan in Shandong Province, was centered on the central and lower Yellow River and named after Longshan, Shandong Province, the first excavated site of this culture. It is dated from about 3000 BC to 2000 BC. The Longshan culture developed a high level of skill in pottery making, including the use of pottery wheels. Longshan culture was noted for its highly polished black pottery and is often referred to as the "Black Pottery Culture". (Figure 2.1) This culture developed under the administration of Jinan city and is widely considered as the rise of Chinese civilization.

Life during this time marked a transition to the establishment of cities. Rammed earth walls and moats began to appear. Rice cultivation was established by that time. During the Longshan culture, Neolithic population in China reached its peak. Then, the population decreased sharply towards the end of the Longshan culture. The decrease in population was paralleled with the disappearance of their fine, black pottery which was found in ritual burials.[6]

Figure 2.1. Longshan Culture Pottery (3000-2000 BC). (Photo: Richard Wertz Exploring Chinese History).

---

[5] Exploring Chinese History, Neolithic and Bronze Age Culture. Richard Wertz http://www.ibiblio.org/chinesehistory/contents/02cul/c03s04.html. Retrieved on 2014.03.20

[6] Exploring Chinese History. Richard R. Wertz http://www.ibiblio.org/chinesehistory/contents/02cul/ c03s04.html. Retrieved on 2014. 03.20

Xia Dynasty

There is a lack of written documents from the Yangshao and Longshan cultures. However, they are referenced in later ancient historical texts and documents describing the Xia Dynasty. The Xia Dynasty 2070-1600 BC is the first dynasty in China to be described in ancient historical chronicles. The Bamboo Annals is a chronicle of ancient China from its early legendary times and extending to 299 BC. The existence of the Xia Dynasty is asserted in the Records of the Grand Historian (c 100 BC) and Bamboo Annals before the Shang Dynasty (1045-256 BC).[7]

Scholars disagree whether or not the Xia Dynasty actually existed and there is conflicting archaeological evidence supportive of its place in history (Mair 2013). Scholars have conflicting views on the matter. Until scientific excavations were made at early bronze-age sites at Anyang, Henan Province, in 1928, it was difficult to separate myth from reality in regard to the Xia. But since then, and especially in the 1960s and 1970s, archaeologists have uncovered urban sites, bronze implements, and tombs that suggest the existence of Xia civilization in the same locations cited in the ancient Chinese historical texts. Documentation suggests indicating the Xia Dynasty was founded by the Huaxia tribe, who were the ancestral people of the Han Chinese (Lung 2011).

At minimum, what is commonly known today as the Xia period, marked an evolutionary stage between the late Neolithic cultures and the typical Chinese urban civilization of the Shang Dynasty.[8]

Shang Dynasty

The Shang Dynasty (c 1600 BC – c 1046 BC) ruled in the Yellow River valley in the second millennium BC and was then followed by the Zhou Dynasty. The accounting of the Shang comes again from the ancient texts such as the Classic of History, Bamboo Annals and Records of the Grand Historian. Archaeological findings outlining evidence for the existence of the Shang Dynasty, c.1600-1046 BC, are divided into two sets. The first set, from the early Shang period comes from sources at Erligang, Zhengzhou, and Shangcheng. The second set, from the later Shang or Yin period, is at Anyang in today's Henan. Importantly, the findings at Anyang include the earliest written record of Chinese past so far discovered. They consist of divination records in ancient Chinese writing on the bones or shells of animals, referred to as the "oracle bones", which date from around 1200 BC (Boltz 1999). (Figure 2.2)

---

[7] Public Summary Request of the People's Republic of China To the Government of the United States of America Under Article 9 of the 1970 UNESCO Convention http://web.archive.org/web/20071215094418/ http://exchanges.state.gov/culprop/cn04sum.html Retrieved 2014.3.21. Redirected to: http://www.studymode.com/essays/History-Of-China-1470580.html 2014.4.16

[8] China The Ancient Dynasties http://lcweb2.loc.gov/cgi-bin/query/r?frd/cstdy:@field%28DOCID+cn0013% 29 Retrieved 2014.03.21

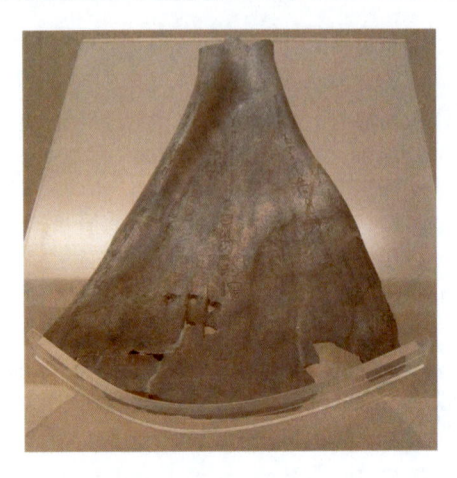

Figure 2.2. Oracle Bone at Shanghai Museum. (Photo:Wikipedia.org Herr Klugbeisser).

Figure 2.3. Bronze Vessel Late Shang Dynasty. (Photo: Wikipedia.org. by Mountain).

There were 31 kings throughout the Shang Dynasty including Tang of Shang to King Zhou of Shang. During the Shang Dynasty people believed that their family members and ancestors became gods when they died and deserved worship. This was in keeping with their worship of different gods including the weather and sky gods and also a supreme god named Shangdi who ruled over the other gods.

The ancient Records of the Grand Historian states the Shang Dynasty moved its capital six times with a final move which led to Yin in 1350 BC. Chinese historians living in later periods were accustomed to the idea of one dynasty succeeding another. However the political situation in early China is known to have been more complicated than the simple sequence of dynasties following one another. As mentioned earlier, some scholars suggest the Xia and Shang refer to political entities that may have overlapped or existed concurrently.

The Shang Dynasty is also referred to as the Yin Dynasty in its later stages. Yang Lu of UCLA and affiliated with the Chinese American Museum of Los Angeles (CAMLA) describes the Shang Dynasty as believed to have been founded by a rebel leader who overthrew the last Xia ruler. In essence, Lu describes the Shang Dynasty as a civilization based on agriculture, augmented by hunting and animal husbandry. Two important events of the Shang period were the development of a writing system as revealed in inscriptions on tortoise shells and cattle bones and the use of bronze metallurgy.

The Shang highly regarded their royal ancestors. Bronze was found in royal tombs. Funerary tablets were kept in the front of temples and rituals carried out in their presence. The tablets were thought to contain the souls of the ancestors. Royal events were announced aloud in the temples to inform the ancestors. As far back as c.1500 BC, the early Shang Dynasty engaged in large-scale production of bronze-ware vessels and weapons. (Figure 2.3) Bronze was commonly used for art in addition to other uses.

The production of bronze necessitated a large labor force that could handle the mining, refining and transportation of copper, tin, and lead ores. The Shang Dynasty royal court and aristocrats required a vast amount of different bronze vessels for various ceremonial purposes and events of religious divination, hence the need for official managers that could provide oversight and employment of hard-laborers and skilled artisans and craftsmen. With the increased amount of bronze available, the army could become better equipped with an assortment of bronze weaponry, and bronze was also able to furnish the fittings of spoke-wheeled chariots that came into widespread use by 1200 BC.[9]

The Shang Dynasty had a fully developed system of writing; its complexity and state of development indicates an earlier period of development, which is still unattested. Their influence, though not political control, extended as far northeast as modern Beijing, where early pre-Yan culture shows evidence of Shang material culture. At least one burial in this region during the Early Shang period contained both Shang-style bronzes and local-style gold jewelry. This influence likely made possible the integration of Yan into the later Zhou Dynasty.[10]

Cities around the capital were referred to as palace-cities and each city was surrounded by a wall. Military and religious centers in addition to nobility residences existed within the walls. Buildings were identical and arranged in a consistent format.[11]

THE RISE OF THE CHINESE KINGDOMS IN SPACE AND TIME AND THEIR IMPACT ON THE DEVELOPEMNT OF THE CHINESE CIVILIZATION

Zhou Dynasty

The Zhou Dynasty (c.1046 BC-256 BC) is described succinctly again by Yang Lu, as the first dynasty to unite most of China under a single government and how, in 771 BC the Zhou king was killed by invading barbarians who were allied with rebel lords. The capital was moved eastward to Luoyang in present-day Henan Province. In essence, because of this shift, historians divide the Zhou era into Western Zhou (1027-771 BC) and Eastern Zhou (770-221

---

[9] Citizen Compendium http://en.citizendium.org/wiki/Shang_Dynasty Retrieved 2014.03.22
[10] ^ Citizen Compendium
[11] Yang Lu UCLA with the Chinese American Museum of LA (CAMLA) http://polaris.gseis.ucla.edu/yanglu/ ECC _HISTORY_SHANG%20DYNASTY.htm Retrieved 2014.03.22

BC). With the royal line broken, the power of the Zhou court gradually diminished and the fragmentation of the kingdom accelerated. Eastern Zhou divided into two sub-periods. The first from 770 to 476 BC is called the Spring and Autumn Period, after a famous historical chronicle of the time; the second is known as the Warring States Period (475-221 BC).

The Eastern Zhou period is thought of as the "shaping period" of Chinese culture. The Zhou were a semi-nomadic clan from the north western fringe of the Chinese world. They replaced the Shang Dynasty. The capital was at Hao, near present Xi'an (Figure 2.4).

The government there was a feudal monarchy. From a social standpoint, the Western Zhou was quite similar to the Shang. The rulers were the nobles with family names and they practiced ancestor worship. Divination marked important decisions or events. Peasants were physically separated from other classes but were a key element. They carried out vital and supportive societal functions such as sowing and reaping. The influential period of the Eastern Zhou was during the time when the uniqueness of China's recorded history begins, with the collections of documents and historical romances. It was also during this time that the decline of the ancient forms of religion and the transformation into Confucianism and Daoism took place. From a social standpoint they created Legalism which is "a loose bundle of thinkers from different traditions rather than a proper school." This social organization was then adopted by other dynasties. It is also in this time that military thought and technology advanced.[12]

The period during the Zhou Dynasty produced what many consider the zenith of Chinese bronze-ware-making. It also covers the period in which the written script evolved into its modern form with the use of an archaic clerical script that emerged during the late Warring States period. Eastern Zhou is also remembered as the golden age of Chinese philosophy: the Hundred Schools of Thought which flourished during a time when rival lords patronized itinerant scholars. The Nine Schools of Thought which came to dominate the others were Confucianism, Legalism (core philosophy of the Qin Dynasty), Taoism, Mohism, the utopian communalist Agriculturalism, two strains of Diplomatists, the sophistic Logicians, Sun Tzu's Militarists, and the Naturalists (Carr 2012). Those who made the greatest impact on later generations of Chinese, were Confucius, founder of Confucianism and Laozi, founder of Taoism and Sun Tzu or Sunzi who wrote the historic and often consulted Art of War.

The Zhou Dynasty was the longest lasting dynasty in Chinese history, with the end of the Zhou period in 221 BC when the first emperor of the Qin Dynasty unified the land on a new imperial basis.

Spring and Autumn Period and Warring States Period

In the 8th century BC, power became decentralized during the Spring and Autumn Period (722 BC-476 BC) which is named after the Spring and Autumn Annals, a chronicle of the state of Lu between 722 and 479 BC. It is known as the earliest surviving Chinese historical text to be based on annalistic principles.

---

[12] Yang Lu UCLA with the Chinese American Museum of Los Angeles CAMLA http://polaris.gseis.ucla.edu/ yanglu/ECC_HISTORY_ZHOU%20DYNASTY.htm Retrieved 2014.3.23

Figure 2.4. One of many structures on ancient Great City Wall, Modern Day Xi'an. (Photo L. Rhodes).

Several of the states rebelled and joined with non-Chinese forces to drive the Zhou from their capital. The Spring and Autumn Period coincides with the falling of the central Zhou power. Hundreds of separate states arose out of that period. Many of them continued obedience to the Zhou kings, if only nominally. Leaders of some of the emerging states began giving themselves royal titles. The new states varied widely in size with some described as small villages and others with forts.

It was during this time, which overlapped with the Zhou, the Hundred Schools of Thought of Chinese Philosophy, mentioned earlier, emerged. With the need to maintain or gain power, various rulers sought advice of the early philosophers and teachers, helping the strategic and philosophical movement develop. Many of China's great classical writings emerged from this period and influenced Chinese culture and civilization for years to come.

During the Spring and Autumn Period, China's feudal system became largely irrelevant. The Zhou Dynasty kings held nominal power, but had real control over only a small royal demense centered on their capital Luoyi near modern day Luoyang. During the early part of the Zhou Dynasty period, royal relatives and generals had been given control over fiefdoms in an effort to maintain Zhou authority over vast territory (Chinn 2007). Incrementally, the power of the Zhou kings waned and the fiefdoms became increasingly independent states.

Gradually, more powerful and larger states absorbed or claimed smaller ones. Most of the small states had disappeared by the 6th century BC leaving only a small number of powerful and large principalities to dominate China. Some became independent from the Zhou and wars broke out. A total of 148 states are mentioned in the chronicles for this period, 128 of which were absorbed by the four largest states by the end of the period. After years of conflict with the most powerful rulers establishing dominance, conflicts between states became prevalent during what is known as the Warring States period. Dates range from 403 BC to 481 BC for the beginning of the Warring States period. Scholars commonly cite 475 BC as the beginning of the Warring States period with 221 BC bringing the period to a close when the Qin Dynasty aggressively took power.

Indicative of the name Warring States Period, intense warfare was prevalent. The warfare and unrest came primarily as a result of competition and aggression among the seven states. The period was known for advances in military technology. The states who made use of their resources to leverage the advances were able to gain superiority. Technological innovations such as casting of individual weapons allowed for improved arming of foot soldiers. Arming individual soldiers was a tactical improvement to previous eras where aristocrats fought from chariots. Fighting from chariots had limitations partially the result of lack of mass production and limits (by class) on who could participate. Thus, with individual casting of weapons, a tactical advantage was given to the states who had the resources and large populations to provide large armies. Partly because of the advanced technologies, smaller states were consolidated into larger states over time. Regardless of the new casting innovations, the chariot however, was able to retain its importance and status for some time. (Figure 2.5)

The various states fielded massive armies of infantry, cavalry, and chariots. Complex logistical systems maintained by efficient government bureaucracies were needed to supply, train, and control such large forces. The size of the armies ranged from tens of thousands to several hundred thousand men (Ebrey 2006). Iron became more widespread and began to replace bronze during this time with most armor and weapons made from iron. The long-range weapon of choice during this period was the crossbow. It had several characteristics making it advantageous: it could be mass produced; it allowed for mass training and could be easily transported. The close-range weapon of choice was the dagger-axe and varied from about 9-18 feet in length.

The legal process began to take shape in Western Zhou times and codification of laws began to appear in city states in the seventh and eights centuries BCE. According to one China expert, Nicola DiCosmo, editor of Military Culture in Imperial China, there were several critical changes to the development of the military and evolution of law. First, the armies increased in size and the infantry came to be the core of the army. By the middle of the fourth century BCE, the riding of horses and formation of a cavalry were adopted from the northern steppe peoples, and this arm of the military became more and more important in later centuries.

All able-bodied males were required to provide labor and military service to the state (women owed labor and service only, except in siege warfare) and all of the states developed systems of household registration to allow government authorities to extract tax, labor, and military resources from their subject populations.

Legalism was a competing and different school of thought (than Confucianism and Daoism) and maintained that man, by nature, had to be controlled by strict rules of law and uniform justice. The imperial form of government adopted Legalism as its philosophical basis. The Legalist philosophy had its greatest impact during the first imperial dynasty, the Qin, evolving out of the Warring States Period.

Legalism was a philosophy emphasizing strict obedience to the legal system. It was one of the main philosophic currents during the Warring States period. It was a utilitarian political philosophy that did not address higher questions like the purpose and nature of life.[13]

---

[13] Legalism http://philtar.ucsm.ac.uk/encyclopedia/china/legal.html philtar.ucsm.ac.uk. Retrieved 2014.03.30

Figure 2.5. Early Bronze Chariot Diagram Display Qin Tomb Museum. (Photo: L. Rhodes).

Three tools for governing under Legalism were the "Fa" or "law or principle"; the "Shu" or "method"; and the "Shi" or legitimacy". The law or principle code was to have been clearly written and made public. Those under the ruler were all equal. "Laws" were to reward and obey or punish accordingly. It was intended that the system of law ran the state, not the ruler. It was said that if the law was successfully enforced even a weak ruler could be strong. The "method" used special tactics and secrets to be employed by the ruler to ensure others did not take control of the state. It was particularly important that no one try to understand or fathom the ruler's motivations, and thus no one could know which behavior might give them an advantage to get ahead, except for following the laws. The "legitimacy" was the position of the ruler, not the ruler himself or herself, that held the power. Therefore, analysis of the trends, the context, and the facts were essential tools for a real ruler. The goal was that all human behavior would increase the power of the ruler or the state.

THE EXPANSION OF THE CHINESE EMPIRE IN SPACE AND TIME AND ITS IMPACT ON THE CHINESE CIVILIZATION

Qin Dynasty to Mongol Rule

The Qin Dynasty (221 BC-206 BC) was the first imperial dynasty of China formed after the conquest of the six other states by the state of Qin, pronounced Ch'in. The name of China is derived from Qin. Its founding emperor was Qin Shi Huang, the First Emperor of Qin. The Qin Dynasty began the unified imperial dynastic role of China and ended in the early 20th century with the ultimate failure of the Qing Dynasty. It originally occupied the strategic Wei River valley in the northwestern portion of the country. It was a short-lived Legalist dynasty of only about 15 years and yet is one of the most famous. Confucianism was suppressed. Emperor Qin insisted on absolute control and Qin was an imperial state in which the government held absolute power, which although harsh, resulted in a unified China.

The Qin Dynasty established the approximate boundaries and basic administrative system that all subsequent Chinese dynasties were to follow for the next 2,000 years. Qin instituted an extremely authoritarian government, ordering all books to be burned unless they were about subjects he thought important. Agriculture, medicine, and prophecy were some of the permitted subjects. Scholars who refused to allow their books to be burned were severely punished, killed or sent to work on what we now call the Great Wall of China. The Wall is one of the architectural monuments initially constructed during the Qin Dynasty. (Figures 2.6) It was eventually completed by connecting sections of a number of existing shorter walls which feudal lords had begun.

During its reign, the Qin sought to create an imperial state unified by highly structured political power and a stable economy able to support a large military (Scott 1995). The majority of the Qin population consisted of peasants over whom the Qin government maximized administrative control. For the most part, peasants were put to work in the fields growing food or harvesting silk. If they attempted to do other things than those tasks assigned to them, they were disciplined or punished. At the same time, the Qin government minimized the role of land owners and aristocrats. By asserting control over the majority of the peasant population, the dynasty was able to embark on large-scale, public-works-type projects in addition to the Great Wall. Roads, canals, irrigation and flood control and bridges were other projects undertaken. Those assigned to work on any project were expected to cooperate and perform their tasks well.

Figure 2.6. Great Wall of China. (Photo: H. Rhodes).

The Qin Dynasty was heavy handed in response to criticism. Criticism of Qin contributed to the severe censorship that led to the burning of books and conversely to standardization of other practices. Many reforms were introduced under the Qin Dynasty. In order to help effectively rule their expansive territory the Qin's government implemented a standardized system of writing, standardized the width of highways, chariots, weights and measurements, laws, and money. Standardization of the highways benefited trade, general transportation, and provided the large-scale military with impressively, strategic and tactical advantages. The code of law was rigorously enforced. Feudalism was ended and a centralized government system was instituted.

Partly due to severe societal conditions along with ever increasing taxes, which were required to pay for many projects and wars, rebellion erupted when the last Qin Emperor, died and the dynasty was overthrown to be replaced shortly thereafter by the Han Dynasty (206 BC-220 AD).

Near present day Xi'an lies the Qin Tomb. The site with over 8,000 life-size terracotta warriors, chariots and horses was initially discovered by local farmers in 1974. Some are still buried. They were made during the time of Qin Shi Huang's rule and intended to protect him after his death. (Figures 2.7 and 2.8) The Terracotta Army is one of China's most significant archaeological discoveries and was designated a UNESCO World Heritage site in 1987. The figures vary in design according to their roles and status or rank.

During a visit to the site in late 2013 we spoke with specialists who told us archaeologists and curators are working to improve scientific technology before excavating additional figures from the site. They hope improved methods will better ensure preservation of the material, colors and paint that shows vividly when first excavated and suffers rapid deterioration when exposed to the air.

Cultural and technological advancements developed and standardized during the brief Qin Dynasty had a lasting impact on subsequent Chinese dynasties.

Figure 7. Terracotta Army Soldiers, Qin Tomb. (Photo: by H. Rhodes).

Figure 8. Terracotta Army Soldiers, Qin Tomb. (Photo: H. Rhodes).

Han Dynasty (206 BC-220 AD)

Following the Qin Dynasty a rebel leader named Liu Bang was successful in leading a civil war and founded The Han Dynasty (206 BC-220 AD). The powerful Han Dynasty was a period of relative stability and prosperity. China was consolidated as a unified state under a central imperial bureaucracy. The Han Dynasty was so important that the term Han is still used today when referring to ethnic Chinese, Chinese language and written characters.

During the Han Dynasty, agriculture, handicrafts and commerce flourished, and the population is estimated to have reached 50 million. During the most prosperous period of the Han Dynasty, Emperor Wu (140 BC-87 BC) expanded the territory from the Central Plains to the Western Regions (present day Xinjiang and Central Asia). Emperor Wu dispatched Zhang Qian twice as his envoy to the Western Regions and in the process pioneered the route known as the "Silk Road" from Chang'an (today's Xi'an, Shaanxi Province), through Xinjiang and Central Asia, and on to the east coast of the Mediterranean Sea. China's silk goods were traded to the West along the Silk Road. As contacts between the East and West increased, Buddhism spread to China in the first century. In 105 an official named Cai Lun invented a technique for making fine paper, leading to a revolution in communications and learning.[14]

The Han demonstrated that China was fundamentally a Eurasian power in their relations with neighboring peoples. The greatest threat to their power was from the north, by the Xiongnu (various nomadic tribes of central Asia). The Han Dynasty was briefly interrupted by the Xin Dynasty (9-23 AD) of the former Wang Mang. The Han were separated into two periods known as the Western Han (206 BC-9AD) and the Eastern Han (25-220 AD). Spanning over four centuries, the period of the Han Dynasty is considered a golden age in Chinese history (Zhou 2003).

The boundaries established by the Qin and maintained by the Han have more or less defined the nation of China up to the present day. The Western Han capital, Chang'an in

---

[14] Law China Digest, http://www.lawinfochina.com/Legal/index.shtm Retrieved 2014.03.30

present-day Shaanxi Province, a monumental urban center laid out on a north-south axis with palaces, residential wards, and two market areas-was one of the two largest cities in the ancient world (Rome was the other).[15]

Poetry, literature, and philosophy flourished during the reign of Emperor Wudi (141-86 BC). The monumental *Shij* (Historical Records) written by Sima Qian (145-80 BC) set the standard for later government-sponsored histories. Among other things, it recorded information about the various peoples, invariably described as "barbarian," who lived on the empires borders. Wudi also established Confucianism as the basis for correct official and individual conduct and for the educational curriculum. The reliance on the bureaucracy by members of a highly educated class grounded in Confucian writings and other classics defined China's statecraft for many centuries.

Under Wudi, China regained control of territories, first conquered by Qin Shihuangdi, in southern China and the northern part of Vietnam. China gained control of the trade routes running north and south of the Taklamakan Desert. In return for its silk and gold, China received wine, spices, woolen fabrics, grapes, pomegranates, sesame, broad beans, and alfalfa.[16]

Disputes among factions, including the families of imperial consorts, contributed to the dissolution of the Western Han Empire. A generation later, China flourished again under the Eastern Han Dynasty (25-220 AD). Ban Chao (32-102 AD), a member of an illustrious literary family, reasserted Chinese control of Central Asia from 73 to 94 AD. Trade, less rigorously controlled than in the first part of the dynasty, expanded, with caravans reaching the new capital, Luoyang every month.[17]

There was also an expansion of diplomacy: fifty envoys from Central Asia were recorded in 94 AD and Japanese envoys visited in 107 AD. The development of paper, water clocks, sundials, astronomical instruments, and the invention of a seismograph in 132 AD attest to the technological and scientific sophistication indicative of this period.[18] The Han Dynasty ended in 220 AD. However, in much the same way that Greece or Rome influenced the West, the Han influenced the East.

Sui Dynasty

After the collapse of the Han Dynasty, there were nearly four centuries of division between competing dynasties, spanning from 220-589 AD before China was reunited again, this time by the Sui Dynasty. The Sui Dynasty was relatively short lived but importantly began the development of southern China. The Sui Dynasty (589-618 AD) reunited China after it had been through a period of fragmentation. However, in the same manner as the Qin Dynasty, they overused their resources and the dynasty eventually collapsed.

---

[15] Department of Asian Art. "Han Dynasty (206 BC-220 AD)". In Heilbrunn timeline of Art History. New York: The Metropolitan Museum of Art, 2000- http://www.metmuseum.org/toah/hd/hand/hd_hand.htm Retrieved 2014.03.30

[16] ^Department of Asian Art, The Metropolitan Museum of Art. Heilbrunn Timeline of Art History

[17] ^Department of Asian Art, The Metropolitan Museum of Art

[18] ^ Department of Asian Art, The Metropolitan Museum of Art

Tang Dynasty

The Tang Dynasty (618-907 AD) established by Li Yuan, united China for nearly three centuries in what is seen as the second high point of Chinese civilization after the Han. Its capital was in Chang'an, present-day Xi'an. The imperial sphere of influence reached Central Asia for the first time. It was a time of general peace and prosperity and was a powerful nation. The Tang Dynasty is often referred to as the Golden Age of Ancient China. Evolving technologies and engineering were advanced during the Tang. Woodblock printing allowed books to be printed in mass production allowing for wide circulation of dictionaries, almanacs and Buddhist scriptures. The Grand Canal was built and helped the flow of merchandise. Toilet paper was invented during this time. The capital city became a major commercial center.

Another major invention of the time was gunpowder. Although it would continue to be perfected over hundreds of years, gunpowder was mostly used for fireworks during the Tang Dynasty. The people believed that fireworks could help to frighten evil spirits. Other inventions included porcelain, advances in mapmaking, gas cylinders for natural gas, advances in medicine, and advancements in clock making.[19]

There was extensive trade between the Tang Dynasty and foreign countries. A contributing factor to the prosperity of the dynasty was its well developed, centralized bureaucracy and policies. The Tang developed and implemented a code of laws and clear administrative functions. Land was taxed and service in the army, for a period of time, was required by farmers in exchange for the rights to their land. After a period of time, the government became weakened as corruption and taxes increased and lands fell into the hands of private land owners.

The dynasty continued to flourish under Empress Wu Zetian, the only empress regnant in Chinese history (Jiang 1998). In 907 the dynasty came to an end when a general took power by removing the last Tang emperor.

Song Dynasty

Following the Five Dynasties and Ten Kingdoms period, The Song Dynasty ruled Ancient China from 960 to 1279 AD. The period during the Song Dynasty was considered to be the most advanced civilization the world had seen. There were many advancements during the Song Dynasty including classical literature, scientific innovation, and improvements to an institution of systems for examinations in order to enter into the Chinese bureaucracy, and advancements using gunpowder for arrows, rockets and bombs. The arts and culture flourished under the Song.

The Song Dynasty came to an end when they allied with the Mongols against their longtime enemies, the Jin. The Mongols helped them to conquer the Jin, but then turned on the Song. The leader of the Mongols, Kublai Khan, conquered all of China and began his own dynasty, the Yuan dynasty.[20]

---

[19] "The Tang Dynasty of Ancient China." Ducksters Technological Solutions, Inc. (TSI) Mar. 2014. Web.30.Mar.2014 http://www.ducksters.com/history/china/tang_dynasty.php Retrieved 2014.03.30
[20] "The Song Dynasty of Ancient China." Ducksters Technological Solutions, Inc. (TSI) Mar.2014. Web.30.Mar. 2014 http://www.ducksters.com/history/china/song_dynasty.php Retrieved 2014.03.30

THE IMPACT OF THE MANDJURIAN AND SUBSEQUENT EMPIRES ON THE CHINESE CIVILIZATION IN THE SCOPE OF SPACE AND TIME

Yuan, Ming and Qing Dynasties

After a long war in which firearms played an important role, the Mongols conquered China and established The Yuan Dynasty also known as the Mongol Dynasty (1271-1368 AD) founded by Kublai Khan, the grandson of Genghis Kahn who had established the Mongolian Khanate in 1206. Kublia Khan adopted many of the customs and institutions of China. The Yuan Dynasty was the first to rule all of China from Dadu, (also known as Khanbalik; now present day Beijing). The Yuan Dynasty was the first time that non-native people ruled all of China. In the historiography of Mongolia, it is generally considered to be the continuation of the Mongol Empire (Prawdin 2005).

Kublai ended the centuries-long situation in which many independent regimes had existed side by side, by forming a united country that brought Xinjian, Tibet and Yunnan under its sway. During the Song-Yuan period, the "four great inventions" in science and technology of the Chinese people in ancient times – papermaking, printing, the compass and gunpowder, were further developed and spread abroad.[21] He was a strong supporter of the Silk Road trade routes which furthered contact between Chinese technologies and those of the west.

Although paper money had been used earlier in China, Yuan was the first dynasty to use paper currency as the main medium of monetary circulation.

The Yuan Dynasty lasted less than a century and was overthrown by the Ming Dynasty (1368-1644) in 1368 after a peasant uprising broke out against the Mongols. The leading peasant Zhu Yuanzhang became reigning Emperor Taizu, establishing the Ming Dynasty in Nanjing. The Ming Dynasty is often called the last of the great Chinese dynasties. It ruled Ancient China from 1368 to 1644 and was to be followed by the Qing Dynasty.

The Ming Dynasty, also called Empire of the Great Ming, was the ruling dynasty of China for 276 years (1368–1644) following the collapse of the Mongol-led Yuan dynasty. The Ming, described by some as "one of the greatest eras of orderly government and social stability in human history" (Reischauer 1960) and the last dynasty in China ruled by ethnic Han Chinese.

The Ming Dynasty was considered an era of significant, large-scale engineering projects which included rebuilding the Grand Canal, impacting trade and the economy and bringing the Great Wall closer to completion. During the Ming Dynasty, a fleet of many ships made seven distant voyages. They passed the Southeast Asian countries, the Indian Ocean, the Persian Gulf and Maldives Islands in addition to exploring as far as Somalia and Kenya. These were the largest scale and longest voyages in the world before the age of Columbus.

Eventually, the Ming was beset by internal power struggles, natural disasters, drought and famine along with threats from the north. The Manchu, a nomadic, warlike people saw the turmoil within China and in the 1640's they invaded and formed the Qing Dynasty (1644-1911 AD). The Qing is known as the last imperial dynasty in China.

In 1644, the Manchus, a semi-nomadic people from northeast of the Great Wall, conquered the crumbling Ming state and established their own Qing (or Pure) dynasty, which

---

[21] Law China Digest, http://www.lawinfochina.com/Legal/index.shtm Retrieved 2014.03.31

lasted nearly 300 years. During the first half of this period, the Manchus extended their rule over a vast empire that grew to encompass new territories in Central Asia, Tibet, and Siberia. The Manchus also established their hegemony over Chinese cultural traditions as an important means of demonstrating their legitimacy as Confucian-style rulers.[22]

The brilliant reigns of the Kangxi (r.1662–1722) and Qianlong (r.1736–95) emperors display a period when the Manchus embraced Chinese cultural traditions and the court became a leading patron in the arts as China enjoyed an extended period of political stability and economic prosperity.[23]

China was among the most advanced economies in the world in the 18th century. It is known to have been the largest and most powerful empire of the world in 1795. Historian Kenneth Pomeranz noticed in the 1990's that at the start of the 18th century, China (or at least the Yangtze valley) and Britain were economically in a similar position, yet within a century and a half, Britain's industrial revolution had taken off. Pomeranz went on to describe how within a century and a half, the British made significant industrial advances while China had not. What accounted for the difference? Pomeranz' argument was complex, but he suggested that the easy availability of coal and the existence of overseas colonies gave Britain an unmatchable advantage.

A long period of peace during the Qing contributed to a sharp increase in population growth with ever more people unable to sustain themselves according to Chinese scholar, Dr. Theobald Ulrich, University of Tubingen. The Qing Dynasty was unable to expand the size and capacity of government in order to cope timely with the changing conditions. By the end of the 18th century increasing problems were prevalent. Monetary inflation and corruption among the officialdom led to numerous peasant rebellions and trade wars. Historians agree that the fall of the Qing Dynasty, when the Xinhai Revolution in 1911 overthrew the Qing's rule, marked the modern era in Chinese history.

IMPACT OF THE BRITISH EMPIRE ON THE CHINESE CIVILIZATION IN THE SCOPE OF SPACE AND TIME AND THE RISE OF THE CHINESE DIASPORA

Opium Wars, Unequal Treaties, and the Exploitation of China

The Qing Dynasty (1644 to 1912 AD), was the last Chinese dynasty preceding the formation of the Republic of China. This dynasty, nearing the end of its reign, was unable to compete with or defend itself against modern military powers and was subject to depredations by the British Empire as well as other foreign powers.

Conflict between China and the British Empire set the stage for how China would be treated by other powers and was initiated when the Chinese attempted to prohibit the importation of opium into China by British merchants.

---

[22] Hearn, Maxwell K. "The Qing Dynasty (1644–1911): Painting". In Heilbrunn Timeline of Art History. New York: The Metropolitan Museum of Art, 2000–. http://www.metmuseum.org/toah/hd/qing_1/ hd_qing_1.htm (October 2003) Retrieved 2014.04.01

[23] ^ Hearn, Maxwell K. "The Qing Dynasty (1644–1911) Heilbrunn Timeline of Art History

The use of opium as a medicine had been known in China since ancient times. It was not until after contact with Europeans that the practice of abusing opium as a recreational drug was introduced (Ebrey 2010). Even as a recreational drug, opium was not a significant problem in China until Britain forced large-scale trade in the drug.

Britain found itself in a quandary in relation to trade with China. Chinese goods such as tea, silk, and porcelain were in demand in Europe but China would only accept silver in exchange for its goods. The Chinese demand for payment in silver caused a drain of hard currency from Britain yet the demand for Chinese products remained high. The requirement for silver by the Chinese was particularly problematic for the British as British currency was based on a gold standard. Trade with China was strictly limited by the Chinese government regarding the method of payment for Chinese merchandise and the locations where trading was allowed to occur. The rules for trade established by the Chinese caused an imbalance detrimental to British financial interests.

To add an additional complication, the Chinese emperor held his power as a "Mandate of Heaven," a concept similar to the European concept of the "Divine Right of Kings." The mandate did not affect low level trading between foreign merchants and the Chinese, but it did affect official contact between foreign powers and the imperial court. Official contact with the Chinese court required gifts in the form of tribute and acknowledgement of the superiority of the Chinese emperor over the client-nation offering the tribute (Fairbank 1953). Acknowledging the superiority of the Chinese was a requirement western powers found distasteful.

The British solution to the trade imbalance was opium. In essence, large quantities of relatively inexpensive opium produced in British India, under the control of the East India Company, were available for export. Opium would be introduced into China covertly by British merchants, in exchange for Chinese silver. Silver, obtained from the trade in opium could then be used to purchase Chinese goods. From the British perspective the problem was solved.

The mechanics of the operation are described by Lapo Salucci in the *Depths of Debt: Debt, Trade and Choices,* as follows: Considering that importation of opium into China had been virtually banned by Chinese law, the East India Company established an elaborate trading scheme partially relying on legal markets, and partially leveraging illicit ones. British merchants carrying no opium would buy tea in Canton on credit, and would balance their debts by selling opium at auction in Calcutta. From there, the opium would reach the Chinese coast hidden aboard British ships then smuggled into China by native merchants. In 1797 the company further tightened its grip on the opium trade by enforcing direct trade between opium farmers and the British, and ending the role of Bengali purchasing agents. British exports of opium to China grew from an estimated 15 tons in 1730 to 75 tons in 1773. The product was shipped in two thousand chests, each containing 140 pounds (64 kg) of opium (Ebrey 2010).

In 1729 the import of opium into China stood at 200 chests annually (Ebrey 2010). At this point in time the Chinese issued their first anti-opium edict, which had no substantial effect on the officially illegal trade. The Chinese issued a second prohibition against opium in 1799. By 1800 the number of chests of opium being imported into China had reached 4,500. The decade of the 1830's witnessed a rapid rise in opium imports and by 1838 the number of chests of opium being imported into China had reached 40,000 (Greenberg 1969).

Due to the removal of significant quantities of silver from the Chinese economy caused by opium trafficking as well as the growing number of opium addicts, the Chinese government began actively enforcing the opium edict. Chinese opium dealers were arrested and foreign merchant's opium stocks were seized (Ebrey 2010).

In response to Chinese attempts to halt the opium trafficking, the British government sent military forces to China to protect the drug trade. These forces attacked Chinese coastal areas forcing the Chinese to agree to British terms. The Treaty of Nanking, at the conclusion of the first Opium War (1839-1842), opened China to expanded trade, including the trade in opium (Ebrey 2006), as well as other concessions which included British control of Hong Kong, fixing low tariffs favorable to the British, and granting extraterritorial rights to westerners in China, a most favored nation status, and diplomatic representation.

The Chinese court refused to accept the terms of the treaty and a Second Opium War (1856-1860) was fought resulting in a second British victory and imposition of the Treaty of Tientsin. Similar treaties, known as the Unequal Treaties, were subsequently made between China and the United States, and between China and France.

The Opium Wars and the Unequal Treaties began the period known as China's "Century of Humiliation," a time of intervention by western powers and Japan in the affairs of China (Kaufman 2010). It was also a time which saw the birth of Chinese nationalism, resentment of foreigners and foreign interests, and a desire to throw off the shackles of foreign domination.

The Chinese Diaspora was a phenomena which began at this time and continued into the 20th century. Starvation and incessant warfare made life untenable for many, especially peasants, and caused large numbers to leave the mainland, seeking work where it could be found. Work existed in a variety of foreign destinations at different times and allowed for expatriate communities to form in other countries. These small communities of Chinese maintained the customs, values, and language of their homeland while also maintaining communication with family members who had remained in China. They also participated in coming political changes in China by providing financial support to people with very revolutionary ideas.

THE ROLE OF THE CONSTITUTIONAL REPUBLIC ON THE CHINESE CIVILIZATION IN SPACE AND TIME AND THE EXPANSION OF THE CHINESE DIASPORA

The Qing Dynasty was failing at the end of the 19th century. Attempts at reforms within the framework of Imperial rule were too little, too late, or ineffective. Imperial Qing conservatism, obstruction, and nepotism stalled critical programs such as the Self-Strengthening Movement to westernize China's military capabilities. Foreign powers saw China as an opportunity for exploitation.

In 1894-1895 Qing forces fought Imperial Japan in the First Sino-Japanese War, a conflict conducted primarily for control of Korea, a country important to both empires and which had historically been a vassal state of china. The modernized Imperial Japanese military efficiently defeated larger and supposedly modernized Qing forces on both land and sea after little over half a year of warfare. The humiliating loss of the war, and control of Korea, caused increased dissatisfaction with the effectiveness of the Qing Dynasty. It also showed the failure of the Qing Dynasty's attempts to modernize its army and navy when compared in actual military engagements with the Japanese. China lost significant prestige with this defeat as well as the resulting regional shift of power from China.

Many Chinese fled their country beginning in the 19th century with starvation and warfare among the primary causes. Additionally, there was also a market for Chinese labor abroad, including the United States, Australia, South Africa and Southeast Asia. Chinese immigrants formed communities in these foreign locations. Despite restrictive and racist laws in some jurisdictions they were able to establish themselves, start families and open businesses. Communication was maintained with families and friends remaining in the mainland. Chinese culture, beliefs and values continued to be observed in the new communities, but many relocated-Chinese shared the desire for a political change in China as well, and provided funds to revolutionaries such as Sun Yat-sen who spoke of making democratic changes in China.

For years, starting after the Opium Wars, foreign powers began to divide China into spheres of influence where foreign business operations ran unchecked and Christian missionaries operated with impunity, regardless of the wishes of the majority of Chinese. Anti-foreign resentments, and anti-Christian sentiments escalated.

The first major revolt threatening foreign interests within China was the Boxer Rebellion (1898-1900). This peasant rebellion, supported by the Imperial Court, was anti-foreign as well as anti-Christian. The Chinese army sided with the peasants. The rebellion was halted by a unified military expedition of the Eight Nation Alliance, an alliance of foreign powers made up of Austria-Hungary, France, Germany, Italy, Japan, Russia, the United Kingdom and the United States. As part of the diplomatic agreement ending the rebellion, the Qing Dynasty agreed to pay an indemnity of 450 million taels* of silver (*Chinese measure of currency) to the foreign powers. The diplomatic agreement ending hostilities is known as the Boxer Protocol, or the Xinchou Treaty, and is considered one of the Unequal Treaties forced upon China.

Many Chinese were ready for change. Revolution was brought to China by reform minded Chinese, including many officers in the military, who had been exposed to western concepts.

In 1911 the Wuchang Uprising, supported by Chinese military forces which had been infiltrated by revolutionaries of Sun Yat-sen's anti-Qing alliance, and the subsequent Xinhai Revolution led to the demise of the Qing Dynasty and the formation of the Republic of China. Qing attempts to raise capital by nationalizing privately financed railroads to pay indemnities demanded in the Boxer Protocol, were only some of the many factors leading to revolt. Ethnic resentment against the Qing was also present because the Qing were Manchu as opposed to the majority Han population.

The Qing Dynasty was replaced by a western style, constitutional government, the Republic of China, provisionally led by Sun Yat-sen. Sun was popular with Chinese who had fled the mainland and established communities in foreign countries. The Chinese diaspora retained strong ties with China and concern about affairs in China and financially supported Sun's efforts. Sun sought to create a republican style government and was concerned with the welfare of the common people and particularly with the equitable ownership and control of farmland.

Sun was soon forced to hand over political power to Yuan Shikai, who had control of the country's largest military force, but Sun continued to work for the betterment of China. Yuan abused his power making deals with foreign governments for personal benefit, but secured his position after a second revolt in 1913. In 1915 Yuan finally declared himself emperor which initiated revolts around China. Yuan stepped down from power in 1916 after which China returned to a nominally representative form of government.

An additional insult to China came with the end of the First World War. Chinese land which had been under the control of Germany was given, in the Treaty of Versailles, to Japan rather than being returned to the control of China. China had not been an aligned country during the First World War, but there had been the recruitment of workers, known as the Chinese Labor Corps, to assist Britain and France with support services and manual labor. Demonstrations were held by Chinese students in Beijing to protest the ceding of Chinese land to the Japanese by foreign governments. Terms such as the May Fourth Movement and New Culture Movement describe movements within China which expressed disillusionment with traditional Chinese values and advocating for the adoption of some western concepts such as democracy and science.

The Republic of China suffered from widening political divisions but was able to conduct the Northern Expedition to attack some of the major warlords who held regional control and plagued much of China. Even after the Northern Expedition, the Republic controlled only limited areas including the Yangtze River Delta. The division between the Kuomintang and Chinese Communist Party increased with the two parties engaging in civil war for control of China. Japan invaded Manchuria (north-east China) in 1931. The second Sino-Japanese War began in 1937 with the Japanese capturing Nanking, the capitol of the republic by the end of that year.

The early 20th century was a time of ideological challenge and conflict for China, where many came to reject their Confucian and traditional teachings for new ideological concepts.

Two major forces emerged as China struggled to find the direction it would take into the 20th century: The Kuomintang (China's National People's Party) and the Chinese Communist Party. A civil war between the two rival Chinese political powers, complicated by the invasion of China by Japan, was not resolved until after WWII when the Kuomintang were forced to flee the mainland for Taiwan, leaving the Chinese Communist Party in sole possession of mainland China.

With the expulsion of the Kuomintang from the mainland the Chinese Communist Party established the People's Republic of China. The Republic of China continues to exist on Taiwan.

THE ROLE OF THE PRC ON THE CHINESE CIVILIZATION IN SPACE AND TIME AND ITS RELATIONS WITH THE CHINESE DIASPORA

With the defeat of Japanese forces by the Allies in 1945, occupying Japanese forces were disarmed and expelled from China. Some surrendered Japanese weapons were delivered by Russia to Chinese Communist forces against the wishes of the ROC. The civil war between the Chinese Communist Party and Kuomintang forces resumed. Communist and Nationalist forces used varying tactics in the civil war and the Communists eventually gained superiority. In 1949 Kuomintang forces withdrew from mainland China and relocated the Nationalist government to Taiwan, formerly the island of Formosa. Some limited hostilities continued and both the Communists and Nationalists made claims to be the sole, legitimate government of China, but the Communists were in de facto control of mainland China. A state of war between the two continued with some limited hostilities. No peace treaty or armistice has ever been signed to formally end the civil war. Both the PRC and the ROC maintain a "one China," policy.

With the withdrawal of ROC forces from the mainland, Mao Zedong, who had come to prominence in the Chinese Communist Party during the years of warfare, declared the creation of the People's Republic of China, taking the leadership role in the new nation. The PRC was initially backed by the USSR but relations between the two nations deteriorated and a split occurred.

Mao's Kuomintang rival, Generalissimo Chiang Kai-shek, maintained his exile government, the Republic of China, on the island of Taiwan. At first, the United States did not support the exiled ROC. It did however, come to the aid of the Nationalists after the outbreak of the Korean War.

During the Korean War, China backed the North Koreans while United Nations forces engaged for the South. The United States played a major part with the UN forces in support of South Korea. The Korean War ended in stalemate with a demilitarized zone dividing the country, but China had established itself as a major regional power with its support of the North.

Mao ruled the PRC until his death in 1976. During the time of Mao's rule several significant programs having disastrous results were initiated, but other actions with results beneficial to China and the Chinese people were also initiated.

The Great Leap Forward from 1958-1961, the Cultural Revolution from 1966 until Mao's death in 1976, and other programs may have been responsible for over 70 million excessive deaths during peacetime (Teiwes 1999).

The Great Leap Forward was a social and economic program initiated by the Communist Party of China which lasted from 1958 to 1961. It was intended to rapidly transform the country from an agrarian state into an industrialized and collective socialist state. The Great Leap Forward occurred during a time of drought and poor weather which, when combined with other factors caused the Great Chinese Famine, also known as Three Years of Natural Disasters.

The Cultural Revolution, starting in 1966, was a program to impose socialist orthodoxy and to eliminate capitalist and non-communist influences within China. The campaign impacted all aspects of Chinese life. During this time the Red Guard terrorized the country, adversely affecting industry, education and transportation. The Red Guard was finally reigned in but aspects of the Cultural Revolution did not come to a complete end until after the death of Mao.

One of the most significant aspects of Mao's reign was not a program but a condition. For the first time since before the Opium Wars, China's sovereignty was secured. Recognition of the new country stalled because of polarization caused by the Cold War, and a pretense was maintained by many nations, led by the United States, that the Republic of China was the sole legitimate government of China. For all intents and purposes, the People's Republic of China was now China. The United Nations finally recognized the PRC as the sole, lawful representative of China to the UN in Resolution 2758 on October 25, 1971. The United States, under President Jimmy Carter, recognized the People's Republic of China as the sole legitimate government of China on January 1, 1979.

Figure 2.9. Joint American-Chinese Lecture; Visiting Professor Harry Rhodes with Prof. Dr. Ling Zhou are teaching at Zhongnan University of Economics and Law in Wuhan, Hubei, China. (Photo L. Rhodes).

Political turmoil and power struggles occurred with the death of Chairman Mao but Deng Xiaoping eventually took charge and working with other, elder party members, embarked China on a program emphasizing openness, economic reform, and guiding the country to a market driven economy. Farming operations were liberated from being collective operations and reforms were implemented in industry as well. The diaspora continued. Changes in US law began allowing more Chinese (through separate quotas for Taiwan and Hong Kong as well as mainland China) to enter the United States.

Other changes in China are less visible but no less important. China offers students in the university system the opportunity to attend universities abroad. Many students and professionals from the PRC come to the United States and other countries to enhance their education, while at the same time, encouraging foreign students and professionals to study at Chinese universities. The result of this program encourages a culture of increasingly, well-educated and motivated scholars with world class educations and an expanded world view. (Figure 2.9)

With the creation of the PRC China found its modern identity.

Conclusion

From its formative, cultural beginnings by the Yellow River, to modern times, China has gone through countless changes through which we find a remarkable and unique history spanning almost 5,000 years. Having the longest continuous civilization on earth, China remains distinct as a complex civilization. She has survived great periods of unrest yet continues to maintain a condition of relative peace for her people and the world. With the early cultural development leading to civilization; technology; standardized laws and governance; inventions; social sophistication; economic stability; challenges of balancing the environment with the demands of development and energy needs; China is positioned to be a leader of civilizational stability and security.

In the 21st century China and its civilization there is in a phase of renewal and transformation from a closed and local power to open and global economic power.

REFERENCES

Allan, S. (2007). *Erlitou and the Formation of Chinese Civilization: Toward a New Paradigm. The Journal of Asian Studies*, 66, 461-496 Cambridge University Press.

Boltz, William. (1999). *Language and Writing*. In Loew, Michael: Shaughnessey, Edward L. The Cambridge History of Ancient China. Cambridge: Cambridge University Press. 74-123

Carr, Brian, et al. (2012). *Companion Encyclopaedia of Asian Philosophy*. New York, NY: Taylor and Francis Library. p.466

Chan, Kwang-chih. *The Archaeology of Ancient China*, Yale University Press, 1986

Chinn, Annping. (2007). *The Authentic Confucius*. New York, NY: Scribner. p. 43

Deady, K. W. & Dubois, M. L. (2004). *Ancient China*. Mankato, MN: Capstone Press.

Ebrey, Patricia Buckley, Walthall, Anne & Palais, James B. (2006). *Pre-Modern East Asia: A Cultural, Social, and Political History*. Boston, MA: Houghton-Mifflin Co. p. 29

Ebrey, Patricia Buckley, Walthill, Anne & Palais, James B. (2006). *East Asia*. Boston, MA: Heughton Mifflin. 378-382

Ebrey, Patricia Buckley. (1999). *The Cambridge Illustrated history of China*. Cambridge: Cambridge University Press.

Ebrey, Patricia Buckley. (2010). *9. Manchus and Imperialism: The Qing Dynasty 1644-1900*. The Cambridge Illustrated History of China (2nd Edition). Cambridge University Press. p. 236

Fairbank, John K. (1953). *Trade and Diplomacy on the Chinese Coast: The Opening of the Treaty Ports, 1842-1845*. Cambridge, MA: Harvard Press. 27-29

Fiskesjo, Magnus & Chen, Xingcan. 2004. *China before China*. J. G. Andersson (editor). *Ding Wenjiang and the Discovery of China's Prehistory*. Stockholm: Museum of Far Eastern Antiquities

Greenberg, Michael. (1969). *British Trade and the Opening of China, 1800-42*. Cambridge Studies in Economic History. Cambridge: Cambridge University Press. p. 113

Higham, Ch. (2004). *Encyclopedia of ancient Asian civilizations*. New York, NY: Facts on File, Inc.

Homer, H. (1938-55). *The history of the former Han Dynasty by Pan Ku.*, (3 vol). Baltimore: Waverly Press.

Jiang, Cheng An. (1998). *Empress of China: Wu Ze Tian*. Monterey, CA. USA: Victory Press

Kaufman, Alison Adock. (2010). *The Century of Humiliation, "Then and Now: Chinese Perceptions of the International Order*. Pacific Focus 25.1. 1-33

Lung, Rachel. (2011). *Interpreters in Early Imperial China*. Amsterdam: John Benjamins Publishing Co. p.5

Mair, Victoria H. w/ Brooks. E. Bruce. (2013). *Was There a Xia Dynasty?* Sino Platonic Papers, No. 238. Pennsylvania: University of Pennsylvania

Morton, W. S. (1995). *China: its history and culture* (3rd ed. ed.). New York: McGraw-Hill Dubs,

Morton, W. Scott. (1995). *China: Its History and Culture* (3rd ed.). USA: McGraw-Hill. p. 49

Mote, F. W. & Twitchett, D. eds. (1998). *The Cambridge History of China.*, In Vol.8, *The Ming Dynasty, 1368-1644, Part 1 and 2*. Cambridge, UK: Cambridge University Press.

Pines, Yuri. (2002). *Foundations of Confucian thought: intellectual life in the Chunqui period (722-453 B.C.E.)*. Honolulu: University of Hawaii Press

Prawdin, Michael. (2005). *The Mongol Empire*. New Jersey: Transaction Publishers

Pringle, Heather. (1998). *The Slow Birth of Agriculture. Science., 20*. Vol 282. No 5393. p. 1446

Reischauer, Edwin Oldfather. (1960). *A History of East Asian Civilization*. Vol 1. East Asia: The Great Tradition. New York, NY: Harvard

Teiwes, Frederick C. & Sun, Warren (1999). *China's Road to Disaster: Mao, Central Politicians, and Provincial Leaders in the Unfording of the Great Leap Forward, 1955-1959*. Contemporary China Papers. Armonk, NY: M.E.Sharpe. 52-55

Wagner, D. B. (1999). *The EarliestUse of Iron in China,* in Young, S.M.M., Pollard, A.M.., Bud, P. et al., *Metals in Antiquity,* Oxford: Archaeopress, 1-9

Zhou, Jinghao. (2003). *Remaking China's Public Philosophy for the Twenty First Century*. Westport: Greenwood Publishing Group, Inc. p. 34

Zhou, Jixu. (2006). *The Rise of Agricultural Civilization in China*. Sino Platonic Papers, No. 175. Pennsylvania: University of Pennsylvania

Part II. Civilizing Culture

In: Chinese Civilization in the 21st Century
Editors: Andrew Targowski and Bernard Han

ISBN: 978-1-63321-960-1
© 2014 Nova Science Publishers, Inc.

Chapter 3

OLD FAITH FOR THE NEW MILLENNIUM: RELIGIONS AND THE CHINESE CIVILIZATION IN THE 21ST CENTURY

Patrick Fuliang Shan[*]
Grand Valley State University, US

ABSTRACT

The purpose of this chapter is to highlight the important role of traditional belief systems in shaping contemporary Chinese civilization. Although all religions suffered in the long yet hostile 20th century, in particular during the Cultural Revolution, their revival in recent decades has been astonishingly phenomenal. An analysis of this latest resurgence displays that spirituality has become inseparable from the Chinese way of life. More importantly, a special probe into Christianity shows its remarkable growth. Of course, ethnic religions are vital for the Chinese state, as any significant event among those believers carries international repercussions. The recent religious renaissance will enable the traditional belief systems to spread continuously among the largest national population and impact China's spiritual redemption, social relations, political affairs, and international relations.

INTRODUCTION

China is not an atheist country; on the contrary, it has its own complex religious traditions. In fact, its ancient civilization has been so intertwined with religion that it cannot be separated from certain belief systems, just as Arnold Joseph Toynbee had long argued for the close tie between religion and civilization. Major global religions have impacted China and enjoyed an inroad into the Chinese spirituality just like Chinese religious traditions impacted other East Asian regions. Furthermore, almost all ethnic groups have their religious practices. Indeed, the altars inside China are full of objects signifying Heaven, God, deities,

---
[*] Corresponding author: Email: patrickshan@hotmail.com.

ancestors, spirits, ghosts, and other worshipping objects. Those supernatural beings suffuse social relationships, outshine individual conduct, penetrate communal ethos, infiltrate political thinking, and impact literal viewpoints. Chinese culture cannot sustain itself without those rich legacies. Religious facilities, such as temples, shrines, ancestor halls, churches, mosques, holy monuments, sacred sites, godly statues, divine objects, or reverent characters, can be found in every corner of the country. Nevertheless, almost all religions endured a hostile and detrimental 20th century, largely due to liberalism, communism, secularism and other ideologies which perceive religion as outdated superstition, if not significantly harmful. Miraculously, after the long period of anguish sorrows, the old religions have enjoyed a dynamic resurgence and have experienced a sturdy renaissance in recent decades. As those age-old beliefs rebound, they have reshaped daily life and will exist as a core value of China's civil life in the new century.

CHINA'S RELIGIOUS LANDSCAPE

China is often viewed as the only uninterrupted and continuous civilization among all cultures. This means that the present religious practices could be traced back to their origins in the remote ancient times. The incessant continuity allows Chinese religions to penetrate into daily life, dominate popular literature, infiltrate communal life, regulate social behaviors, saturate material refinement, and impact administrative management. The old belief is so ingrained inside the culture that the Chinese did not even coin a term of "religion" [*zongjiao*] as we are familiar with today. The current phrase of "religion" was created when the modern translators encountered Western religions. Traditionally, the Chinese used "teaching" [*jiao*], "rituals" [*li*], "sacrifice" [*ji*], or others to depict their religious activities, their sacred doctrines, and their social implications.

First of all, "three ways to one goal" is appealing to most Chinese who practice the three major religions in a syncretic approach (Fitzgerald, pp. 568-569). These include Confucianism, Buddhism and Daoism which are intertwined and integrated to shape a colorful kaleidoscopic world. This intermingled attitude might be disconcerting to Westerners, because they have a monotheistic religion and their God prohibits idol-worshipping. Nevertheless, the practitioners of those three religions in China see their way as natural and normal. In their spiritual realm, the lack a jealous God, who denounces the existence of his rivals, allows the Chinese to comfortably worship Heaven, honor spirits, respect ghosts, venerate deceased relatives, tolerate new religions, and accept new deities.

To many Westerners, it is hard to deem Confucianism as a "true" religion, because of the virtual absence of a commonly worshipped deity. For more than two millennia, however, it has defined Chinese culture, shaped Chinese religious activities, and impacted Chinese spiritual life. Confucianism accepts the worship of Heaven, relies on the mandate of Heaven, believes in fate, places faith in supernatural spirits, and honors deceased ancestors. Because Confucianism emphasizes the use of rites to regulate human relations, Herbert Fingarette claims that it sees "human community as holy rite" (Fingarette, pp. 1-17). Although some view Confucianism as agnosticism or rationalism, no one denies its religiosity and its religious tenets. For this reason, most Western scholars offer a detailed discourse over Confucianism whenever they introduce world religions (Zaehner, pp. 357-373). Peimin Ni asserts that Confucius was "a spiritual leader" (Ni, pp. 57-98) because his teachings are quite religious. Jeffrey N. Wasserstrom claims that Confucius "has occasionally been elevated to the status of a saint or a godlike figure, with temples being devoted to him ... and his hometown of Qufu being transformed into a pilgrimage site" (Wasserstrom, p. 10).

Daoism was originally more a philosophy created by Lao Zi whose *Dao De Jing* [The Classic of the Way and Power] is its canon. Daoism promotes the pursuit of the Way, a belief in natural life, the advocacy of simplicity, the approval of non-action [*wuwei*], and the exclusion of deep social engagement (Lao Tzu, pp. 1-85). Yet, through particular phases of evolution, Daoism turned out to be, as Ronnie L. Littlejohn puts it, "one of the most ancient of the world's spiritual structures" (Littlejohn, p. 1). Not only did Lao Zi become the object of worship, but other deities were also installed. In the Daoist pantheon, innumerable deities are to be found. Furthermore, Daoism reassures immortality through personal endeavors and by assistance of divinities. It champions the lengthening of one's life via making cinnabars, practicing alchemy, engaging in martial arts, and many other techniques. Ultimately, religious professionals [*daoshi*] are to organize events, guide activities, train converts, and construct shrines.

Buddhism was imported from India but has been a widely accepted religion in China. The reason of its total indigenization is its offering fills a spiritual gap left by China's native religions. For example, Buddhism offers salvation in the next life and grants an opportunity of entering the eternal joyful realm [*nirvana*]. Nevertheless, Buddhism experienced a dramatic metamorphosis as Sinified Buddhism became Mahayana Buddhism, diverging from the original, fundamental teachings. Buddha is worshipped as a deity and Guanyin [Bodhisattva] is viewed as a savior. Guanyin's gender was changed from an original male to a compassionate female. According to late Harvard University professor John King Fairbank, China once experienced a Buddhist Age (Fairbank, pp. 72-73). Yet, as time passed, many new denominations emerged such as the Tiantai Sect that emphasizes intellectual pursuit of Buddhist wisdom, the Chan Sect that stresses meditation and inner pursuit, and the Pure Land [*Jingtu*] Sect that pushes for immediate salvation through prayers to Amitabha Buddha and Guanyin. Today, Buddhist monasteries can be found in almost all counties throughout China and serve as the centers of Chinese style spirituality (Chen, pp. 134-170).

Figure 3.1. The Nanhai Chan Buddhist Temple in Runan, Henan Province. (Public Domain).

The religious landscape in China is quite complicated since many different beliefs co-exist to compete for faithful followers. Because of this multi-faceted characteristic, Chinese religious life tends to retain its own features. As previously mentioned, the syncretic approach enables the Chinese to practice many religions simultaneously. As an educated man, a Chinese in his office is a Confucian, as he respects his superiors and endeavors to fulfill his duties. When he returns home, he might be a Daoist as he intends to relax to enjoy a natural way of life. Occasionally, he might visit a Buddhist temple to burn incense and pray for benefits. The syncretism works for most people, even though religious professionals strongly champion for a single faith and advise people to keep away from other religions.

Second, most Chinese religions have evolved, at least from the historical perspective, from philosophy to religion. Even now as a belief system, a religion still carries on its philosophical teachings. In many ways, Chinese religion functions as a philosophical-religious tradition, or a humanist belief, or a philosophical religion, or an ethical faith.

Third, Chinese religions tend to be stratified for different social classes to keep ties with many religions, although people tend to retain a particular link with one religion. For example, most upper class members are traditionally associated with Confucianism. Some educated men might keep a strong tie with Daoism. Yet, many uneducated people simply practice all the religions.

Fourth, Chinese religions are in general tolerant to other faiths, even though occasional conflicts occur. The lack of a monotheistic deity helps many religions not only co-exist peacefully together, but also prompts them to absorb each other's teachings. Throughout Chinese history, there has not been a Western-patterned religious war.

Fifth, the large size of the huge territory is porous to regional practices and lenient to communal faith, allowing locals to worship different and diverse provincial deities. In other words, some gods or goddesses are the objects of worship in certain confined areas, beyond which they will not be honored. For example, the Goddess, Mazu, in Fujian, Taiwan and other coastal regions, is much venerated and glorified as a protector for seafaring peoples. However, Mazu is alien to Northern Chinese. Mazu, according to local annals, was a local woman during the Song Dynasty in Fujian who died in the sea. Somehow, she turned out to be an almighty goddess. This verifies the statement that Chinese religion is amorphous and adaptive, allowing provincials to acquire new deities and to adopt additional divinities.

Sixth, the spiritual and human realms can communicate with each other and establish relations. Because of this belief, Chinese literature, ancient or modern, is rife with human-spirit interactions. Indeed, the human and ghost stories always attract a large audience and enthrall readers.

Seventh, a hierarchy exists in the spiritual world. Heaven is the supreme object for all to worship. Below it, however, spirits, ghosts, wraiths, and apparitions are numerous. Some of them are roaming human souls which result after physical demise. Many of those souls assume diverse identities as either ghosts or spirits, but some turn out to be deities, such as the Luo River Goddess who was the daughter of legendary king, Fuxi. The goddess drowned in the Luo River and thus turned out to be the river goddess.

Eighth, Confucianism stands out as extraordinary among all, because it served as the backbone of Chinese civilization as the state religion of the Chinese Empire until the early 20th century. In many ways, Confucianism determined Chinese social relationships, political hierarchy, and cultural structure. For about thirteen centuries prior to 1905, the Civil Service Examination System involved testing a candidates' knowledge of Confucian classics. As a result, imperial officialdom was dominated by Confucian elites to such an extent that one Western scholar termed it "literacracy" to highlight the scholars' rule. This institutionalized Confucianism allowed its religious teachings to permeate "every fiber of Chinese society" (Yang, p. 244).

THE SETBACKS IN THE 20TH CENTURY

Vincent Goossaert and David A. Palmer assert that China's modern religious history started in 1898, when Kang Youwei and Liang Qichao launched a reform movement under the cultural influence of the West. Although the movement failed, it initiated a battle assailing traditional religions. Kang and Liang intended to destroy temple cults in order to build Confucianism as a reformed religion. In the ensuring years until 1912, the government confiscated the assets from temples of various religions and used them for the schools. According to Goossaert and Palmer, this confiscation and destruction symbolized "the first all-out assault on religions in the name of modernization" (Goossaert & Palmer, p. 44, p. 49). Traditional religions suffered their first setback. Nevertheless, this did not ensure that Confucianism would prevail; in fact, it did not. The abolition of the Civil Service Examination System in 1905 was a heavy blow which pushed Confucianism to the margin. Accordingly, the collapse of scriptural Confucianism led to significant religious, social, political and other changes during the span of the 20th century (Elvin, pp. 352-389).

In such a historical background, the birth of the anti-superstition movement became inevitable. As Western influence intensified, Chinese religions were seen as superstitious, unscientific, and self-deceptive. Many intellectuals, who were exposed to Western culture, relegated traditional religions to be charlatan imposters. During the New Cultural Movement or the May Fourth Movement in the late 1910s, numerous scholars called to wipe out religions in order to embrace Mr. Sai (science) and Mr. De (democracy). In particular, they turned their rage against Confucius and blamed Confucianism for all existing evils. "Down with the Kong family store!" was the slogan for that generation of intellectuals who saw Confucianism "as the root of all the problems in China" (Ni, p. 54). Novels and stories were published to make fun of traditional beliefs. While condemning Confucius, they introduced rationalist philosophy, extolled scientific attainments, and championed individual autonomy.

The Chinese intellectuals, inspired by this so-called scientific mentality, moved on to denounce all religions in the 1920s and launched a decade long anti-religious movement. In 1922, the Antireligious Alliance was established and violent actions followed (Goossaert & Palmer, p. 51). Some scholars regard this movement as an impact of Marxism, yet the movement attracted a large number of intellectuals and students from all over urban areas, and even some from the rural regions. Needless to say, it caused damages to all the old faiths. Fortunately for the religions, this raging movement did not become an ever-lasting and rampant one, as it faded away from the historical arena abruptly after its swift rise.

After the collapse of the Qing Empire, the governments of the Republic of China, both the Northern Warlord regime and Chiang Kai-shek's state, were not hostile to religions, even though some individual officials embraced anti-religious attitudes. Mao Zedong's communist movement, however, was more aggressive and injurious to religions. In the 1920s, when Mao initiated the peasant movement in Hunan, he started to target religions and blamed them as being "supernatural (religious authority)" and an oppressive force. According to Mao, religions, "ranging from the king of Hell down to the town and village gods belonging to the Nether world, and from the Emperor of Heaven down to all various gods and spirits belonging to the celestial world" were all superstitious, repressive and onerous. When Mao waged a war against "the local tyrants and evil gentry," he vehemently attacked religions (Sommer, pp. 305-307).

Yet, Mao did not advocate an immediate eradication of all religious beliefs, even if after he seized power in 1949. In the following decades, Mao, like other communists, regarded the religion as a spiritual opium, but at the same time he intended to confine religious believers and limit their propagation rather than eliminate them. As a result, a national association for each religion was established in Beijing in the 1950s, and their branches and sub-groups were built throughout the country. Mao's laws specified that any citizens under eighteen years of age were not allowed to be new converts of any religion because of immaturity. At the same time, propaganda machines depicted religion as harmful and unscientific. The believers of religion under the Maoist regime were confined to small communities, and the number of their co-religionists tended to be tiny.

According to C. K. Yang, Mao's reign of twenty-seven years caused the decline of theistic religions, yet it also led to the search for a national devotion to the communist ideal. In other words, Mao's rule created a spiritual vacuum but helped communism become a new faith. The myths and retrospection of communist martyrs had a certain religious quality. A new member of the Communist Party usually experienced ecstatic enlightenment from his former confusion and entered a sudden spiritual condition. For their communist ideal, many pledged loyalty and expected the fulfillment of a classless society. Like many other religions, communism inspired emotional devotion and requires tenuous faith (Yang, pp. 378-404).

The most disastrous move against religions in modern Chinese history occurred during the Cultural Revolution (1966-76). Religions were designated as part of the so-called "four olds" [*sijiu*] – old customs, old habits, old culture, and old thinking. The Red Guards, the youths who vowed to defend Mao, were encouraged to destroy the four olds (Spence, p. 575). Many religious monasteries, shrines, churches, statues, and other worshipping sites were seriously damaged or even totally eradicated. Religious or holy scriptures were burnt, religious professionals were forced to recant their faith and their normal gatherings were terminated (Overmyer, p. 108). In fact, quite a few religious believers were put into labor camps for ideological reform. According to one estimate, about half a million Chinese died during those violent years of the Cultural Revolution and among them were religious believers.

It is noteworthy to mention that the Mao Cult during the Cultural Revolution reached its apex and could be, according to Laurence G. Thompson, seen as a new state religion. China was flooded with Maoist busts, badges, photos, portraits, paintings, and others. Mao's "Little Red Book," a collection of Mao's sayings, was in everyone's hands (Thompson, p. 138). Mao was hailed as "the Great Leader," "Great Teacher," "Supreme Commander," "Great Helmsman," and "the Red Sun" (Schoppa, p. 351). The Chinese prayed to Mao's portraits or statues before they had meals, offered self-criticism, and criticized others. They sang quasi-religious songs to glorify Mao as the person who was closer than parents and bigger than both sky and earth. They pledged obedience to Mao and promised to make sacrifices to his revolutionary cause. "Revolutionary asceticism and violence" were promoted and led to a strange political religiosity of "state ritual, the Mao Cult, self-cultivation and state-sponsored moral education." According to one estimate, 2.2 billion Maoist portraits and as many Maoist badges were produced and 40 million volumes of Mao's works were published (Goossaert & Palmer, p. 169, p. 187, p. 188).

Naturally, the Mao Cult faded into the historical backstage after Mao's death which formally marked the end of the Cultural Revolution. Gradually, the religious situation seemed to return to the pre-Cultural Revolution era as the government continued to manage the religious affairs, restrain believers, and curtail the number of converts. Nevertheless, the Cultural Revolution pattern of violence did not reoccur. Of course, the particular relationship between the state and religion could be viewed as a special episode of the communist rule, as the former (state) was in charge of the latter (religion), manipulated the latter and directed the latter. Indeed, political vicissitude has significantly impacted religious life until today.

THE ON-GOING RELIGIOUS REVIVAL

Chinese religions suffered enormously during the Maoist years particularly during the ten year tumult and tragedy of the Cultural Revolution. Soon after the pandemonium and after Deng Xiaoping initiated his reforms, religions in China started to enjoy a phenomenal revival, a speedy recovery, and an astonishing dissemination. Temples were renovated, shrines rebuilt, congregations held, seminaries reopened, rituals performed, festivals reorganized, and all kinds of "religious activities came bubbling to the surface" whenever and wherever conditions permitted. As the new century arrives, it seems that religions are an inseparable component of Chinese life, at least to a certain portion of the population. According to the two recent surveys conducted in 2001 and 2007, the percentage of those Chinese who specified their religious status as "none" dropped from 93% to 77.1% (Stark & Liu, p. 282, p. 286). In other words, at the threshold of the 21st century, nearly one quarter of the Chinese, more or less, practice a certain religion.

The reasons for the religious resurgence are many, but a careful review demonstrates several important factors. First of all, the loosened grip by the government over individual life was the foremost cause. As Deng Xiaoping's reforms were enforced, a new political and social environment was created. The former totalitarian control of citizens was replaced by a relatively liberal administration, which offered religions room to revive. When Arthur Waldron offered his interpretation of the recent religious revival, he boldly declared that "communism today is dead ... leaving in China a great void that some shared belief must fill" (Waldron, p. 325). Indeed, the overall control by Mao made the communist belief a quasi-religion, but Deng's reform changed it. This created a vacuum in the ideological realm as the spiritually hungry citizens endeavored to seek an alternative to fill the hollow space. For millions of individuals who suffered during the Cultural Revolution, they began to question their past behaviors, figure out the meaning of life, and cross-examine the existing faiths. This new inquiry naturally led many of them to religious life.

The economic growth inevitably contributed to the religious revival. As Deng's reforms resulted in a market economy and led to a free yet private ownership of enterprises, many religious believers became business owners who could sponsor the construction of new temples, the building of new religious sites, and the erection of new sacred monuments. As more sponsors gathered and more money collected, religious organizations could hire more hands for further expansion and quicker propagation. More importantly, religious leaders could make use of their donations to publish tracts, pamphlets, and scriptures for more readers and possibly more converts. Many religious organizations have worked with local officials to build holy sites, historical relics, and religious shrines to attract tourists as the officials need more revenues and the monks more souls. Indeed, in the two decades after the 1980s, almost all former religiously related historical sites were renovated and expanded, and they now are attracting a large number of visitors on a regular basis.

The outside influence upon the religious revival should not be ignored. During the Cultural Revolution, Chinese traditional religions in Hong Kong, Taiwan and Chinese diasporas were not impacted by the Maoist anti-religious violence. As the Maoist era ended and as China opened to the outside world, the Chinese from those outside communities went back to the mainland to help rebuild religious sites. For example, in Runan County, Henan Province, the famous Chan temple had laid in silence for decades. This temple, known as the Nanhai Chan Temple, however, was expanded with grandiose buildings, impressive statues, and spacious squares with millions of dollars from the Taiwan Chan association. Other overseas Chinese also devoted uncountable amounts of financial support to various projects in many provinces for the restoration and expansion of religious sites. All these efforts were easily carried out, because the virtual absence of language barriers and close affinity between the two partners.

The new technology and communication tools assisted the religious revival. Differing from the Maoist era during which people relied on the postal office to deliver letters for long distance communication, telephones were widely used in the Deng era. In the post-Deng era, more Chinese now use emails, cell phones, iPods, and the Internet for swift communication. Some Chinese view the new network communication as the most rapid, most wide-spread, and most direct mode to spread religious messages. Indeed, the Internet enables the religious missions to enjoy low costs and easy accessibility. More importantly, it possesses its own flexibility to sidestep legal jurisdiction, to traverse national boundaries, and to circumvent administrative supervision, and to eschew official manipulation (Lei, p. 56).

Figure 3.2. The Nanhai Chan Buddhist Temple in Runan, Henan Province, which was built recently with investments from Taiwan. (Public Domain).

The revival of Confucianism could be seen in a number of ways. Even though its religious status is not officially granted, its teaching on belief in heaven is still held by most Chinese. Ancestor worship, a central tenet of Confucianism, now emerges as a dominant cultural phenomenon in daily life in particular in the rural areas. Ancestor temples and clan halls are being built as the centers of family gatherings. In society, Confucian values are promoted for reaching personal ties and communal relationship. On the national level, the state publicly fosters Confucian ideals in order to establish a harmonious society [*hexie shehui*]. In recent decades, the Confucian classics, the Five Classics and Four Books, and in particular *The Analects*, have sold very well. Many have opened Confucian classes to attract interested learners. As the government emphasizes the Great Renaissance of the Chinese Nation, Confucianism fits the needs of the country to glorify the unbroken and continuous civilization. To reach out in the international community, the Chinese government has sponsored more than 300 Confucius Institutes to facilitate international cultural exchanges. To some Chinese, the newly built or restored Confucian temples are more a religious site rather than an educational spot.

Daoism is often regarded as a weak religion, because its doctrines are viewed to be too individualistic and anti-social, and its philosophy too abstract. Yet, Daoism is on rise in Chinese society. Some statistics could be employed to review the trend: in 1982 about twenty-one Daoist shrines were open for worshippers and visitors. The number jumped to 1,200 in 1995 and 1,600 in 1998. The total number today is far larger. The Daoist priesthood is not only restored, but also strengthened with newly trained professionals. Various Daoist denominations have enjoyed rapid growth, in particular the "Daoist living at home" that plays a unique role in the spread of the religion (Lai, pp. 425-426).

The revival of Buddhism is the most phenomenal upshot as it has become a newly risen prominent traditional faith. Buddhist temples have been refurbished and opened to the public to attract millions of believers and visitors. All the old denominations have reemerged to be a part of daily life. Professionals have been trained and assigned to various posts at temples to spread Buddhist teachings. Donations from believers have facilitated the construction and maintenance of religious sites. For most visitors, the mercy of the Buddha and the Bodhisattvas offers solace and comfort. The rich have pleaded for protection while the poor have prayed for blessings. Indeed, this religion offers peace and benediction while those beseechers are increasingly facing a huge disparity between the haves and the have-nots (Luo, v. 2, pp. 505-506).

Popular religion (or folk religion), which differs from the above-mentioned orthodox or well-structured religions, are also booming. On one hand, this reveals the multi-faceted nature of Chinese religiosity; on the other hand, it demonstrates the long traditional syncretic practices. Popular religion is not confined to one source of religious ideas but combines concepts from several religions and absorbs nutrients from all existing religions. Very often, it takes in mythical notions, acquires distinctive rituals, and adopts strange ideas from local culture. In many ways, popular religion has become an inseparable element of China's religious landscape, as it has penetrated into daily routines by conducting *fengshui* geomancy, presiding weddings and funerals, envisaging prophecies, foretelling divination, functioning as a moral force, participating in philanthropic events, and facilitating a tie connecting mainlanders and overseas Chinese communities (Lin, pp. 86-91).

Figure 3.3. A Buddhist temple in Shanghai. (Public Domain).

CHRISTIANITY IN CHINA

In the long history of Christianity in China, there were four waves of introduction. Nestorian Christianity arrived in the Chinese Empire as early as 635 during the Tang Dynasty. During the Yuan Dynasty (1279-1368), Catholic missions spread Christianity in China. From 1582 to 1724, about one thousand Jesuit missionaries worked diligently to win converts. In the 19th century, in particular after the Opium War, Protestant missions entered China for evangelicalism. Of course, the four waves encountered interruption but ever since the modern era, Christianity has become an inseparable ingredient of China's spiritual life. Henrietta Harrison's research of a Catholic village in Shanxi Province reveals an uninterrupted history of Christianity in that community for about three hundred years (Harrison, p. 2).

The monotheistic teaching inevitably clashed with traditional faith in multiple cases. The Boxer Uprising of 1900 targeted the Christians indiscriminately. Tragically, two hundred fifty foreign missionaries were killed and thousands upon thousands of Chinese converts were slaughtered. After the catastrophe, the changing political situation, new mission strategies, and Chinese Christians' efforts for indigenization enabled Christianity to enjoy a golden age in the first half of the 20th century. By 1949, around five million Chinese Christians lived in various regions of the country (Shan, pp. 33-47). Yet, the communist rule has proved to be a challenge. In the early 1950s, Mao Zedong's government organized the Protestants into one group which would be managed, supervised and guided by the government. This organization was called the Three Self Patriotic Movement for self-support, self-government and self-propagation (Bays, 2012, p. 160). The Catholics were organized into another group called the Catholic Patriotic Association. Foreign missionaries were driven out and the contact with the outside coreligionists was cut off. Under such a pressure, some believers became the so-called Red Christians, including Y. T. Wu [Wu Yaozong] who became the leader of the Three Self Patriotic Movement (Gao, pp. 338-352). Those who challenged the government were persecuted, jailed, and forced to labor on reform farms. Wang Mingdao (1900-1991), who refused to co-operate, suffered persecution for decades (Harvey, p. 115). According to the government arrangements, two nation-wide religious organizations symbolize the shaping of two denominations of Christianity: the Protestant Church [*xinjiao*] and the Catholic Church [*tianzhujiao*]. To many Chinese, these two are two completely different religions. The reorganization of Protestant believers resulted in the elimination of various minor denominations with just one officially recognized Protestant group under one umbrella of one national association.

Although the Cultural Revolution was not to target the Christians, it deeply impacted Christianity as it was criticized as a tool of imperialism and as such, it was relegated into the realm of the "four olds." Many churches were destroyed, congregations suspended, and new conversions became impossible. Many Christians were "suspected of counterrevolutionary activities," and the "outside world was without news of Christians in China for about ten years; the church there was effectively buried, but with the hope of resurrection" (Charbonnier, p. 443).

Indeed, this hope was not dashed but was reached in the post-Mao years, as the revival of Christianity has been under the way. Arthur Waldron remarked in 1998 that the renaissance of Christianity in China was "of a vigor that is astonishing ... more vigorous than at the height of Jesuit influence in the seventeenth century or at the peak of Protestant evangelization in the 1920s" (Waldron, p. 325-327). The old churches were rebuilt, new cathedrals constructed, and numerous converts flocked to congregations. Because there was no direct religious link with the outside world, Chinese theologians such as Ding Guangxun [K. H. Ting], Zhao Zichen [T. C. Chao] and many others developed a unique interpretation of Jesus through their meticulous scrutiny of the Bible. For example, Zhao views Christ as "universal love" and "moral perfection;" thus God is not a static reality rather a dynamic force seeking a more perfect expression and fulfillment. Ding coined the concept of the Cosmic Christ and views him as the focus of a spiritual journey. In a speech in 1991, Ding argued that the Cosmic Christ is no more a weapon to fight a theologian battle, but a personal synthesis of a spiritual journey. The Cosmic Christ is a point of attraction and the ultimate focus in human history (Tang, pp.1520-1525).

Because of government control and the multiple layers of approvals for the establishment of a new church, many believers circumvent the administrational procedures to build their own holy churches without governmental certification. Without official endorsement, this kind of congregation is termed as "the underground church" [*dixia jiaohui*]. It is there where the faithful believers congregate, hold prayers, read the Bible, and offer help to each other. The lack of well-trained professional ministers poses an issue because of its conflict with the government and other underground churches. Very often, the underground church is viewed by the government as a heresy or an evil sect and is subjected to political persecution.

In the vast rural areas, as Daniel H. Bays observes, Christianity has become a folk religion because of the nonexistence of professional theologians. In 1982-83, a sectarian group emerged as "the Shouters," because the followers indeed shout at their services. In recent years, more radical groups with an estimate of a few million followers are active, such as the Established King Sect, the Lord God Sect, the Narrow Gate in the Wilderness, the Three Grades of Servants, and the Lightning out of the East (Bays, 2012, pp. 194-196). The leaders of those groups employ their appealing charisma, use their leadership skills, adopt fascinating tenets from the Bible, and convert people. Xi Lian claims that these moves "offer intimations of the future of popular Christianity" (Lian, 2010, p. 222).

Figure 3.4. A Christian congregation in Wenzhou, Zhejiang Province. (Public Domain).

The booming Christian enterprises dramatically remolded the Chinese religious landscape in some special regions in particular. For example, Wenzhou in Zhejiang Province symbolizes this significant transformation. During the Cultural Revolution in Wenzhou, church buildings were destroyed and very few residents practiced Christianity. After the tragedy, the revival was a splendid scene. As the Wenzhou economy prospered, in the 1980s alone, more than five hundred churches were built. Local entrepreneurs who turned out to be the so-called Boss Christians [*laoban jidutu*] provided financial support to assist the church growth. By the beginning of the 21st century, there are as many as one million Protestant Christians in more than 2,000 churches in Wenzhou. This phenomenon turned the city into the largest urban Christian hub in all of China and some scholars straightforwardly call it "China's Jerusalem" (Cao, p. 1, pp. 24-30).

The non-existence of the contacts with foreign churches could be acceptable to the Protestants, but it poses a serious problem to the Catholics who are supposedly to be loyal to the Pope and to be guided by him. The Vatican does not have a diplomatic tie with Beijing and often the Vatican and Beijing appoint rival bishops in various dioceses. The Beijing government only regards its own appointees as the legal religious leaders. This clash between the two sides often result in the arrests of "illegal" bishops and their co-religionists, a move which is seen by the international community as religious persecution and violation of human rights. Although in the recent years, the Vatican and Beijing have started to negotiate over some issues, the Vatican still recognizes Taiwan as the legal government of China. Unless Beijing changes its current policy to treat Catholics more leniently or the Vatican becomes more flexible in its relation with China, bilateral diplomacy may not be reached in a short time.

Although confined under governmental control and without guidance from professional theologians, the growth of Christianity is a salient progress. One writer recently stated that "Christianity has probably become China's largest nongovernmental organization (Osnos, p. 315). The exact number of Chinese Christians might never be easily obtained, as many underground churches do not register with the government. The often cited figure stands at fifty million in these days, including both Catholics and Protestants, yet the real number could be far larger as some estimate it as 100 million (Wielander, p. 3). No one can foretell the future, but it is still safe to assert that Christianity will continue to grow and play a more remarkable role in the coming century. "The Christian conquest of China" (Madsen, 2003, p. 286) might not be soon realized in the immediate future; a South Korean model, where more than thirty percent of population practice Christianity, may be an East Asian paradigm for its big neighbor.

ETHNIC MINORITIES AND RELIGIONS

Although Han Chinese make up an overwhelming majority of China's population, fifty-five other ethnic minorities, whose population demographically stands at ten percent of the total, all have their own special origins, particular languages, and more importantly unique faith systems. Ethnic peoples can be found everywhere through the country, but most of them remain in their ethnic regions, prefectures, counties, townships, or villages which are designated as ethnically autonomous. The fact that the ethnic areas occupy over half of China's territory deserves serious attention. Of course, within those domains, ethnic minorities practice their religions. The government has enforced a series of religious policies to grant ethnic autonomy, respect traditional holidays, honor religious rituals, and prize local customs. Consequently, religions play a vital role in shaping ethnic culture, daily subsistence, and communal ties.

The religious vista of ethnic minorities is variegated yet colorful. The geographical location could be seen as a determinant of this religious landscape. Most of the northwestern ethnic minorities are believers of Islam, as a part of Richard Foltz's interpretation of the Islamization of the Silk Road (Foltz, pp. 89-109). From Tibet to Inner Mongolia and even farther to Northeast China [Manchuria], Lamaism is the major belief. In Southwest China, most practice animistic religions, but some are believers of Buddhism or Daoism. In the Southwest, some ethnic groups confess in Christianity, such as the Bai, Lisu, Lahu, Wa, Nu and Dulong. Those who practice Christianity aver that their religion was the corollary of missionary ventures in the past century. An overview of the ethnic religions highlights two important faiths: Islam and Lamaism. Those two have impacted Chinese political life, ethnic relationship, and religious transformation. At the same time, they have exerted an influence upon the global community. Without a doubt, both Islam and Lamaism will continue to draw global attention in the new century.

At the beginning of the 21st century, the total population of Islamic believers in China was around thirty million. Their ethnicities include: the Hui, Uighur, Kazakh, Kyrgyz, Tajik, Tartar, Khalkhas, Dongxiang, Salar and Bao'an. The Hui are Chinese descendants whose population is over ten million. The Uighurs, about ten million, are Turkish speakers mainly living in Xinjiang. Over one million Kazakh, of Turkish origin, also reside in Xinjiang. Other smaller groups, either Turkish, or Mongolian origins, or even one Iranian (Tajik), are concentrated in Northwestern provinces. Like all Muslims in other countries, the believers inside China confess faith in a single deity, Allah, read the Holy Koran, fast during Ramadan, observe Islamic festivals, pay pilgrimages to Mecca, and form their own communities. In the post-Mao years, more mosques have been built for worshippers, more religious training centers have opened, and more pilgrims have gone to Mecca. Most believers in China are Sunni and retain a special tie with the Arab World. In the recent decades, among the Uighurs, some extreme activities, such as moves for separatism, have cause serious concerns (DeAngelis, p. 167). Even worse, some Uighurs have openly challenged the authorities and have even resorted to actions which the government has labeled "terrorism", occurring in Xinjiang, Beijing and more recently in the southwestern city of Kunming on March 1, 2014. Although the government terms these as the three forces, terrorism, extremisms, and separatism, the problem continues to persist and will cause further international concerns.

The Hui are physically indistinguishable from Han Chinese as they are descendants of the long intermarriage between remote Western or Central Asian ancestors and Han Chinese. Yet, the Hui's religious faith separates them far apart from the Han. Whenever any sensitive anti-Islamic events occur, the Hui and other Muslims respond vehemently. For example, in 1989, two Chinese authors, portrayed Islamic minarets as phallic symbols and distorted the Muslims' pilgrimage to Mecca as an occasion of homosexual contact. Protests immediately spread across the whole country. Consequently, thirteen million copies of this book were confiscated and burned. One Hui author, Zhang Chengzhi, in 1991 urged the Hui to hold their faith and use the Manchu persecution of the Hui in the 19th century as a case to propagandize and promote their beliefs. Zhang asserted that God had chosen the Jews in Europe yet selected the Hui in China to reveal a truth that blood is the seed of religion. He implied that the Muslims should strengthen their belief and not be afraid of any persecutions (Luo, v. 1, p. 302).

Islam has existed in China for thirteen centuries and has exerted an impact on the shaping of Chinese civilization. The Chinese endorsement makes it flourish but occasional conflicts have made its believers suffer. The sizable population of thirty million among ten ethnic minorities means that Islam has been successful in its propagation and conversion. This nation-wide residential demography of its believers will enable the religion to be an inseparable component of Chinese religious life. The wide dispersal of its believers through the land in particular in the Northwest will continue to attract national as well as international attention in one way or the other.

Figure 3.5. Chinese Muslims (the Hui) celebrate an Islamic festival. (Public Domain).

Lamaism, also known as Tibetan Buddhism, is a prominent religion among seven ethnic groups: Tibetans, Mongols, Tu, Yugu, Naxi, Qiang, and Dai. The land where these ethnic groups reside covers a large chunk of territory inside today's People's Republic. Among the various sects of Lamaism, the Gelug Sect (Yellow Hat) and the Nyingma Sect (Red Hat) are the most famous. However, it is the Gelug that dominates Tibetan Buddhism and its leader, the Dalai Lama, is the head of the religion. In fact, the Gelug affirms that the Dalai Lama is the reincarnation of the compassionate Buddha and thus he is worshipped as the holy one (Luo, v. 2, p. 650). The Gelug emphasizes monastic life for professionals, stresses the pursuit of spirituality in a sequential manner, and underscores the intent of seeking wisdom. Lamaism belongs to Mahayana Buddhism, a dominant denomination of the religion in East Asia, which has developed to fit the needs of local culture and has enjoyed rapid growth because of its flexibility and adaptability.

Lamaism endorses the vital role of its spiritual leader, the Dalai Lama, a title granted by the Mongol ruler in the sixteenth century. In the past century, this religion went through dramatic changes, in particular after the collapse of the Qing Empire that loosened the political grip over the Tibetan region. In 1950, the communists sent troops into Tibet in the name of liberation and the reforms which followed remolded Tibet. Tibet was granted the status of an autonomous region and the 14th Dalai Lama (1935-) was invited to live in Beijing until 1959 when a failed Tibetan rebellion was crushed by Mao. Ever since then, the Dalai Lama has lived in exile. Nevertheless, his long efforts for Tibetan autonomy have earned him an international reputation, which enabled him to win the Nobel Peace Prize in 1989. In recent years, negotiations between Beijing and the Dalai Lama are under way but thus far have not panned out well. Occasionally, riots have happened in Tibet, which were labeled by Beijing as the religious extremism and political separatism. Outside China, Beijing always lodged strong protests to any country that invites the Dalai Lama for a visit. Although Beijing views the Tibet issue as an internal and domestic issue, pledges financial aid to monasteries, and builds better communication lines, such as the newly built railway in Tibet, the Tibetan issue will continue to draw attention from the global village.

THE UPCOMING PROSPECTS OF RELIGIONS

It is hard to predict the future trends of religious developments, but we may still assume that several potentials will continue in the new millennium from our knowledge of past experience. In terms of the relationship between politics and religion, Chinese style political control will continue to confine religions within certain boundaries. Unless radical political transformation occurs, the current state-religion tie may persist. This means that complete freedom of religious practices may still be guaranteed by the constitution, but it may hardly be a reality in practice. As a result, political liberty, individual freedom, human rights, and religious persecution inside China might continue haunting the global media as a hot topic whenever the religious issue is put on the table.

Under government management, Chinese religions, according to Fenggang Yang, will bring forth three different religious markets with three various colors: red, black and grey (Yang, pp. 41-46). The red market refers to those practitioners who cooperate with the government, abide by the existing rules, and operate under the supervision of the authorities.

In the eyes of the officials, the red market is completely legal and permissible. The black market designates those who challenge the government, resist the administrative regulations, hold rituals secretly, establish congregations without endorsement, and occasionally yet openly organize protests. Naturally, the black market from the governmental perspective is illegitimate and obnoxious. The grey market, however, exists between the red and the black markets. It appears under the camouflage of certain guises such as cultural events, social gatherings, tourist attractions, scientific experiments, and health trainings. The grey market contains non-religious elements, yet may suddenly turn to be a regional or even national movement. The Falun Gong's activities started in the early 1990s under the name of *qigong* practices, but turned out to be a national organization. Whether Falun Gong is a "practice," or a religion, or a cult, scholars have debated but have not reached an agreement (Madsen, 2007, pp. 182-191). At the very least, it was initiated in the grey market and attracted sixty million practitioners in 1999 before it was banned by the government in the same year.

In the new century, just as it was in the past millennium, Han Chinese will continue their tradition of practicing religions in the coalesced model, which is termed by Western scholars as syncretism. Some may question those individuals' sincerity in adopting a faith and others may even regard it as a superstition. Others still may consider it a pragmatist religion for a particular practical purpose. This syncretic approach, as a tradition, will continue to make China's religious milieu colorful, multifaceted, and tolerant. This broad-minded but moderate condition will not make Chinese believers bigoted, uncompromising, or intolerant. Rather, this blended practice turns practitioners to be more flexible, more forgivable, and more rationalistic. Ultimately, it may be a benefit to all religions to peacefully co-exist.

As it occurs in many countries, the secularization of religions will persist in China. More people study religions as a source of moral inspiration than purely for purposes of religious piety and obedience to a certain religious order. The ethical values, a shared core of all religions, require humans to be well-mannered, refined, and respectful to others. This essential moral will live on. On the personal level, Daoist and Buddhist promotion of vegetarianism has become a fashion in the recent years as "this worldly asceticism" (Goossaert & Palmer, p. 286). *qigong* practices, often seen as the component of Daoism, as a secular way to preserve health will endure even though the Falun Gong model is banned. The physical exercise and body cultivation are to work for public health. In the decades to come, the commercialization of religious events and festivals will enable more to integrate religions with business. As Andrew Targowski argues, a new religion (secular one) of the Global Civilization focusing on super-consumerism and business will emerge and some Chinese will definitely move toward that direction (Targowski, 2014).

As modernization is often interpreted as Westernization, the deepened modernization inevitably brings Christianity closer to China's modernizers, particularly in the urban areas, including intellectuals, entrepreneurs, and others. One survey has shown that about 70% of a group of college students assumed that Christianity would "enrich social culture, help Chinese people to understand the West and increase Sino-Western cultural exchange" (Goossaert & Palmer, p. 302). In such a milieu, many Chinese intellectuals have become "Cultural Christians" [*wenhua jidutu*] who celebrate Christmas and other holidays and live up to the values of the Bible, although they may not stick to a particular church. The Cultural Christians have forged an identity and have developed a supportive network that could be both religious and political, as they have demanded political rights (Lian, 2013, p. 71). Nevertheless, it is hard to predict to what extent those Cultural Christians will play a role in

Chinese social and political life as an enduring force. To say the least, they have already demonstrated vigor in the cultural life.

The ever expanding new technology will continue to assist the Chinese to absorb religious teachings through several communicational means, notably the Internet. The network has become the microphone of God or other deities and has popularized religious tenets, becoming a new foundation of conversion. The online video website, You-Tube, website, and others are often used to spread religions. The fact that most Chinese now own cell phones and that the number of Chinese Netizens makeup more than half of the population inevitably expose the Chinese to new approaches of propagation. Perhaps, the Chinese exposure to electronic religious teachings will turn them to be engaged in the digital religion which is a traditional belief but circulated through the most advanced and effective technology.

It is evident that ethnic minorities are returning to or holding firmly onto their own traditional religions. Among the fifty-five ethnic minorities, the religious revivals have become the most prominent phenomenon. The rise of the ethnic religions time and again ties them with the international community, in particular Muslims with Central Asia, West Asia and the Arab world. Tibetan Buddhism (Lamaism) naturally poses an issue to the Chinese government as its spiritual leader is living in exile. All these factors compel China to deal with international politics and oblige China to negotiate with many nations. Whenever a terrorist attack occurs, or an ethnic unrest happens, it always touches the inner nerves of the top leadership in Beijing. The special relation between ethnic religions and global politics will remain to be a tough issue.

CONCLUSION

The amazing and on-going religious resurgence should not be ignored because it will re-determine the course of Chinese civilization in the new millennium. This phenomenon proves that religion will not naturally die out or automatically disappear as many had envisioned some decades ago. This affirms that religion is not irrelevant to modernization or antagonistic to science. It confirms that religion is not simply opium; rather, it is a spiritual victual to nurture peoples' hungry hearts and satisfy the innermost needs of man. Facing high-speed modernization and waves of technological renovations, the intelligent man often feels powerlessness. As the booming economy brings forth the sharp disparity between the rich and the poor, social conflict inevitably emerges. In recent years, the high rate of unemployment is alarming as millions could not find an ideal job for their expertise. Rural migrants endure hardship and college graduates take manual laborer's work. Many notice the limitation of man's power. Naturally, a supernatural being or a powerful almighty can offer solace, comfort, and peace. Therefore, the religious renaissance is a natural course in recent Chinese history.

The long, commonly held view that religion is outdated might be passé itself. On the contrary, Chinese religions have returned triumphantly. This might confirm the validity of Samuel Phillip Huntington's assumption of a civilization clash, as the world returns to different cultural zones with a traditional religious belief system serving as the core value for each zone. Whether Chinese civilization will collide with others is still unknown, because

Chinese religions, unlike others, are multiple, mutually interactive, and syncretic. With the co-existence of so many religions, one can hardly label China as the Confucian zone, or the Buddhist zone, or the Daoist zone, or any other zone. The complicated situation cannot allow the Chinese to fashion the notion of "the Chinese Grace" with which they feel a burning desire and a duty-bound obligation to convert others or to assume an unshrinkable responsibility to spread their faith. Rather, this system of co-existing religions, after all, will urge the Chinese to carry on their humanistic tradition in order to establish their own "harmonious society," to improve their human relationships and rebuild their own civilization.

REFERENCES

Bays, Daniel H. (2012). *A new history of Christianity in China.* Wiley-Blackwell.
Cao, Nanlai. (2011). *Constructing China's Jerusalem: Christians, power, and place in contemporary Wenzhou.* Stanford, CA: Stanford University Press.
Charbonnier, Jean-Pierre (2007). *Christians in China, A.D. 600 to 2000.* San Francisco: Ignatius Press.
Chen, Kenneth K. S. (1968). *Buddhism: the light of Asia.* Hauppauge. NY: Barron's Educational Series, Inc.
DeAngelis, Richard C. (1997). "Muslims and Chinese political culture," *The Muslim World*, (April 1997), 151-168.
Elvin, Mark. (1996). *Another history.* Canberra: University of Sydney Press.
Fairbank, John King. (1999). *China: a new history.* Cambridge, MA: Harvard University Press.
Richard, C. Foltz. (1999). *Religions on the silk road: overland trade and cultural exchange from antiquity to the fifteen century.* New York: St. Martin's Griffin.
Harvey, Thomas Alan. (2002). *Acquainted with grief: Wang Mingdao's stand for the persecuted church in China.* Grand Rapids, MI: Brazos Press.
Fingarette, Herbert (1998). *Confucius: the secular as sacred.* Prospect Heights, IL: Waveland Press, Inc.
Fitzgerald, C. P. (1996). *China: a short cultural history.* New York: Praeger Publishers.
Gao, Wangzhi. (1996). "Y. T. Wu: a Chinese leader under communism," in Daniel H. Bays, *Christianity in China: from the Eighteenth Century to the Present.* Stanford, CA: Stanford University Press, 338-352.
Goossaert, Vincent & Palmer, David A. (2011). *The religious question in modern China.* Chicago and London: The University of Chicago Press.
Harrison, Henrietta. (2013). *The missionary's curse and other tales from a Chinese catholic village.* Berkeley, CA: University of California Press.
Lai, Chi-Tim. (2003). "Daoism in China today, 1980-2002," *The China Quarterly*, (no. 174, Jun. 2003), 413-427.
Lao Tzu [Lao Zi]. (1997). *Tao Te Ching* [Dao De Jing]. Catham, Kent, UK: Wordsworth, 1997.
Arthur Waldron. (1998). "Religious revival in communist China," *Orbis*, vol. *42*, no. 2, Spring, 325-334.

Lei, Chunfang. (2013). "Shijie zongjiao fazhan de jige xin dongxiang" [Several new trends of development for the world religions], *Zhongguo zongjiao* [Chinese Religions], (no. 12, 2013), 55-57.

Lian, Xi. (2013). "Cultural Christians and the Search for Civil Society in Contemporary China," *The Chinese Historical Review*. vol. *20*, no. 1, May, 70-87.

Lian, Xi. (2010). *Redeemed by fire: popular Chinese christianity in the twentieth century*. New Haven, CT: Yale University Press.

Lin, Guoping. (2009). "Minjian zongjiao de fuxing yu dangdai zhongguo shehui" [The Revival of Popular Religion and the Current Chinese Society], *Shijie zongjiao yanjiu* [The Study of World Religions], (no. 4), 81-91.

Littlejohn, Ronnie L. (2009). *Daoism: an introduction*. London & New York: I. B. Tauris.

Luo, Jing. (Ed.). (2005). *China today: an encyclopedia of life in the People's Republic*, vol. *1*, vol. *2*, Westport, CT: Greenwood.

Madsen, Richard. (2003), "Chinese christianity: indigenization and conflict," in Perry, Elizabeth and Selden, Mark (2003). *Chinese Society: Change, Conflict and Resistance*, New York and London: RoutledgeCurzon, 271-288.

Madsen, Richard. (2007). "Understanding Falun Gong," in David B. H. Denoon, *China: contemporary political, economic, and international affairs*, New York: New York University Press, 182-191.

Ni, Peimin. (2010). *Confucius: making the way great*, Shanghai: Shanghai Translation Publishing House.

Osnos, Evan. (2014). *Age of ambition: chasing fortune, truth and faith in the new China*, New York: Farrar, Straus and Giroux.

Overmyer, Daniel L. (1998). *Religions of China: the world as a living system*, Prospect Height, IL: Waveland Press, Inc.

Schoppa, R. Keith (2011). *Revolution and its past: identities and changes in modern Chinese history*, 3rd edition, New York: Prentice Hall.

Shan, Patrick Fuliang. (2009). "Triumph after catastrophe: church, state and society in post-Boxer China, 1900-1937," *Peace and Conflict Studies*, Winter, vol. *16*, no. 2, 33-47.

Sommer, Deborah. (1995). *Chinese religion: an anthology of sources*, New York and Oxford: Oxford University Press.

Spence, Jonathan. (1999). *The search for modern China,* 2nd Edition, New York: W.W. Norton.

Stark, Rodney & Liu, Eric Y. (2011). "The religious awakening in China," *Review of Religious Research*, vol. *52*, no. 3, 282-289.

Tang, Edmond. (2007). "The cosmic christ: the search for a Chinese theology," in Roman Malek (Ed.), *The Chinese faces of Jesus Christ*, vol. 3b, Sankt Augustin, Germany: Monumenta Serica Monograph Series, 1515-1526.

Targowski, A. (2014). *Global civilization in the 21st Century*. New York: NOVA Science Publishers.

Thompson, Laurence G. (1996). *Chinese religion,* 5th edition, New York: Wadsworth Publishing Company.

Wasserstrom, Jeffrey N. (2010). *China in the 21st century: what everyone needs to know*, Oxford, UK: Oxford University Press.

Wielander, Gerda. (2013). *Christian values in communist China*. Oxford, UK: Routledge.

Yang, C. K. (1991). *Religion in Chinese society: a study of contemporary social functions of religion and some of their historical factors*, Prospect Heights, IL: Waveland Press, Inc.

Yang, Fenggang. (2006). "Zhongguo zongjiao de sanse shichang" [The Three Color Markets of Chinese Religions], *Zhongguo Renmin Daxue Xuebao* [Journal of Renmin University of China], no. 6, 41-46.

Zaehner, R. C. (1997). *Encyclopedia of the world's religions,* New York: Barnes & Noble.

Chapter 4

CHINESE CIVILIZATION AND CONTEMPORARY POP CULTURE IN THE 21ST CENTURY

Shan Li[*]
Sichuan University, Chengdu, China

ABSTRACT

The *purpose* of this investigation is to analyze relations between Chinese traditional and contemporary pop-cultures paying particular attention to the impact of the strong forces of globalization in the 21st century on the latter. The *methodology* is based on an interdisciplinary big-picture view of civilization as a complex system of art, literature, music, customs, architecture and other. Among the *findings* are: a 5000 year long traditional culture has had a strong presence in contemporary China; however, younger generations are strongly impacted by Western Civilization. *Practical implication:* To understand contemporary China one must understand its 5000 yearlong civilization. Particularly one must see it as evolving through four stages: establishment and development, suffering and confusion, revival and transformation; the last stage is taking place in the 21st century. *Originality:* this investigation, by providing an interdisciplinary synthesis of numerous factors expands the scope of the traditional approach to the issues of relations between Chinese traditional and contemporary cultures.

INTRODUCTION

In the former chapter, we placed emphasis on the course of Chinese religion in the 21st century. For this part, we will focus on the cultural aspects in China through the cultural track of Chinese tradition, the description of modernization and rising western-oriented pop culture in China, and the repercussions of the clash between tradition and contemporary cultures. The purpose of this investigation is to define the central issues of the current and future trends of Chinese traditional and contemporary pop culture. The methodology is based on an interdisciplinary big-picture view of the Chinese traditional culture and western-oriented pop

---
[*] Shan Li" <lishan@scu.edu.cn>

culture and their developments and interdependency. By providing the interdisciplinary and civilizational approach, we believe this investigation has the two-fold implication of being both practical and social.

LEGACY OF 5000 YEARS LONG CHINESE CULTURE

Culture implies the overall way of life for a particular group of individuals, which refers to human behaviors and the symbols that give significance to these behaviors, changing constantly with the social development. Generally speaking, every society has a different culture.

Chinese culture is one of the world's oldest cultures for its attribute of openness. It originated from the Xia Dynasty (c.2070-1600 B.C.) more than 5000 years ago, according to some of Ancient Chinese historians. Henceforth, through various dynasties, Chinese culture carried itself forward and absorbed numerous cultural elements from foreign cultures such as Buddhism, forming a splendid ancient Chinese culture. It is important to understand Chinese history and society for anyone who wants to understand Chinese culture.

From Qin-Han Period to the late Qing Dynasty, up to the Revolution of 1911, China was a traditional agricultural society, owning a unique economic system, political system, value system, social structure and it created an integral secular culture which was composed of science, art, literature, architecture and other aspects. All of the above are the essential elements of Chinese culture, but not all of these have been preserved to this day due to historical factors. From the later Qing Dynasty, the flood of Western culture occurred in China on a large scale through colonial invasion, which caused a tremendous impact on Chinese culture. Facing the challenge of Western culture, Chinese scholars never changed the system and structure of Chinese culture in order to maintain its own characteristics, and instead of learning from the West actively, they managed to achieve cultural transformation and revival in the suffering acculturation process. All these attempts made new creations that further enriched the meanings of Chinese culture, not only successfully preventing the legacy of Chinese culture from dying off, but exercising a profound influence on the modernization of Chinese society as well. Chinese culture, as it was, has always been a culture of the Chinese nation.

In ancient China, the economic system usually manifested itself as a subsistence-based agrarian economy, with a kind of social structure that combined great tradition and little tradition. (King, 1999, p.10) Due to this fact, a compound peasant society constituted by scholars and farmers had taken shape. People who lived in the society were strictly divided into a leisure class and working class, and the latter always lacked political consciousness which was the inevitable consequence of despotism. Nevertheless, this changed gradually after the Revolution of 1911 due to the overthrow of the absolute monarchy.

The Chinese value system is the most plentiful part of Chinese culture, extremely delicate and complex, containing a great many of concepts and beliefs. For example, Confucianism (Figure 4.1) shaped a vast majority of the personality structure of the Chinese as a system of philosophy and moral rules. It made people gentle, abundant in empathy, and helped them to live a formal life (Hweng-Ming, 2012, p.2-8). Over the past thousands of years, Confucianism's position in China is equal to the religions in the western countries. There is no denying that Confucianism is one of the precious legacies of the 5000 year long Chinese culture. It can be said that the Chinese value system is far more stable than its economic and political system.

Figure 4.1. Confucius (557-479 BC), the Father of the Chinese way of wise thinking. (Photo: http://www.chinakongzi.org).

Social structure influences cultural transmission directly, and the examination system along with family values are two important concepts of the Chinese social structure. The former promotes social mobility with a set of standardized procedures, while the latter delivers the social values to individuals by enculturation and socialization as the most primary social unit. They are also preserved until now as valuable legacies, still playing significant roles in modern Chinese people's lives. Compared with the ever-changing social stratum structure, these concepts have remained stable.

In this special environment, the secular culture of ancient China was created, of which Traditional Chinese Medicine as well as the Great four Inventions are among the most famous of the symbols of ancient China for most foreigners. The aforementioned Traditional Chinese Medicine was connected with the words such as Herbology, Acupuncture and moxibustion, longevity preservation and so on. Although it seems mysterious, the essence of Traditional Chinese Medicine is the generalization and summarization from practical experiences, which is the common characteristic of ancient Chinese Science.

Chinese art and literature contain plenty of aspects, rather than merely forms of amusement. To take music as an example, in ancient China, ordinary people confirmed that music can influence the harmony of the universe. Therefore, music was taken as an important way to communicate with "Tian"[1]. And at the same time, literature played a role as a mirror, which reflected the social reality and the common value of the general public, not merely reconstructing a temporal, historical context to some extent, but also owing great practical meanings, such as *A Dream of Red Mansions* (Figure 4.2).

Figure 4.2. Lin Daiyu (also spelled Lin Tai-yu, Chinese: 林黛玉; Pinyin: Lín Dàiyù) is one of the principal characters of Cao Xueqin's classic Chinese novel *Dream of the Red Chamber*. She is portrayed as a well-educated, intelligent and beautiful young woman. (Photo: Wikipedia).

As for architecture, Chinese wood frameworks are unique in the world which embodied the value and the aesthetic of Chinese people. In most cases, Traditional Chinese Architecture highly praised harmony (Figure 4.3) and order relating them to the concepts of nature and

---

[1] It is an important concept of traditional Chinese philosophy. In general, it refers to the highest criterion of the universe.

human society. The use of the axial layout pattern is a remarkable feature, and the Forbidden City was the best example.

Figure 4.3. Harmony in Chinese traditional architecture is present in its contemporary settings like this hotel and planimetria building. (Photo: thedesignsoc.com and, plusmood.com).

The above list is just a few sides of Chinese culture, and there are still other things, such like costume, cuisine and so on, shaping a particular way of life and personality structure altogether. This is the legacy of the 5000 years long Chinese culture.

How Traditional Chinese Culture Is Applied in the 21ST Century

Traditional Chinese culture is, in the narrow sense, a complex system of spiritual concepts composed of values, moral codes, and behavior standards, which gradually formed the long-term social and economic development of China and then eventually came to dominate the minds of most all Chinese people. It was nearly closed-off culturally before the

May 4th Movement of 1919 which was a great turning point of Chinese history. At that time, China had been relegated to a semi-colony and had been enslaved to a series of humiliating treaties, facing unprecedented challenges from the West.

Under the great impact of Western culture, it can be said that the disadvantages and weaknesses of traditional Chinese culture had been exposed day by day, and their value system, based on Confucianism, lost its appeal in the process of industrialization and urbanization. Some scholars even launched a criticism termed the "New Culture Movement" on traditional Chinese culture from numerous perspectives, which brought irreparable damage to the traditional culture due to the extreme nature of the criticisms. However, although the traditional Chinese value system had been destroyed by Western culture, the Western value system never took root in the thought of Chinese people.

Thus, during the period of social transformation, a new kind of person, one between the traditional culture and the modern one, appeared. They turned to traditional culture, trying to mix the best elements from the East and the West jointly for a new operative and functional synthesis. (Yeo-Chi, 1999, p.82). On this occasion, traditional humanism presented by Confucianism had been well preserved until now, which advocated the establishment of a well-disciplined, stable, multi-level society with high moral values. This was reflected in the moral codes and social concepts of the Chinese.

As for Chinese moral codes, the core is improving self-cultivation for adjusting to the standards of "Tian". This requires people to pursue a personality of individual perfection and to become a noble person of good morality with an integration of the soul and actions, or of a person's inner quality and outward appearance. This was kept by family education and folk tradition, which is also applicable to modern Chinese people.

The Chinese social concepts take the "Tianxia" as ultimate goal while "Datong and Taiping" [2] are the supreme ideals. (Mu, 2012, p.20) The way to realize these concepts depends on every individual, so the function of education attracts public interest. Furthermore, since the family is the most primary educational unit of society, the idea of attaching importance to family value was commonly recognized. If applied in the modern times, the idea will arouse new educational methods while handling the loneliness among the elderly in economically developed countries.

The way for the Chinese to get along with each other is to find a way to deal with the most pressing questions faced by humanity, most outstanding, the relationship between humans, nature and "Tian". The only basis is to build on the faith of "kindness in human nature". The only goal is achieving the harmonious state of "the unity of the Tian and Humanity" that contains the thoughts of harmony and balance, both of which are highly praised by the Chinese at present, especially the government. Nowadays, it is extended to the Human-oriented Scientific Outlook on Development.

All of the above are the heritage of Traditional Chinese culture and have become one of the required courses for China. The government and many NGOs are also advocating this in different ways. Although Chinese culture is ever changing with time, there is always something which has hardly changed. To this day, Chinese scholars have never stopped exploring about the values of traditional Chinese culture, and how to apply them to the modern society is still a major task.

---

[2] "Tianxia" refers to all the people and the land under heaven. "Datong and Taiping" refers to an ideal society in perfect harmony.

THE IMPACT OF MODERNIZATION OF CHINA ON CHINESE TRADITIONAL CULTURE

China has a rich traditional culture, always a source of wealth to every Chinese descendant, which had a continued influence until now. The modernization of China has had a large number of impacts on the tradition. The Chinese have experienced many changes, from the process of agriculture to industry, to the change from monarchy to democracy and from a culture focused on relationships to one of achievements. In this section, we emphasize the analysis of a series of reforms in the process of Chinese modernization, including the aspects of culture, conception, economy, society, technology and politics. With four hallmark historical periods, Chinese culture has experienced a conspicuous transformation.

The first important transformation took place during the May 4th Movement, in which there occurred the conflict between Chinese traditional culture and Western culture, the rise of democracy, more attention to popular culture and the criticisms aimed at tradition. Because of the social reform, especially after the May 4th Movement in 1919, plenty of the material legacies faded away, while the mental ones remained. Based on the movement, China ushered in the course of modernization.

The New Culture Movement took place last century, which brought cultural and historical significance for endless interpretation, in which Chinese people changed their style of literature composition and expressional habits. The New Youth journal, the leading publication in the movement, laid the blame for the causes of China's weakness on Confucian culture. As a result, Chen Duxiu called for "Mr. Confucius" to be replaced by "Mr. Science" and "Mr. Democracy." Another outcome was the promotion of written vernacular Chinese. Hu Shih proclaimed that "a dead language cannot produce a living literature." In theory, the new format allowed people with little education to read texts, articles and books, instead of those which were only understood by scholars and officials. And almost at the same time, students with a full knowledge of foreign education returned to China and entered the Chinese education system. Due to these forces, new institutions shocked the traditional system.

As the conception of modernization has given rise to the awareness of freedom and democracy, at the same time, from the conservative and dogmatic form to the much more liberal and multiple one, the idea of marriage and family has switched gradually.

The second period was ushered in after the establishment of the newly formed republic of China. Under the impact of Soviet Union, the culture of the Working Class thrived. But since the Cultural Revolution, which excessively stressed the mainstream ideology, Chinese traditional culture has suffered an unprecedented destruction. Until the Third Session of the Eleventh Central Committee of CPC in 1978, with the themes of bringing order out chaos, emancipating the mind and so on, especially the epistemological foundation of Deng Xiaoping's philosophy that "practice is the only criterion for testing truth", Chinese traditional culture has gotten a new chance to revive.

The third remarkable era was due to Deng Xiaoping's (Figure 4.4) policy of Reform and Opening up. Pop music from Hong Kong and Taiwan, movies and fashionable dress brought the concept of vogue to Mainland for the first time. Chinese rock music, which is represented by the famous singer Cui Jian, led a new way to express one's personality. The Spring Festival Gala and TV series has spread the pop culture.

Figure 4.4. Deng Xiaoping 2004-1997), the Father of Renewalling China in the 21st century.

And the unparalleled flourishing of the publishing industry has provided a high-efficiency access to share information and diffuse cultural fashion. After the economic reforms, the Chinese Supreme Leader, Deng Xiaoping, focusing on agriculture, industry, national defense, science and technology, helped China to abolish the planned economy pattern and establish socialist market economy.

The overall industrialization, especially the development of heavy industry, turned the country to a powerful one, and with economic development, the Chinese people's living conditions has been significantly improved.

In the fourth stage, that after the nineties, the Chinese ushered in the popularization of the Internet and mobile devices. The guiding ideology of urbanization was concerned about folk culture and initiating the protection of an intangible cultural heritage and native culture, so that the traditional culture was endued with new vitality. In addition, because of the increasing economic strength, the Chinese government focused on enhancing the national cultural soft power as the second economic entity of the world. More crucially, it is especially emphasized that all the people should have access to equal cultural services in the cultural development in China. As for the culture industry, the single economic entities moved on to multiple industrial chains. Like the Disney Corporation which produces amusement parks, movies, cartoons, and a plethora of associated merchandise, the Oversea Chinese Town Group in China, whose innovation of the management system has improved to a new level, is a new driving force and has promoted its high speed running engine, which is marked a great success now. In its enterprise systems, some famous brands are well-known, such as Konka, Splendid China, Windows of the World, Happy Valley China, OCT Grand Hotel, and so on[3]. (Today's OCT, 2010)

Besides the economic benefits, another trend is the combination of industry and culture, which provides new leisure and art patterns for the places constructed at the ancient factories, like the famous Dashanzi Art District (Factory 798 or 798 Art Zone) in Peking. DAD was once officially named Joint Factory 718 (Figure 4.5), which began as an extension of the "Socialist Unification Plan" of military-industrial cooperation between the Soviet Union and the newly formed People's Republic of China. From 1995, after several artists moved their workshops in this area, it ushered in an artistic rebirth. Here, abundant original expositions took place, genius young artists created new works and numerous clubs found their places. Today, it is already an irreplaceable factory complex of art creation and public leisure with a unique industrial style.

Figure 4.5. The 798 Art Zone, or Dashanzi Art District, is a part of Dashanzi in the Chaoyang District of Beijing that houses a thriving artistic community, among 50-year old decommissioned military factory buildings of unique architectural style. (Photo: Wikipedia).

As for the society, because of the developing industry and economy, the life of general people has been transformed. In the cities, a new and reasonable government and much more public facilities have been established. The citizens gradually have gained legal-right protection awareness. In the rural area, thanks to the new agriculture technology, the production output has improved to a new height. From the end of 19th century, a new phenomenon has appeared that a large number of rural people have moved into cities, and now take part in industry production. China is experiencing its process of urbanization.

---

[3] From: The official website of Overseas Chinese Town Enterprises Cooperation, http://www.chinaoct.com.

What's more, the modernization theory suggests democracy follows with the development of a modernized state, which remolds the Chinese regime in a sense, giving birth to a model called Democratic Centralism. Despite some problems still existing in the political system, the overall course has progressed to a great extent. Under the influence of globalization, the world system takes on a new look, while China consciously occupies a critical position. The Chinese government has scored great achievements in pursuing its independent foreign policy of peace. It also has joined plenty of inter-government organizations and engaged in economic and cultural exchanges all over the world. In 2014, China's diplomacy will concentrate on neighboring countries, with aims of changing the nation into stronger regional power. From here we can see that China now has greatly attributed to world peace and development, and enjoys a high prestige in international affairs, which is unprecedented compared with the past, old China.

Through several reforms of Western model, the modernization of China has benefited the country as it rises as a world power in the 21st century.

THE RISING WESTERN-ORIENTED POP CULTURE IN TODAY CHINA

The rising western-oriented pop culture has rich connotation. In a narrow sense, pop culture relates to art, literature, pop music or the new lifestyle of young people. And in a generalized sense, pop culture includes much more meanings, as the new media, the consumer conception and common values. So pop culture perhaps means culture that most people share and know about. Since modern times, foreign cultures have been critical of the Chinese native culture, permeating with all aspects of social life.

There is a common sense that stereotypes connect the social values and social judgments about other people. Since these stereotypes are mainly communicated by media, the changes of communication channels will probably be followed with the changes of stereotypes, the most important in which is the emergence of the computer and Internet (Figure 4.5).

Figure 4.5. In the first several years of the Internet's existence in the 20th century in China it was used for research and was not popularized. In the beginning of 1990s, when browsers became available, PCs became a necessity for life and came into the ordinary family for the first time. (Photo: http://www.cmiea.org/upLoad/news/month).

In the first several years, the Internet was used for research was not popularized. In the beginning of 1990s, PCs became necessity for life and came into the ordinary family for the first time. Since then, they have continued to change the ways of communication. Nowadays, with some dominant apps like QQ, Wechat, and Skype, Chinese people share a new social mode based on the Internet, which renovates the way people get along with each other.

Furthermore, the computer is a multifunctional device which facilitates daily life. Thanks to the portability, people can use only one machine for complex works. But on the other hand, because of that, it is likely that some industrial products which have the coessential functions such as TV, radio, cinema, will become weakened.

Different from closed times, the Internet now offers people a platform that contains various information. This means a great ability of screening information is crucial for today's world, instead of collection. For instance, as a student who needs some details of referral, the difficulty is no longer how to find relative documents, but to distinguish their authenticity in the information explosion era.

In addition, with the complicated merchandise both real and virtual, the Internet catalyzes new economic form and consumption. People can go shopping and complete the payment online. In this sense, the virtual world and the real world have been connected. Furthermore, not only can the shopping website provide economic benefits, but so can the entertainment industry like online games, advertising businesses and so on, among which the online games can even create an industry chain with abundant derivatives. Therefore, the Internet is not just a tool for life, but it is also becoming a strong entity motivating economic development.

Finally, along with the information society, a new democratic pattern called Cyber Democracy or E-democracy has appeared. This refers to a form of government in which all the citizens are presumed to be eligible to participate equally in the proposal, development, and creation of laws. This enables the free and equal practice of political self-determination. At present, Weibo, a primary social networking service in China, plays a leading role in Chinese E-democracy. Many government departments have Weibo accounts, through which they can announce the official news and communicate with the public at any time. A typical example is that the trial of Bo Xilai's hit case was broadcasted synchronously by Weibo.

Pop culture also has had a deep influence on general people's lifestyles. Some high technology domestic appliances have become available to families and have caused some change. The film is a good example. Watching films dose not only mean entertainment, but it also can give a vista to the Western world. Chinese people can know about and understand the history, politics and lifestyle in other countries by watching their movies. In addition, television has become one of the necessary parts of family life.

Watching TV is a new way to communicate with families. During the spring festival, almost every family sits together and watches the Gala Evening to celebrate the New Year. Nowadays, the TV shows and some videos add much more interactions with audiences. The programs serve as a multiple and individual way to suit different needs.

Another important part of W pop culture is music. Different from the Europe Classic music and Chinese traditional music, pop music is an absolutely new style of music composition. For example, rock music, with its fast pace and crazy passion, makes the Chinese people, especially the young, fall in love with it. Through this unprecedented style of music, people can understand some of the thoughts and attitudes of Western culture. Now, many pop music designers in China have been composing a large number of colorful songs and melodies.

At last, because of the pop culture, the style of clothing shows a new developmental direction. The Western style of clothing emphasizes the convenience and individual to a higher degree. After the First and the Second World War, the American clothing style became the leader of world fashion. Under this clothing trend, the Chinese have shown a new and special taste in clothing. Until recently, after the clothing revolution, Chinese designers combined Western fashion and Chinese aesthetics together, finding out a new way of Chinese clothing design.

The Western-oriented pop culture has brought changes to the concept of consumption as well. A key moment in the emergence of shopping as popular culture is the development of the department store in the late 19th century, which now has evolved into large-scale supermarket providing all kinds of products. (Storey, 2007, p.148) It has become a familiar feature of city shopping. This kind of institution functions economically and at the same time socially. And together with advertising, they symbolize the start of the present-day consumer society. The principal of consumption is also influenced by foreign culture. Originally, the Chinese were much more frugal and conservative, while Americans dared to premature consumption. In America, consumption loan is a universal phenomenon, and now, Chinese people share a similar idea, especially in the purchase of houses, cars or something costly like iPhones. Most people have agreed with the saying "high incomes, high consumption level and high quality of life", even though sometimes, they don't get such high incomes. Financing among ordinary people is another feather in this aspect. In the past, financing was considered as a luxury for the rich. But nowadays, many ordinary people who have a certain amount of savings consciously manage their property. Therefore, financial services, as a newly sprouted business, has begun to flourish.

Art, contenting the spirit of the nation and the ethos of the time, is the eye of life. As for Western art, its painting style, which is an individual style with numerous schools, came into China and made a difference. After the invention of the camera, painters have shown more interests in catching feelings, and explaining the happiness or sorrows in people's life. This is different from the classical painting style, which tries to copy reality. During the 20th century, there were a number of famous painters in Western world, such as Claude Monet, Pablo Picasso, Dali and so on. Their paintings and even their life experiences gave an example to Chinese painters and artists. Picasso and his impressionism art shows a new painting style to express the experiences of love, a country's history and even the people's life. From the 1980s to now, Chinese painters have created many beautiful and fashionable paintings, which have been marked in Chinese history.

As a sort of art, the sculpture was also deeply influenced by Western pop culture. From 1990s some Abstractionism sculptures began to appear in the streets in china. It is a new annotation of instantaneous movement or expression.

Also, the architecture of the cities have also changed a lot because of pop culture. The 19th century is all about industry and technology. People's taste turned from the glorious, complex, and colorful into the unified, industrial and less decorate. The Bauhaus represented the aesthetic of this period. Bauhaus architecture is shown everywhere around the world nowadays. The Chinese construction style is also enormously affected, and as a result, the grey colored walls and cube buildings are everywhere in big cities in China such as Beijing, Shanghai and Shenzhen. Perhaps Western pop culture has given Chinese people a new taste of art. It asks that the Chinese artist attempt to combine the traditional style and the new expression method together, leading Chinese art to a new direction.

THE REPERCUSSIONS OF THE CLASH BETWEEN TRADITIONAL AND CONTEMPORARY POP CULTURES IN CHINA

Pop culture has extensive connotations, which include the aspects of culture, economy, education, technology and diet. At present, contemporary pop culture permeates almost every facet of people's life. As a result, acts without consideration can have some repercussions for traditional Chinese culture.

Pop culture has had a deep influence on Chinese traditional festivals. In Chinese culture, there are many different festivals to celebrate, such as the Spring Festival (Figure 4.7), Dragon Boat Festival, Lantern Festival, Mid-Autumn Festival and so on. The traditional festivals are representative of the culture and people's spirit. Celebrating traditional festivals are very important for the preservation of culture. Nowadays, some Western festivals have come into China and have greatly impacted Chinese traditional culture. For the young people in China, some traditional festivals are not necessary to celebrate any more, and they have been replaced by Western festivals. For example, most young people prefer to hang out with their girlfriends or boyfriends on Valentine's Day rather than celebrate the Magpie Festival. The ancient romantic love story in China is out of fashion. In addition, the Mid-July Days is another example: Today's young Chinese, especially those who live in cities, know less about the ways to remember ancestors in old way. They show much more interests in Western festivals--Halloween and the Christmas for instance.

Figure 4.7. The Traditional Spring Festival in Chinatown of Seattle is celebrating the Chinese New Year 2011 and cultivating the national ancient tradition whichnowadays is mostly practiced in the Chinese Diaspora (Photo: Wikipedia).

Another characteristic in contemporary culture is utilitarianism, which reigns supreme in today's China. In China, this ideology faces dissimilation, and as a consequence,, only the distorted content that "the worth of an action is determined only by its resulting outcome" is accepted by the public. Most of the time, this "outcome" refers to economic benefits. This helps explain why Chinese intangible cultural heritages are inevitably in danger. Kunqu opera, Guqin art, Hakka folk songs, Mongolia Changdiao and so on, all these treasures of the colorful national culture of China are gradually forgotten in a "money talks" society because of their unprofitable character. As for a lucrative industry like tourism, human nature always gives way to economic profits. This will lead to a phenomenon of following suit blindly and homogenization. A typical example is the constructed ancient town, which refers to the imitation of a few originals such as Lijiang. All of these share the same construction styles and many other characteristics, like old streets, big houses with courtyards and similar souvenirs; however, they should have been more distinctive.

Under the impact of pop culture, education has changed significantly as well, due to the damage done to the traditional Chinese education system and the academic culture. In ancient China, education was the way to know benevolence, righteousness, propriety (decorum) and wisdom. Starting from the 19th century, Chinese education began to include Chinese, math, physics, chemistry and so on, which transformed from diffuseness to specificity. Since then, studying English has become a very important part of the Chinese education system. Children in China begin to learn English from primary school, even kindergarten. English is becoming the common language around the world. The education system in modern China makes Chinese traditional language face tremendous challenges. Some traditional expressions and literature are missing.

For a long time, science and technology have been regarded as a double-edged sword. Now digital products, a symbol of contemporary progress, flood into people's daily life, which can be both convenient and impeditive. This could be explained through a new symptom called "dependence on digital products". This account describes a group of people who carry their mobile phones with them all the time for purposes such as listening to music, checking e-mails and playing games. If one day they could not use any digital products, they would be uncomfortable. This "digital product addiction" is no doubt harmful for communication and personal health both physically and mentally. People stare at their own small screens, ignoring the real interpersonal relationships, which is opposite to the Chinese traditional philosophy of life. What is more, digital products as a new fashion could attract unreasonable consuming behaviors, especially for young people, the proof of which is the hot sale of iPhones and iPads in China. To get a fashion product, people are willing to pay a high price, although it probably far exceeds their income level.

Perhaps even the eating habit is also an aspect. China has a long and rich food culture. On the one hand, Chinese people have their own original traditional foods, such as dumplings, hot pots, yuanxiao and so on. On the other hand, there are different cuisines in different regions of China. But now some Western foods have become the favorite of young people. The fast food culture is a great part of contemporary pop culture in which KFC and McDonald's are two paradigm cases. The fast food culture is suitable for the high speed lifestyle in a metropolis, and it is becoming a common fashion of cities. Under the influences of this sort of pop culture, young people lose the interest in traditional food. Convince, fast, and easy are the key principles of our food culture nowadays, so that most Chinese people hardly ever cook by themselves.

Without doubt, through the indigenization, Chinese traditional culture also assimilates some elements of pop culture. Only based upon their tradition and modernity will China be able to stand firmly in the upheaval of the times.

Figure 4.8. The National Stadium *Bird's Nest* for the Olympic Games in Beijing 2008, reflects the way Chinese architecture has modernized and complied to the international style in the 21st century. The design (by Herzog & de Meuron), which originated from the study of Chinese ceramics, implemented steel beams in order to hide supports for the retractable roof; giving the stadium the appearance of a bird's nest. Leading Chinese artist Ai Weiwei was the artistic consultant on the project. (Photo: Wikipedia).

THE FUTURE OF CHINESE CULTURE

Contemporary Chinese culture is not a perfect system, and is still transforming day by day. Chinese people should take their traditional culture as the base, trying to discover the relationship between tradition and modernity, and find a way to develop Chinese culture without blindly copying the West, which should be modified under the requirements dictated by the present and future.

In the first aspect, the future of Chinese culture is globalization. At present, China is a powerful political and economic entity, recognized by the world leaders (Figure 4.8).

The richness and uniqueness of Chinese culture is an important element of Chinese civilization, and also is a part of the wealth of the entire human civilization. In the contemporary environment, pop music, fashion clothes and the newest movies synchronously have appeared in Chinese society. The world fashion culture is assimilated into people's life much more quickly and easily. For example, some international brand TV shows have entered Chinese pop culture: the Voice of China, the If You Are the One, the Where to Go, and Papa rise a new phenomenon. At the same time, Chinese culture is also on the global stage. Chinese art styles, just like the pop music, performance art and installation art, are gradually having a great international influence. Chinese movie stars march towards Hollywood, and thanks to them, a lot of Chinese elements are going into the global stage.

Furthermore, the future of Chinese culture must involve protecting and developing tradition. After the 1990s, China has more measures to protect and develop the traditional culture than ever before.

Figure 4.8. World leaders like presidents Vladimir Putin (Russia) and George W. Bush (USA) recognize Chinese impact upon the world during the APEC (Asia-Pacific Economic Cooperation) Summit in China, October 19-21, 2001, (Photo: Wikipedia).

Figure 4.9. Traditional Chinese painting has the permanent place in Chinese culture, regardless of contemporary and future tastes. (Photo: Wikimedia.org).

Protecting tangible and intangible cultural heritage, the new culture plan, and the lists of folk artists are important parts of such measures. At the same time, Chinese traditional culture has become more and more industrial, central and interactional. The new system of culture is asking Chinese tradition to change itself into a new style which is combing culture, technology and economy together. This new operational mode allow Chinese tradition to show new glamour for instance the little theatre Xiangsheng in Tinajing, the teahouse culture in Chengdu, the Peking Tianqiao art and so on.

Figure 4.10. China's pavilion during the Shanghai World Exposition in 2010 is an example how traditional architecture can be traced in the Chinese contemporary architecture (Photo: archdaily.com).

Finally, the future of Chinese culture will likely show an individual trend. After the appearance of the internet and mobile devices, information has spread quickly. Selecting information has become much easier and is now more individual. Chinese culture has shown new energy nowadays; art and fashion bring new freedoms and colors. A grassroots culture has come into people's daily lives. No doubt, Chinese stars show their charisma on the global stage, organizing charities or non-commercial activities. Some of them have become image ambassadors and have had great influence around the world, showing the positive energy of the Chinese. Above all, Chinese culture needs to be rooted in traditional culture, and be able to adapt to international standards. Chinese culture is delivering a unique spirit to the world, showing the China dream and sharing the wealth with everyone in the global village.

Conclusion

To understand Chinese civilization and contemporary pop culture in the 21st century, it is necessary to understand China's historical process and context. In history, the development of Chinese civilization has undergone four major stages: establishment and development, suffering and confusion, revival and transformation.

In ancient China, the history of Chinese civilization began 5000 year ago. During the Tang Dynasty (618-907), glorious cultural achievements were made in various respects. During this time, foreign culture was introduced into China by national war and cultural exchange, becoming elements of traditional Chinese culture and part of a 5000 year long Chinese cultural legacy of Chinese cultural tolerance.

From the mid-19th century to the founding of the PRC, the course of traditional Chinese culture was interrupted by culture aggression coming with the military aggression from the West. The essence of the clash was between tradition and modernity, which had made Chinese culture lost in suffering and confusion. Most of the material legacies, like the economic and political system have faded away, while the mental ones, such as the value system which has been imprinted on the Chinese people's minds, remain till today.

Since the founding of the PRC in modern times, the conflicts between tradition and modernity still exist; different civilizations renew and regulate themselves through dialogue with each other. In China, the traditional culture represented by Confucianism has experienced a revival in the process of modernization once more, and is seeking integration with the rising Western-oriented pop culture as well.

In brief, in the course of globalization and modernization, affected by both Chinese traditional culture and Western culture, Chinese culture has shown some new features. The spiritual world handed down from the tradition has combined with the lifestyle coming from modern culture, and has made new creations and international impacts. But nowadays Chinese culture is still in the transitional period between tradition and modernity, which is not a complete culture form. Therefore, how can Chinese culture enrich and develop itself by carrying out modernization while at the same time absorb the valuable merits of foreign culture? This problem is not a topic noted merely by scholars but the general public as well.

REFERENCES

Hweng-MingKu. (2012). *The Spirit of the Chinese people.* Nanjing: Yilin Press.
KingYeo-Chi. (1999). *From tradition to contemporary.* Peking: China Renmin University Press.
MuQian. (2012). *Nation and culture.* Peking: Jiuzhou Press.
Ruzhen Jiang. (1999). *The historical explanation and the modern value of Chinese traditional culture.* Shanxi: Shanxi Education Publishing House.
ShiquZheng. (2009). *A study of Chinese national spirit.* Peking: Beijing Normal University Publishing Group.
Storey John. (2007). *Culture studies and the study of popular Culture.* Peking: Peking University Press.

Part III. Civilizing Infrastructure

In: Chinese Civilization in the 21st Century
Editors: Andrew Targowski and Bernard Han

ISBN: 978-1-63321-960-1
© 2014 Nova Science Publishers, Inc.

Chapter 5

CHINESE CIVILIZATION AND THE STATE OF INFRASTRUCTURE IN THE 21ST CENTURY

Guo Yang[*]
Northeast Forestry University, Harbin, China

ABSTRACT

The *purpose* of this investigation is to define the central issues of the current and future trends of Chinese traditional and contemporary civilizational infrastructure. The methodology is based on an interdisciplinary big-picture view of the Chinese traditional infrastructure and contemporary civilization infrastructure and their developments and interdependency. Among the *findings* are: That there have been 5,000 years of brilliant Chinese civilization that has left a valuable heritage for China which has acted on the recent conditions and developments for the future. With this heritage, education has gained recognition through an inherited knowledge infrastructure, and development of information and transportation infrastructures. This has created a condition for further development of Chinese civilization. The infrastructure of Chinese civilization has a far-reaching effect on the development of Chinese modernization, both urban and rural. The heritage of Chinese civilization has made China achieve outstanding results in transportation, science, education, culture and space, and further development of knowledge, information and transportation infrastructure inevitably has brought power and new prosperity for Chinese civilization. *Practical implications*: Through the analysis of the impact of Chinese civilization upon Chinese society, this research will provide prospective directions of Chinese civilization particularly in the scope of its infrastructure. *Social implications:* The findings of this research will enhance one's knowledge about the history of Chinese civilization and awareness of China today and her future. *Originality:* This research is based on collecting relevant and independent objective secondary data. It offers a comprehensive overview and original insights into the infrastructure of Chinese civilization. Furthermore, it employs an interdisciplinary approach to pinpoint the infrastructure of the state of Chinese civilization in the 21st century.

---

[*] Corresponding author: email yangguo198731@126.com.

INTRODUCTION

Chinese civilization has a long history; it has been around for 5,000 years. The most important reason for its survival and longevity is "unity". This unity is seen in the written language, the moral and ethical standards, and the political organization of the culture. Chinese civilization has irreplaceable characteristics and values as a world civilization. This is not only the case for Chinese history and culture, and for the splendid achievement of Chinese civilization, but also for the unique thinking and language of the Chinese, the cultural system and the thought tradition which seems to contain infinite wonders. The corresponding infrastructure is vital in social production, scientific study, and the spreading of cultural achievements.

Until the fifteenth century, Chinese civilization's science and technology were in a leading position in the world. There is a tight connection between these achievements and the Chinese advanced education system. Ancient education is the foundation of the continuation and development of Chinese civilization. With the progress of social civilization, it has experienced three phases:

1. The first stage was from ancient times to the Chun Qiu (春秋770BC~476BC) and Zhan Guo (战国476BC~221BC) Dynasties. This was the formative period of education.
2. The second stage was from the Chun Qiu and Zhan Guo Dynasties to the Western Han Dynasty (西汉202BC~9AD). During this period education grew.
3. The third stage was from the Western Han dynasty to Sui (隋581AD~619AD) and Tang (唐618AD~907AD) dynasties; in this period, Chinese civilization matured in growth and education was closely combined with politics. (Dong, 2013)

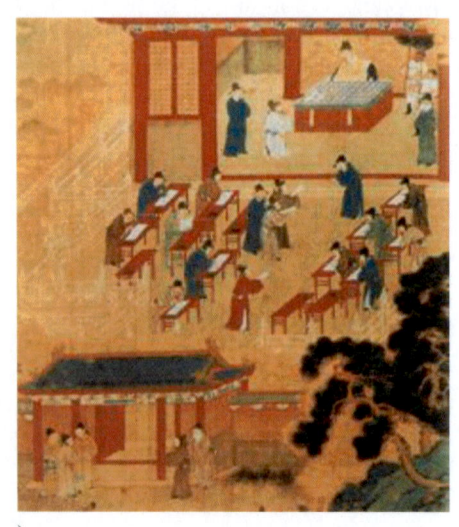

(Source : www.wikipedia.org).

Figure 5.1. The imperial examinations in the Ming Dynasty (明1368AD~1644AD).

The imperial examination system (Figure 5.1) that was produced in the Sui dynasty had a significant importance in the history of ancient Chinese civilization. It had a great influence on Chinese politics, society, academics, culture and education in the feudal society. The imperial examination system played a very important role in moving Chinese culture southward during the Song (宋960AD~1279AD) dynasty. In the long march of history of Chinese education, reading offered an avenue for students to have an official career and change of fate. From the initiation of education to imperial examination, most of the activities were held in a college or school. Yue Lu (岳麓) Academy was founded in during the Northern Song (北宋960AD~1127AD) dynasty; it was one of the four famous academies, and is the most commonly represented school. It was the first Imperial Academy that appeared during the Han (汉202BC~220AD) dynasty and was one kind of the ancient Chinese universities located in the capital.

Aside from the knowledge infrastructure, remarkably, Chinese people are the inventors of four great inventions: papermaking, printing, gunpowder and the compass. In the Eastern Han (东汉25AD~220AD) dynasty a reformation and innovation for papermaking was carried out by Cai Lun (蔡伦). This greatly improved the yield and quality of the paper that had been produced. Because of this, the use of paper spread throughout China, instead of the traditional use of bamboo and silk. After the invention of paper, printing also arose from the need to publish books. In the Northern Song dynasty, Bi Sheng (毕昇), a carver, invented the movable type printing, which was a significant revolution in the history of printing. *Gunpowder* was discovered in those times. The invention of gunpowder led to the invention of fireworks and early gunpowder weapons in China. *Gun powder* was widely used in the military during the period of the Song and Yuan (元1271AD~1368AD) dynasties. The earliest *compass* appeared in the period of Zhan Guo. People used the properties of a magnet to indicate north and south; they called it Si Na (司南). In the Northern Song dynasty, a famous scientist, Shen Kuo (沈括), using his predecessors' experience, found the existence of the magnetic declination and made a convenient and exact compass applying the artificial magnetization method.

These four great inventions of ancient China have become a strong force for promoting the development of science and civilization in the world. They were great inventions that shocked the world and in the two thousand years of their existence, they have obtained consistent approval everywhere. (Xu, 2004). As the German philosopher, Karl Marx, pointed out: "*Gunpowder, the Compass* and *Printing*", they announced the coming of bourgeois society. *Gun powder* liquidated the knight class; the *Compass* opened up the international market and established colonization, while *printing* became the tool of Christianity. Overall, *printing* became the most powerful lever for promoting the development of spiritual civilization.

THE INFORMATION INFRASTRUCTURE

Looking back in history and the way information was disseminated among Chinese people, one can find that there are broad fields and rules. In the process of information transmission in ancient China, the earliest way of information communication was verbal communication. This kind of dissemination was the main mode of communicating in ancient Chinese society (Wu and Wang, 2001). The earliest form of a systematic written language in China was called an Oracle. (Figure5.2).This allowed information to be spread to distant places by using texts and symbols on a medium. The creation and application of the written word allowed dissemination to be freed of time and space limitations; this marked the beginning of a new era: the transmission of words.

With the continuous development of human society, the means of communication has also undergone a long evolution. There are four main ways that the transmission of information occurred in ancient times:

- The You Yi pass, signal fires passes, Pigeon passes and others. The You Yi (邮驿) transfer was generated during the Zhou (周 11th century B.C~256BC) dynasty.
- In order to meet the needs of the political and military activities among kingdoms, the government set a Yang Zhi (阳置) (Yi Zhan (驿站)) every 15 kilometers along the main road for good horses and firm carriages. It was responsible for passing governmental documents, receiving the coming and going officials and delivering goods. Through this, a relatively complete system was formed. The subsequent dynasties adjusted this system only slightly. The system had a large influence on the modern postal system.
- People in the Western Zhou (西周11th century B.C~771BC) dynasty used signal fires to transfer information. There were beacon towers successively placed at particular distances apart from one another. These beacon towers were guarded by soldiers. When the enemy was coming, a solider would light a fire in their tower to signal the other towers, and one by one this passed on information. The beacon towers in the Han dynasty were broad, and management was very strict. It has been said that every 2.5–kilometers there was a Sui (隧), every 5–kilometers there was a Dun (墩), every 15–kilometers there was a Pu (堡) and every 50–kilometers there was a village. Fire passed information quickly. This method of transferring information was still in use during the Ming and Qing (清1636AD~1912AD) dynasties. Yan Tai (烟台, Eastern China) got his name for the beacon towers developed during the Ming dynasty. "The fire plays governors" is a famous story in Chinese history.(Zhu, 2002)
- Others forms of transmission included "Mailbox" transmission and "Kite" transmission. "Post" was a kind of water transportation; people placed a letter inside of a bamboo tube, then they would let it float along the river; this passed information on to others.

Transmission is just a tool. Its content is fundamentally expressed by words. Humans entered a new era of the "information superhighway" in the 21st century. Since the 1990s, this new technology spread to public life. The technologies that were spread were things such as digital technology, computers, multimedia and the Internet. Human society is entering a new era of the "Information Superhighway" after the "Mass Media Age" which innovations included mainly the television, newspapers and the radio.

(Source: www.wikipedia.org).

Figure 5.2. Oracle[1].

TRANSPORTATION INFRASTRUCTURE

Throughout the economic and social development of China, transportation was essential for a civilized society to get rid of chaos and establish order. With population growth, transportation becomes more and more important (Coyle, Novack and Gibson, 2010). China has a long history and profound culture of transportation, which has been very important to the history of transportation. Transportation in ancient China can be divided into two different stages: the "Walking Era" and the "Carriage Era." People socialized by walking due to lower technology until around 2100 BC. The "Carriage era" was from about 2100 BC to the Industrial Revolution at the end of the 19th century. It has been characterized by animal power instead of human power as the main way of transportation.

Road and water transport were both considered the basic means of transportation in ancient China. There was a well-developed road system in the Zhou dynasty. Frequent wars between kingdoms in the Chinese Chun Qiu and Zhan Guo dynasties sparked the development of carriage technology. Some kingdoms had thousands of carriages.

---

[1] Oracles were thought to be portals through which the gods spoke directly to people. In this sense they were different from seers (manteis, μάντεις) who interpreted signs sent by the gods through bird signs, animal entrails, and other various methods.

(source: www.wikipedia.org).

Figure 5.3. Zhao Zhou Bridge in the Sui Dynasty.

After Qin Shi Huang (秦始皇) united six countries, he built up two central roads running through Xian Yang (咸阳, Northwestern China). One went from the east to the Bohai Sea (The extreme north of the eastern China) and the other from the south to the Jiang Su (江苏, Eastern China) and Zhe Jiang (浙江, Eastern China). During the Han dynasty a certain level of construction and maintenance of the roads had been reached, and opened up the "Silk Road" to central Asia and west Asia. Chang'an (长安, Northwestern China) city, during the Tang Dynasty, had a population of more than 1,000,000. Because of this the construction and management of urban and rural roads were improved from the Song to the Qing dynasty. Guang Xu (光绪) built the first highway (the total length of 108 Li) from Long Jin (龙井, Northeast China) to Nan Guan (南关, Northeast China) during his reign as Emperor in Guang Xi (广西, Northeast China). Zhao Zhou (赵州) bridge, developed during the Sui dynasty, (Figure 5.3) became an outstanding example of bridge technology because of the principles of mechanics used and its beautiful Chinese style.

The ancient Chinese had a long history of using water traffic tools for water transportation. They used treasure ships of the Ming dynasty, the Grand Canal of the Sui dynasty, and the "Silk Road" and the "Grain Transportation". All of these showed that the ancient Chinese led the world for a long time in inland navigation and navigation technology. The Qin(秦221BC~207BC) and Han dynasties, the Tang and Song dynasties, and the Yuan and Ming dynasties formed three nautical climaxes with the use of the sail, the invention of the compass and advanced shipbuilding technologies. In particular, the Beijing (北京, Northern China) - Hangzhou (杭州, Eastern China) Grand Canal that was initially built in the Spring and Autumn, and completed during the Sui dynasty, played an important role in material transportation and promoting the exchange between the north and south for centuries.

As Chinese marine technology matured, strength and the will for peace were manifesting in the navy voyages outside of China. One example was Zheng He's (郑和) voyage (as it is depicted Figure 5.4). Some think that Zheng He's activities contributed to navigation and Marine culture worldwide, and promoted the exchange of navigation technology between Chinese and Arab regions, especially the scope of a large fleet, the ability to travel far distances, efficient navigation technology, excellent organization, effective logistics, well-organized port facilities, and precious Marine crystallization. Zheng He's seven expeditions (Table5.1) to the western seas allowed for Chinese civilization to spread to South Asia, East Africa, the Persian Gulf, the Pacific Ocean, and the Indian Ocean, and resulted in bringing in all kinds of plants, animals, medicines and raw material to China. His activities greatly broadened the Chinese horizon, enhanced the understanding of oversea cultures for Chinese during the Ming Dynasty, and promoted the exchange of Chinese and foreign culture. His expeditions composed a new chapter in the history of exchange between the Chinese and foreign civilizations and had a far-reaching influence on China's cultural presence in the world (Fan, 2005). Also, the "Silk Road" that began during the Han Dynasty and flourished during the Tang dynasty also strengthened the economic and cultural exchange between China and the countries surrounding the South Sea.

Table 5.1. Zheng He's seven expeditions

Order	Time	Regions along the way
1st voyage	1405–1407	Champa, Java, Palembang, Malacca, Aru, Samudera, Lambri, Ceylon, Qiulon, Kollam, Cochin, Calicut
2nd voyage	1407–1409	Champa, Java, Siam, Cochin, Ceylon, Calicut
3rd voyage	1409–1411	Champa, Java, Malacca, Semudera, Ceylon, Quilon, Cochin, Calicut, Siam, Lambri, Kayal, Coimbatore, Puttanpur
4th voyage	1413–1415	Champa, Kelantan, Pahang, Java, Palembang, Malacca, Semudera, Lambri, Ceylon, Cochin, Calicut, Kayal, Hormuz, Maldives, Mogadishu, Barawa, Malindi, Aden, Muscat, Dhofar
5th voyage	1417–1419	Champa, Pahang, Java, Malacca, Samudera, Lambri, Bengal, Ceylon, Sharwayn, Cochin, Calicut, Hormuz, Maldives, Mogadishu, Barawa, Malindi, Aden
6th voyage	1421–1422	Champa, Bengal, Ceylon, Calicut, Cochin, Maldives, Hormuz, Djofar, Aden, Mogadishu, Brava
7th voyage	1430–1433	Champa, Bengal, Ceylon, Calicut, Cochin, Maldives, Hormuz, Djofar, Aden, Mogadishu, Brava

(Data source: www.wikipedia.org).

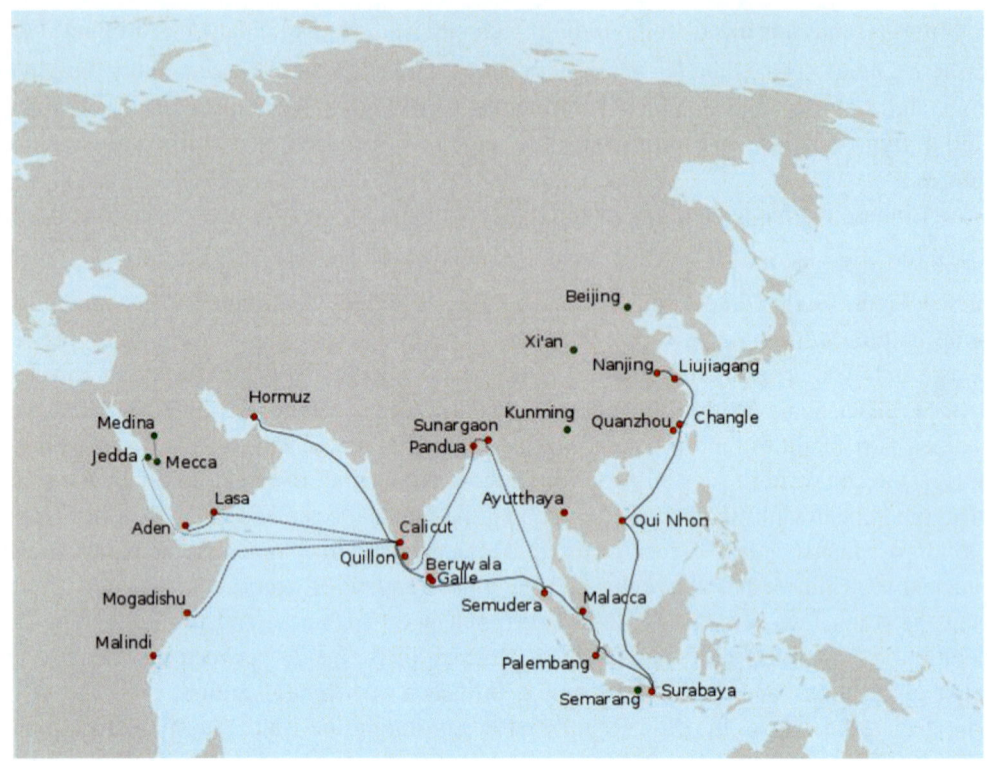

(source:www.wikipedia.org).

Figure 5.4. Zheng He's voyages down the western seas.

HOW TRADITIONAL CHINESE CIVILIZATION INFRASTRUCTURE IS APPLIED IN THE 21ST CENTURY

From a Traditional to a New Socialistic Civilization Infrastructure in Rural Areas

The fifth plenary session of the sixteenth central committee for the Communist Party of China was held in Beijing from the 8th to 11th of October in 2005.The fifth Plenary Session of the Sixteenth Central Committee put forward that society should advance the construction of a new socialist countryside according to the general requirements of enhanced labor productive forces, higher living standards, improved living styles, sustainable environmental practices and better administration. This important decision was based on a new stage of city-countryside relations in China, where industry promoted agriculture and cities helped the countryside. Building a new socialist countryside was a major project that involved economic, political, cultural and social construction. The movement of building a new socialist countryside was primarily focused on the following four aspects:

- Rural education infrastructure,
- Rural information infrastructure,
- Rural roadways and water channels.

- Taxation, which supported the development of these infrastructures (by cancelling the agriculture tax completely, helping farmers with subsidies for growing superior seed and subsidies for purchasing agricultural machineries and general subsidies for agricultural supplies).

Protecting Ancient Villages

The guiding Party's document pointed out that the countryside renewal should highlight the characteristics of the countryside, local characteristics and national features, and protect historic ancient villages and the ancient houses in new countryside developments.

The traditional village was known as "the DNA of the Chinese nation". The protection of the traditional village not only protected ancient architecture, but it also drew attention to the mixture and evolution of local culture and modern civilization.

The reconstruction of rural civilization was considered during the new developments. The protection of ancient villages frequently had the following problems: the number of villages was so large and it was difficult to fully protect them, there was not enough funding. The renewal of ancient villages often triggered commercial tourism as a benefit for the local community, but often caused the destruction of traditional architecture.

Hence, as the protection of ancient villages became more and more urgent, the renewal needed to look at the relationship between new rural needs and the protection of ancient villages in their current perspective. For now, the patterns of Chinese ancient village protection mainly relies on the police, especially with respect to the museums in the Jin Zhong (晋中, northern China) region. There are also a variety of forms of protection in Wu Yuan (婺源) of the Jiang Xi(江西)province (Eastern China), echoing the forms of Li Jiang, (丽江, southwestern China) an ancient city as well as a new town, and the forms of the inhabitants in Jiang Su, Zhe Jiang and other places.

Traditional Civilization Infrastructure in the Municipal Areas – The Chinese Urbanization Process

China is the only ancient civilization that has kept its historical continuity. This civilization has been maintained for 5,000 years. Chinese urban history can be divided into three stages (similarly to other developed nations):

- Agricultural Wave
- Industrial Wave
- Information Wave. (He, 2009)

Although scholars in academia have different views on the center of the world's agricultural origin, they all agree that China is one of the origins of agricultural centers if not the primary origin. With the development of agriculture, the number of cities increased, and the trend of the rural population moving to big cities was continuously growing. While the industrialization of China was not yet finished by the dawn of the 21st century, the major developed countries of Western Civilization began to enter the Information Wave. With the transformation of industrialization in China to the Information Wave, new changes also took place in cities. Time will tell whether "Digital Cities" are the right path compared to the 5,000 years of traditional Chinese Civilization.

The Protection and Application of Traditional Civilization Infrastructure in the Process of Urbanization

Today, great changes have taken place in many Chinese cities during the process of Chinese urbanization. This is due to large-scale construction, which very often demolishes traditional buildings. After numerous demolitions and rebuilding, thousands of new buildings and cities now have the same monotonic style, and the historical features have begun to fade away.

Cities as material entities of architectural culture accumulation reflect the continuity of history and the traditional culture of the nationality in that region, as well as form a distinctive and attractive art complex. The protection of the historic cities, ancient architectural structures and various cultural relics can only promote a distinctive Chinese urban charm.

THE STRATEGY OF THE MODERNIZATION OF CHINA FOCUSING ON THE CIVILIZATION INFRASTRUCTURE

China as the Outsourcing Power for the Western Civilization

"Made in China" is a general term for Chinese products sold around the world. The essence of this saying is that the expanding market shares in the international market because of the competitive advantage of lower prices from cheap labor. "Made in China" has a relation with extensive use and consumption of Chinese products in the world. This globally famous phrase, "Made in China", is impossible without the world's understanding of many manifold commodities that are the product of China.

Since China's reforms and opening to the world market, China has sped up the pace of the international market and the global production network. More and more manufacturing activities of multinational companies are moving to the China. China started off by producing toys, clothing, shoes, hats, textiles and other light industrial products. Now they provide all kinds of manufactured goods. China went from a light industrial products provider to "the world manufacturing base" during the last 20 years.

This change has largely been due to the aggregation and precipitation of the international movement across-borders. This is seen in elements such as labor, capital, technology, information, and so on. The formation of the world's manufacturing base usually is accompanied by the transfer of foreign assembly of products being moved to China. This precipitation and increased production volume gave many foreign enterprises a better world market share and profit. After the United States, China is the second largest economy today. Chinese–made products fill every corner of the world. If one walks into a foreign supermarket, one will find that there are a variety of products with the label, "made in China," such as towels, hair dryers, cosmetics, mobile phones and so on. Perhaps this is reason that China is considered the World's Factory.

But China's status as the World's Factory in some ways does not conform to the economic development trend of modern society, China is just a processing factory, and makes goods, while core technology remains firmly in the hands of foreign companies. For instance, many people desire to purchase Apple's iPhone; in fact, Apple's iPhone catches people's attention due to the core of continuous technological innovation, and they so far are standing in the forefront of technological progress in the world. Apple's products are very popular largely because they are inexpensive due to being "Made in China." When Steve Jobs (Apple's CEO) took a MacBook Air (thin as Air) from the envelope, many people were shocked, and ever since this product has entered into the Chinese market. It has become the main laptop used for business in China.

The key to the success of "Made in China" is giving foreign companies technological superiority (in the case of Apple); the Chinese enterprises only assemble the corresponding parts, and then sell them. But, perhaps, one day China will be able to be a completely independent manufacturer.

China Transforming from Dependent Manufacturers to Independent Manufacturers and the Repercussions on the Civilization Infrastructure

Today and in the Future

From the founding of PRC (People's Republic of China) in 1949 to 2008-2014 China has become the second largest economy in the world. China is the largest developing country in the word; the main gap between China and the developed countries is in the application of intellectual property rights in science and technology. Currently, China is a big manufacturing country; many products are the best or ranked among the best in the world. But the goods which China has created by itself are limited. To get from being a subordinate manufacturer to being an independent manufacturer, China must display its resources as the world's biggest market, and use its knowledge, wisdom, and skills to create its own engineering solutions to improve labor productivity, reduce costs, improve the technical level of its products, strengthen the combination of production and research, pay attention to the cultivation of innovative talents, apply intellectual property laws and brand value, be decisive in the taking-off process from "Made in China" to "Created in China", and finally achieve the great rejuvenation of the Chinese nation.

The innovation that China should take on is not only technology and products "created in China," but it should also draw inspiration from the heritage and tradition of the Chinese culture that has existed for five thousand years. In the wonderful opening ceremony for the Beijing Olympic Games 2008, the performance was a most convincing demonstration of Chinese traditional culture as a symbol of China's face such as the Beijing Opera (Figure 5.5), Fou Yue (缶乐), Kung Fu (功夫) and landscape painting.

The international media of the Olympic Games broadcasted Chinese elements and culture all over the world and reminded everyone that China is rising and becoming a world power again, as it used to be 500 years ago. Recently many Confucius Institutes have been established around the world, demonstrating a decisive motivation for the Chinese government in trying to expand its international influence. Confucius Institutes numbered at 1,089 in March 2014 in 121 countries. The Confucius Institute has become a symbol of Chinese "soft power" and a transnational mind rising in contemporary China. The Confucius Institute wants to improve the understanding of Chinese language and culture for people in other countries, developing friendly relations between China and others, promoting the development of multiracial culture, and contributing to construct a harmonious world.

China today is playing an increasingly important role in international affairs. Chinese participation is essential for gaining solutions to major world affairs. With the rise of emerging powers, people can find that political and economic order is changing from the dominance of the Atlantic to Pacific hemisphere, where China is the emerging power. The world of the 21st century is moving on to a new equilibrium of profound adjustment.

Firstly, the influence of Chinese culture in the world has increased. Chinese civilization lasting for 5,000 years has been rejuvenated in the era of economic globalization, and it is compatible with other civilizations, which will enhance the interaction and fusion of the world's civilization and complement each other, and perhaps promote the coming of an era of harmonious civilization all over the world. With the ascension of Chinese foreign investment volume and quality, there is an all-around deepening development of relationships between China and other countries. Chinese traditional culture gives a unique charm in which different cultures can coexist and have a harmonious development. For instance, Chinese food can be found in almost every city of the world.

Secondly, China through its strength in supplying inexpensive goods is making contributions to the prosperity and development of the world's economy. The continuous, rapid, coordinated and healthy development of the Chinese economy has given and will continuously give the international community more opportunities and greater space in cooperation.

THE EXAMPLES OF MODERNIZED CHINESE CIVILIZATION INFRASTRUCTURE IN TODAY'S CHINA

Computers in Schools and Universities

The popularity of computers has increased during the last 30 years in China which has about 17% of the world's population (Tan, 2011). It has not only profoundly changed the face of China, but shocked the world. The developed countries and some developing countries have promoted the application of information technology in education since the late 20th century. The Chinese government also seized this historic opportunity and formulated the corresponding measures and carried out productive work.

In 1984, Deng Xiaoping put forward "the popularization of the computer to grab the next generation from birth", since then the application of information technology for teaching has continuously been promoted in primary and secondary schools. The number of schools that had computer electives as a course was only five in 1982, but the number grew to 26, 294 by 1994, and it reached 40,851 by the end of 1996. At present, all provinces of China have courses in computer education to varying degrees. The network of satellite broadband transmissions and the Internet are currently in primary and secondary schools across the whole country.

A preliminary environment for Network teaching has been formed. According to the statistics of the Ministry of Education, about 16% of China's primary schools, 46% of junior high schools, and 77% of high schools have built varying campus networks. About 25% of the primary and secondary schools have access to the Internet in a variety of ways. The number of primary and secondary schools that have at least 100M bandwidth has reached 20,000 today. There were 5.12 computers per 100 students on primary school campuses, 7.78 computers on secondary school campuses, and 13.45 computers on the high school campuses by the end of 2011.

The database of the National Basic Education Resource was recently built, which evaluates 7 categories and 36 subjects. Knowledge points refer to a total of 4,129 disciplines. The database covers the content of multiple textbooks for grades 1-9.

The internet is effective in China; usually the main line has the capacity/speed of about 1000MBaud/s, and 100 MB/s. Such networks as CHINANET, which is a campus network, not only provides DNS, WWW, FTP, VOD, MAIL and other basic services, but also provides various kinds of office and teaching application systems, such as the electronic document exchange system, Tsinghua comprehensive educational administration system, high-quality goods curriculum network development platform, etc. Meanwhile, the schools also are continuously enriching the online resources, providing electronic database resources such as electronic science and technology periodicals, the database of master and doctor students' theses, electronic books, and so on (Zhang, 2010).

(Source: www.wikipedia.org).

Figure 5.5. Beijing Opera performance in the opening ceremony of Olympic Games 2008.

Bullet Trains

Since the 1960s (Japan, France, and later Germany) many countries started to develop high-speed railways. China also carried out a large number of scientific and technical researches in the design and construction technology of high-speed railways, bullet trains, and basic theories of operation management and key technologies.

On October 12, 2003, the first Chinese high-speed rail, "Qing-Shen (秦沈) passenger line", was completed and opened to public traffic. On December 1, 2013, the Jin-Qin (津秦) railway passenger line was opened to public traffic. After the efforts of nearly a decade, the total Chinese mileage of the high-speed rails (Figure 5.6) has reached 11,028 kilometers. China has become a country that has a very comprehensive technology and strong integration ability, as well as the longest mileage, the highest speed and the largest scale of constructing in high-speed railway.

There are 16 countries that have completed and operated high-speed railways. These countries are China, Spain, Japan, Germany, France, Sweden, the UK, Italy, Russia, Turkey, Korea, Belgium, the Netherlands and Switzerland. It can be seen that most of these countries are developed. Compared with the developed countries, the development of the high-speed railway in China started relatively late, but has grown quickly. Chinese mileage of high-speed railway will reach 19,000 km by 2015, and it will be more than 120,000 km by 2020. The net of rapid passenger transportation will basically cover provincial capitals in China and other cities which have more than 500,000 people.

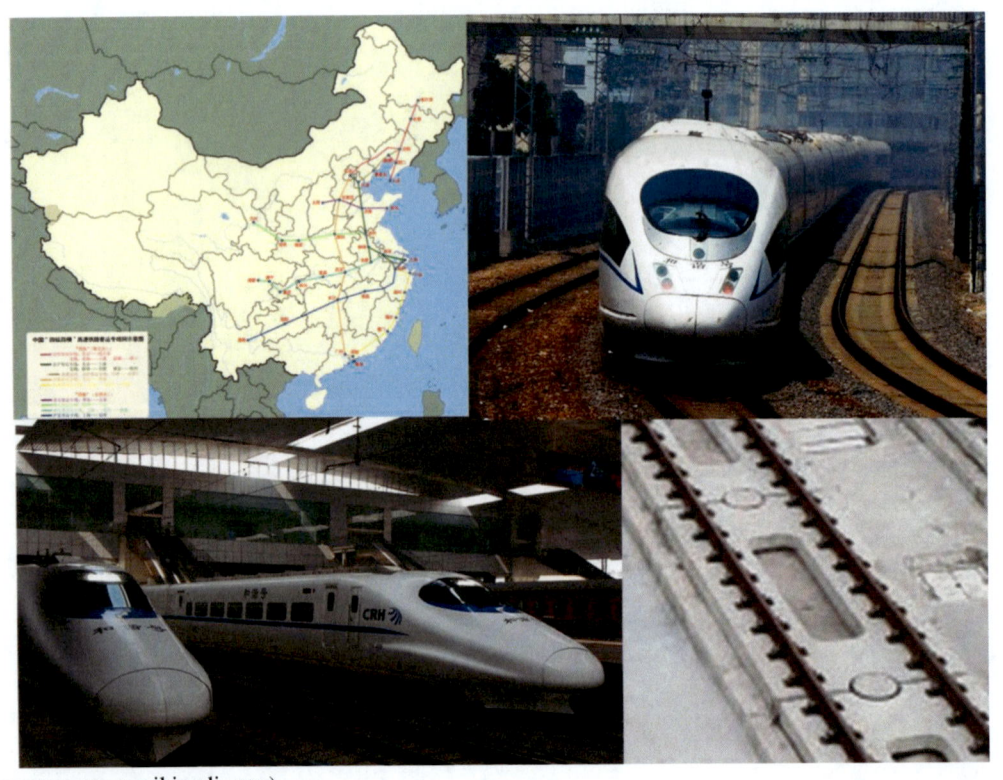

(source: www.wikipedia.org).

Figure 5.6. Chinese high-speed rail.

Table 5.2. The Chinese Airline Infrastructure Statistics in 2012

Total	International Routes	Domestic Routes	
2,457	381	2,076	Number of Regular Civil Aviation Routes (line)
3,280,114	1,284,712	1,995,402	Length of Regular Civil Aviation Routes (km)
31936	2,336	29,600	Passenger Traffic (10000 persons)
5,450,342	1,565,170	3,885,173	Freight Traffic (ton)

(data source: 2013 Statistical Yearbook of China).

Airlines

The airlines originated during the 1920s in China. After entering the 21st century, the Chinese economy ensured sound and rapid development. The national economy had high-speed growth for decades and air transport demanded similar growth. This led the construction of civil airports to have a developmental climax. By the end of 2012 (Table 5.2), the number of civil airports reached 180. In 2012, China had 3,589 civilian aircrafts and 2,457 flight routes; the cumulative flight distance was 3,280,114 km, carrying approximately 319.36 million passengers and goods of about 5,450,342 tons. The United States has accumulated the largest aviation system in the world during the past hundred years. It has more than 19,750 airports, with 3,356 of them belonging to the national air system. Compared with the sheer scale of the airports in the United States, Chinese current airports remain highly short of demand. The development of air transport system has a long way to go. (Wang and Yan, 2010)

The Chinese space industry started in 1970. It was marked by successfully launching China's first man-made earth satellite, "East is Red", on April 24th 1970. China became the fifth country that could independently develop and launch artificial earth satellites in the world. China's first lunar lander, named Chang'E 3, was successfully launched on December 2nd, 2013. On December 15th, 2013, the Moon lander separated from the patrol unit of "Chang'E 3." The patrol unit of "Yutu" (玉兔) (Figure 5.7) successfully reached the surface of the moon. By December, 2013, China developed and launched 238 artificial earth satellites of various types; the rate of successful flights has been more than 95%.

Roads

With the establishment and perfection of the socialist market economic system, Chinese highway traffic entered the track of rapid and healthy development after adopting a policy of reform and opening up. The total mileage of Chinese highway is in continuous growth. It was only 80,800 km long in 1949, but after 40 years it has reached 4.2375 million kilometers long. Chinese highway construction embarked on a track of accelerated development beginning with the first highway "Shanghai–Jiading" (上海, Eastern China - 嘉定, Eastern

China) which opened in 1988. It remedied the zero breakthrough in the Chinese mainland. The trunk highway system, reaching the total size of 35,000 kilometers, was built in 2008. "Five vertical and seven horizontal" roads on the map mark the formation of a skeleton for the Chinese highway system (Figure 5.8).

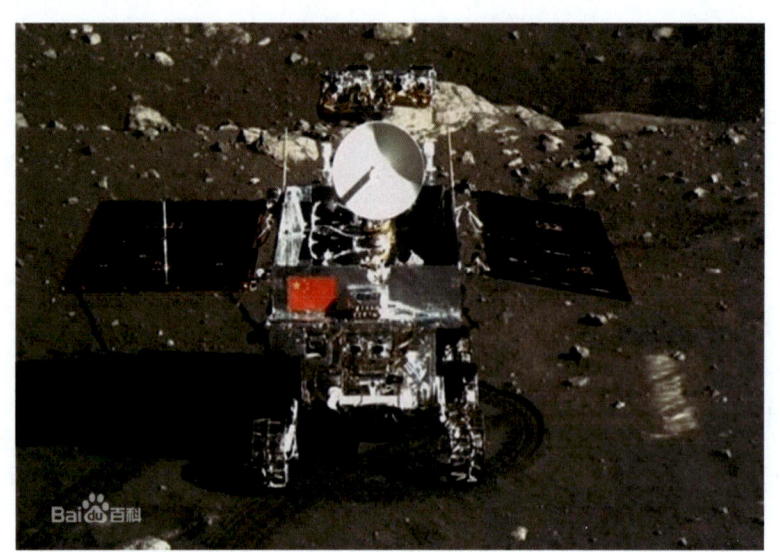

(Source: http://baike.baidu.com).

Figure 5.7. "Yutu" lunar rover.

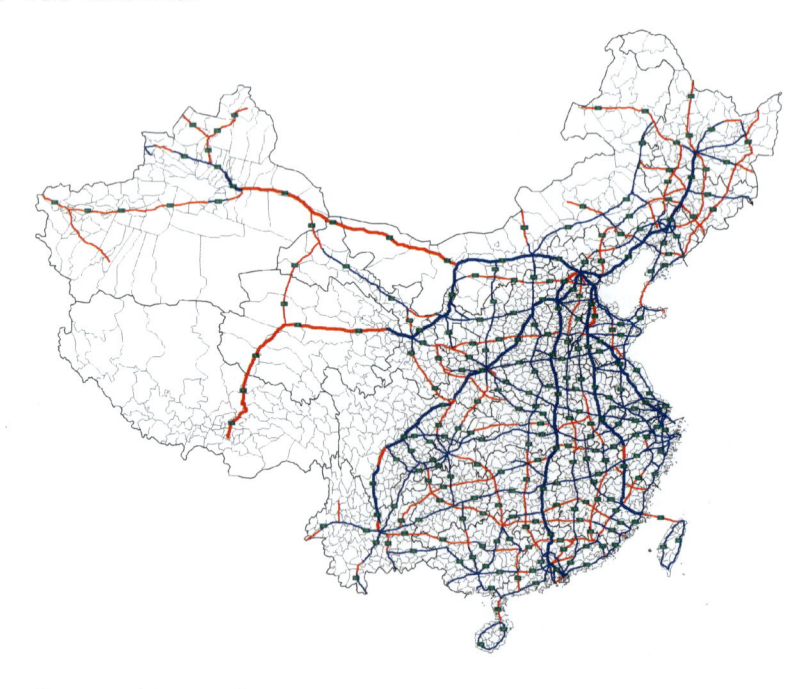

(Source: http://www.cngaosu.com/).

Figure 5.8. Chinese highway network.

Chinese highway mileage reached 96,200 kilometers by 2012, only second to the U.S.A. China became the second-largest country in terms of highway infrastructure. Highways in China can be characterized by the leap-forward in development and can meet the needs of the economy. Developed regions in Eastern China have the same level of density as the United States and other developed countries. The Chinese road network has already been formed. But because of the large Chinese population (by 2012, the total number reached 1.35404 billion), there is only 0.003 km per person on the highway. Obviously, the Chinese road infrastructure cannot yet fully meet the needs of the social and economic development that occurred during the 21st century.

THE FUTURE OF THE CHINESE CIVILIZATION INFRASTRUCTURE

The Future of the Chinese Knowledge Infrastructure

China is a developing country with a large population and limited natural resources. Development of its knowledge economy has become an inevitable choice. In order to cope with the tide of the era of knowledge economy, it became increasingly important to strengthen the national knowledge infrastructure. The center of education and R & D (Research and Development) are the most important departments of the knowledge economy era. Education and R & D infrastructure will be the highlight of the Chinese knowledge infrastructure. A network is necessary for any department; through a network, people in all aspects of economic activity can easily obtain and apply the knowledge they need, which should be the top priority of the Chinese knowledge infrastructure. This network should have access to the World-wide Knowledge Infrastructure and not keep China in isolation.

The Future of the Chinese Information Infrastructure

Since the 20th century, information technology spread with rapid pace into the economic and social fields. It triggered a worldwide information revolution. In order to adapt to the accelerated development of global information, the Chinese government also attached great importance to information technology and spared no efforts to push forward the pace of infrastructure construction. With positive efforts of all aspects in China, national information infrastructure began to take shape and a network infrastructure significantly improved. (Table5.3)

Table 5.3. Chinese information infrastructure in 2012

indicators	The total length of cable(Km)	The capacity of mobile telephone exchange (Ten thousand)	Internet access ports (Ten thousand)
2007	5,777,000	85,486.1	8,538.3
2012	14,806,000	182,869.8	26,835.5

(Source: MII's statistical bulletin of national telecommunications).

However, the domestic society is in the preparation stage of creation of the Chinese Information Society. In the meantime, Shanghai and Beijing took the lead in this scope. The "2006-2020 National Development Strategy" published in 2006, pointed out that "by 2020, the strategic objectives of the development of China's information technology were: to popularize the integrated information infrastructure, strengthen information technology, enhance the capability of independent innovation, optimize the level of protection of national security information and substantially improve the national economy and social information, make remarkable achievements in the development of new industrialization model, and increase the National IT application capacity significantly.

All these should lay a solid foundation for the information society. During the following years, China needed to do a lot of preparatory work, in which the infrastructure construction and improvement is most critical. Meanwhile, cloud computing, networking, 4G and other new information technologies could be popularized and applied within the whole society.

The Future of the Chinese Transportation Infrastructure

China is a typical continental country. Therefore transportation plays an important role in supporting the national economy and social development. The Chinese economic miracle is contingent on the great progress of Chinese transportation. The future pattern of the Chinese transportation infrastructure will face a transformation from the traditional to the modern mode of sustainable development, , will promote coordinated development of highways, aviation and other kinds of transportation, and will establish a modern comprehensive transportation system that has a flawless regulatory system of traffic safety and security.

CONCLUSION

Chinese civilization has a history of 5,000 years; therefore, traditional and modern infrastructure in the process of the current and future development embodies this precious heritage. This study, based on interdisciplinary and overall view of Chinese traditional infrastructure and contemporary infrastructure, as well as the development and the present situation of interdependence, reached the following conclusions:

1. The legacy of the Chinese civilization is enormous, spanning 5,000 years. The mode of Chinese education has been profoundly affected by the imperial examination system.
2. Chinese civilization infrastructure reflects the change from walking and riding horses and chariots to develop and advance transportation, which today are harmonious effects of the early development of Chinese settlement in the urban and rural communities throughout its vast territory.
3. The infrastructure of Chinese civilization makes improvement while developing. Along with Chinese reform and opening up, China rapidly became the outsourcing post of Western Civilization and wants to transform from a subordinate manufacturer into an independent manufacturer, which also will improve the infrastructure of

Chinese civilization, which is exemplified by "Created in China" and high-speed trains and aviation.
4. The infrastructure of Chinese civilization is not yet completed and needs further developments, particularly in the scope of knowledge and engineering infrastructures.

REFERENCES

Coyle, John J., Novack, Robert A. & Gibson, Brian. (2010). *Transportation: a supply chain*. Perspective: Kentucky: Cengage Learning.

Dong, Kunyu. (2013). Newly explore the division Chinese ancient education history. *Journal of Hebei Normal University (Educational Science Edition)*, (*5*), 25-29.

Fan, Jinmin. (2005). The position of treasure voyages in world's navigation history. *Jiangsu Social Sciences*, (*1*), 201-204.

Fu, Xiaoyun. (2008). attach importance to the protection of history culture in city development. *Science & Technology Information*, (*4*), 147.

He, Yimin. (2009). Agriculture, industry, and information: three of China city historical periodization. *Academic Monthly*, (*10*), 139-141.

Huang, Yuehao. & Rao, Xiaojun. (2010). The method of vernacular village protection--a case study of Wangkou village. *New Architecture*, (*5*), 27-31.

Landes, Davis S. (1999). The wealth and poverty of nations: why some are so rich and some so poor.New York: W.W. Norton & Company

Li, Dan. (2012). An analysis of the status of "world factory" in China. *Commercial Culture*, (*4*), 140.

Li, Shaohui. (2013). Conservation of traditional villages expect "organic recovery." *China Reform Newspaper*, (*11*), 1 3.

Lu, Li. (2010). The technology changes and ethical reasoning of China's ancient transportation. *Jiangxi Social Sciences*, (*4*), 225-230.

Luo, Yang. (2010). Four patterns of ancient village protection. *Art of Design*, (*4*), 8.

Qu, Lingyan. (2004). Key points on urban historic area's conservation planning. *World Regional Studies*, (*12*), 40.

Shi, Yaobo. (2011). Role change of China role in international division of labor. *International Economic Cooperation*, (*8*), 28-30

Tan, Haoqiang. (2011). Process and inspiration of the computer in China. *Computer Education*, (*9*), 1-4

Tao, Jinjue. (2013). Problem research of world factory contemporary China. *Northern Economy*, (*11*), 51-53.

Wang, Xiaolei & Yan, Xuedong. (2010). Proceedings of international conference on engineering and business management. *Scientific Research Publishing*.

Wei, Yuejun. (2011). The status quo and countermeasure to infrastructure construction in China. *Journal of Beijing Forestry University (Social Sciences)*, (*6*), 46-49.

Wu, Jianqi & Lin, Shusheng. (2001). A brief view of the way of ancient Chinese information transmission. *Journal of Harbin Institute of Technology(Social Science Edition)*, (*3*),126-128.

Xia, Rongmin. Wang, Qin. & Su, Lina. (2011). A study on the trend of construction and development of the Chinese national knowledge infrastructure. *Agriculture Network Information*, (*11*), 19-21.

Xu, Xiaowang. (1998). Study on the development of imperial examination and southeast culture. *Southeast Academic Research*, (*6*), 84-90.

Xu, Xuelin. (2004). Review of "origin, development, spread and world influence of China's four great inventions." *Academic World.*

Zhang, Jun & Gao, Yuan. (2007). Why China own good infrastructure? *Economic Research Journal*, (*3*), 4-19.

Zhang, Xueyi. (2010). Thought on construction of computer network in campus. *Communications Technology*, *43*(3), 81-55.

Zhu, Xiaoli. (2002). The modes and approaches of ancient Chinese information transmission. *Modern Information.*

In: Chinese Civilization in the 21st Century
Editors: Andrew Targowski and Bernard Han

ISBN: 978-1-63321-960-1
© 2014 Nova Science Publishers, Inc.

Chapter 6

IS CHINA ON THE WRONG PATH OF THE U.S. AGRICULTURAL DEVELOPMENT IN THE 21ST CENTURY?

Agnieszka Couderq[*]
Orange Alternative Foundation,
Vice-President, Poland

ABSTRACT

The *purpose* of this essay is to examine the Chinese Civilization and the limits to its current development, taking into consideration the most critical aspect for human survival: access to fresh air, water and food. The *methodology* consists of comparing the past US agricultural and rural development in the 20th century and its present-day consequences with the model adopted by China since the beginning of their economic reforms in 1979. Among *the findings* are: since 1980 China has followed the US model of rapid urbanization and industrialization of its agriculture. Similarly to the US it is now facing very serious and undesirable side effects of this strategy such high pollution of air, soil and water as well as cultural losses due to the destruction of the village based cultural fabric. In addition, urbanization compounded by growing incomes has led to negative changes in dietary habits of the Chinese, resulting in a diabetic epidemic. *Practical implication*: Chinese leaders need to muster up sufficient political will to immediately introduce necessary strategic changes which will address the water crisis through a variety of policies in sectors ranging from agriculture to education. *Social implication*: Without water, very soon the Great Chinese Dream will become the Great Chinese Nightmare undermining the very foundations of the current political and social system. *Originality:* This analysis, taking in account the ecological impact of Chinese economic development on its most vital resources, emphasizes the natural limits of growth of the Chinese Civilization.

[*] nuren@inpoland.pl

INTRODUCTION

The purpose of this essay is to examine the Chinese Civilization and the limits to its current development, taking in consideration the most critical aspect for human survival: access to fresh air, water and food. The availability of these three resources is a precondition for human existence, not to mention its culture or political and social relations.

In his ground breaking book, *Collapse: How Civilizations Choose to Fail or Succeed* [1], Jared Diamond identifies five factors that contribute to the collapse of civilizations: hostile neighbors, collapse of essential trading partners, environmental problems, climate change and failure to adapt to environmental issues.

One of the oldest domains of the human activity which deals with air, food and water, and happens to be intrinsically related with the last three factors defined by Diamond is, of course, agriculture.

After 1978, China has been faced with different choices for its urban vs. rural and agricultural development. In this essay I will compare the path of development chosen by China's government with the agricultural strategy that has been underway since the 1930s in the United States to look for significant similarities and differences.

In this analysis of key importance will be the fact that China and the US are two countries with a total area of comparable size (i.e. about 10 million km2), yet the Chinese population is bigger than its American counterpart by a factor of three.

Another key issue which I shall consider is the freshwater availability and the current water pollution levels in both countries. According to data for 2011 on the CIA's World Fact Book site, the total renewable water resources in the US and China are comparable in volume (2,840 cu km vs. 3,069 cu km, respectively). However, due to the population size, China's freshwater availability per capita is at one third of that in the US. Furthermore, the freshwater pollution in China at 3.78-tons/cubic km is already twice the US level at 1.14 tons/cubic km [2]. The above considerations are of extreme importance as the US style of agricultural development has proven to be extremely harmful, among other negative impacts, for freshwater resources. In short, the increased efficiency of food production in the US has been obtained only in exchange for higher levels of water pollution.

In light of the differences between China and the US in the population size and freshwater availability, I herein propose a thesis that the closer the Chinese agricultural development model is to that which is practiced at present in the US, the faster China's development will be limited by the most vital human choice: *to Drink or to Eat?*

Being faced with such a *"no-way-out"* alternative will necessarily mean, for the Chinese civilization just like for the American one, a period of dramatic upheavals that in the end *will shatter* the present social and political order.

HISTORIC OVERVIEW OF THE U.S. AGRICULTURAL DEVELOPMENT

Urbanization of the United States

As a country developed over the course of the last two centuries by settlers, the United States started on its economic development primarily as an agricultural economy. The last two hundred years saw not only a spectacular increase in the country's population but also a dramatic transformation of its rural and urban environments and its approach *to farming as a traditional activity with its inherent social and family values.*

Still at the beginning of the 19th century, the US population totaled 5.3 million people, and city dwellers accounted for only about 300 thousand. This disproportion began to change with the advent of industrialization of the nation in the mid 1850s, and today one of its most immediate consequences is *the near total disappearance of the farming population. The statistics for 2010 show that for the total population of 311 million people, under 1 % are actually citing farming as their primary occupation.*

The farm depopulation trend was somewhat offset by the appearance of rural communities, whose subsistence, however, has not been tied directly to farming. Not surprisingly then, *rural America is dominated today by a service oriented economy* such as gasoline stations, retail distribution, restaurant and banking services. Even so, percent-wise, when compared with the total US population, the rural (defined as farming and non-farming) population has been in constant decline (see Figure 6.1).

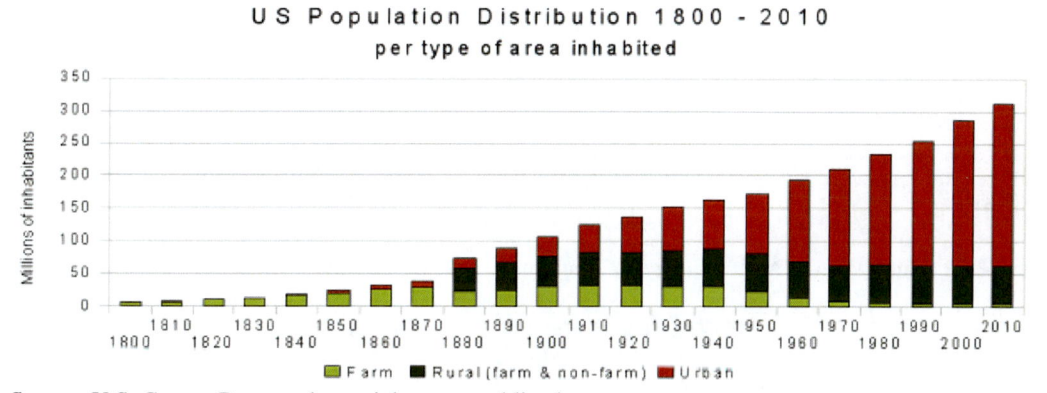

Source: U.S. Census Bureau, decennial census publications.

Figure 6.1. US Population Distribution 1800 – 2010 per type of area inhabited.

According to the Bureau's statistics as of December 2010, about *82% of the population* of the United States live in the urbanized *area,* which represents *about 2% of the land area* of the United States. The rural area inhabitants correspond, therefore, to less than one fifth of the total population (about 18%).

Elimination of the U. S. Farming Jobs

The biggest drop in the farming population was observed in three decades: the 1950s, 1960s and 1970s. Along with the drop in the farming population, the number of farms had been dwindling from its peak in 1935 at 6.8 million until it leveled off at 2.2 million at the beginning of 1990, and has remained at this number ever since.

The decline in the number of farms also necessarily implied a decline in the number of farming jobs available in the US. The labor force employed in farming has shrunk from over 10 million jobs in the 1930s to slightly over 2 million in the 2010s (see Figure 6.2). This *evaporation of 8 million jobs* was accompanied by a corresponding drop in the number of workers employed per farm.

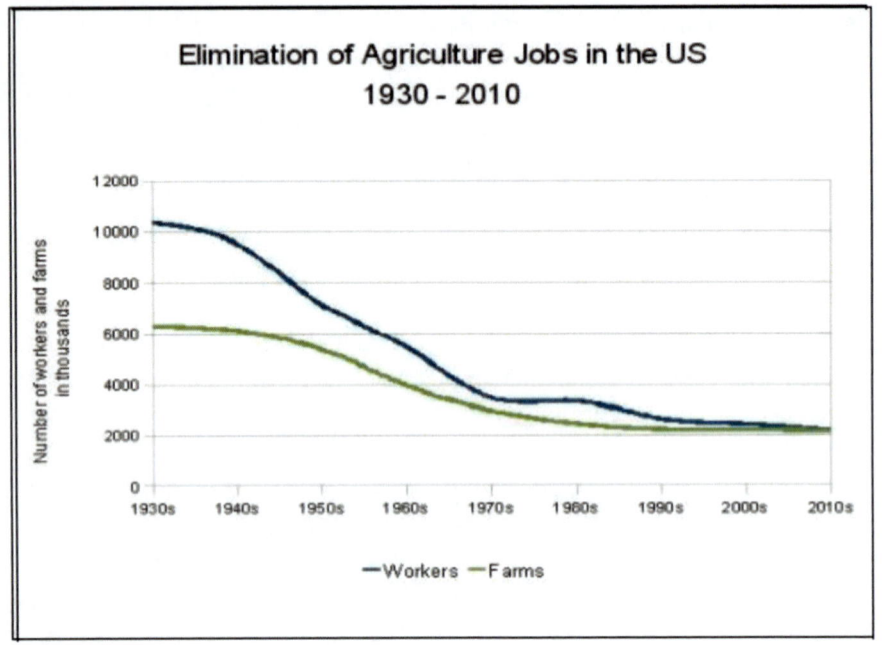

Source: *Agricultural employment: has the decline ended*, Patricia A. Daly, Monthly Labor Review, BLS.

Figure 6.2. Elimination of Agriculture related jobs in the US in the period 1930-2010.

Source: www.agcensus.usda.gov

Figure 6.3. Land distribution of the US farms per economic sale class in 2012.

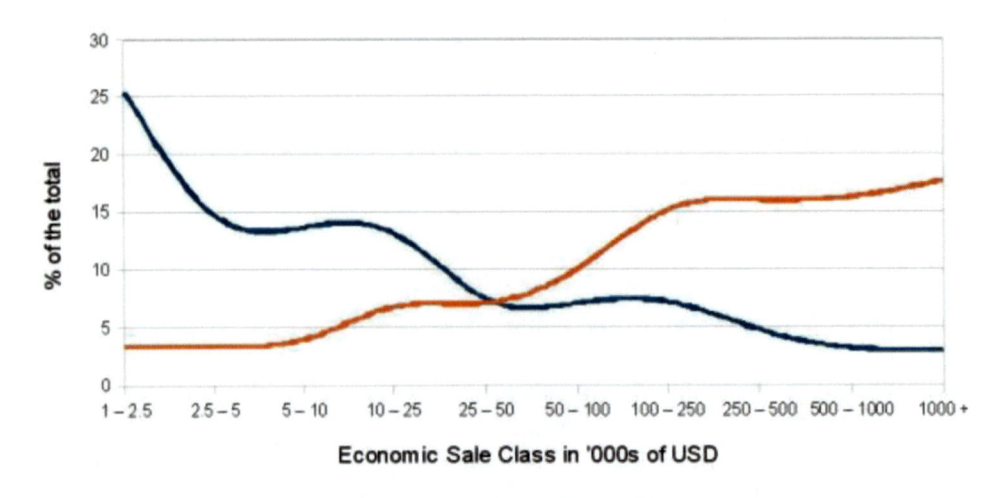

Accelerating specialization and capitalization of the farming sector allowed for massive farm buy-outs and consolidation. Those in turn led to an increase in the *average farm size* to about *159 hectare (ha)*. Today, *3% of farms representing the class of annual sales above 1 million USD hold together nearly 18% of US farming land*, while 82% of farms representing annual sales under 100 thousand USD own less than 35% of the total farming land in the US (see Figure 6.3).

As consolidation continues, the share in the total US agricultural output of the biggest 3% of farms has increased since 2002 from 47% to nearly 60% in 2012.

In view of the growing food demand, which is due to the expanding population of the US, all of the above reductionist and consolidating processes were only made possible by major transformations in the farming activity itself.

The Hidden Truth behind the Growth of Efficiency in U.S. Agriculture

Economies with large-sized farms not only led to large-scale mechanization but also to greater density per ha of commercial fertilizers and pesticides. This resulted in a dramatic *six-fold increase in the efficiency of food production*. As a result, today's American farmer feeds about 155 people worldwide. In 1960, that number was 25.8.

On another hand, even though one farmer's efficiency grew in terms of the number of people fed, since the beginning of the 1970s the *relative rate of this increase has been continuously dropping* notwithstanding sharply rising farm expenditures (see Figure 6.4). Thus the marginal cost of feeding one more person has been persistently growing. Put in simple words, for an average US farmer, the accomplishment of being able to feed one person more is becoming increasingly expensive. The growth of marginal costs is leading to higher consumer prices for food products, a fact widely known to anyone in the US shopping for food on a regular basis.

Efficiency Growth in the US Agriculture vs Farm Expenditures
(Absolute and relative increase in the number of people fed by one farmer)

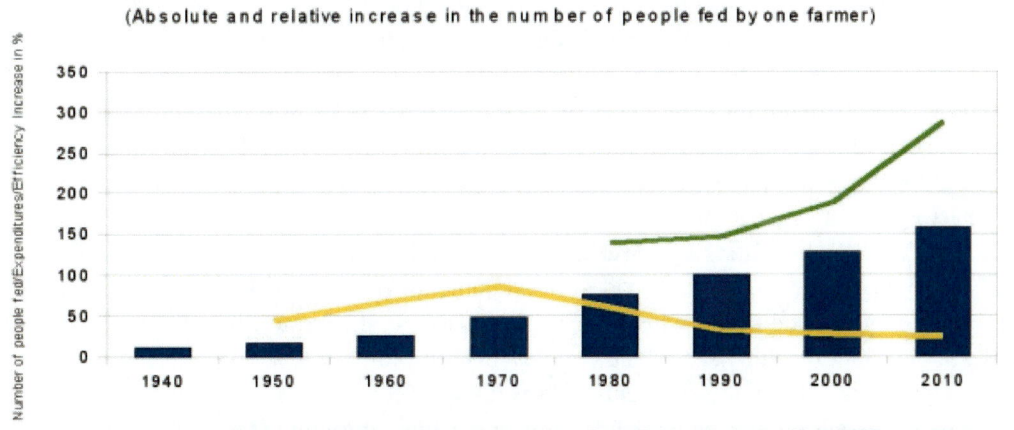

Source: United States Department of Agriculture.

Figure 6.4. Efficiency growth in the US agriculture vs. farm expenditures.

The explanation for both the increase in efficiency as well as the falling rate of this growth lays in the transformation of the farming process itself. Large farms are not like smaller farms on a bigger scale. They are like factories, churning out a single or a limited choice of agricultural products. Large farms almost always have to specialize in a few cash crops, abandoning the traditional idea of crop rotation (hence the greater need for fertilizers). Farm animals are raised in industrial conditions, away from their natural environment in conflict with their natural instincts. For example the share of industrially raised hogs in US pork production grew in less than thirty years from 30% to the present level of nearly 92% (see Figure 6.5).

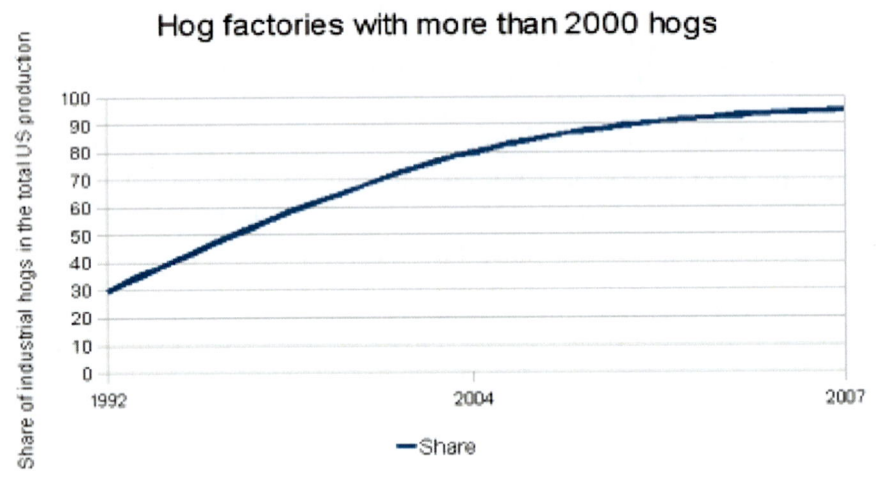

Source: USDA.

Figure 6.5. Share of industrially raised hogs on the US Market. Hog factories with more than 2000 hogs.

The use of these modern agro-industrial technologies is "packed" with so-called "negative externalities". The drive to efficiency and profit maximization has pushed the so-called "agro-businesses" to set aside environmental preoccupations, leading to the overuse of chemical and pharmaceutical products such as fertilizers, pesticides, antibiotics and growth hormones (see Figure 6.6 and 6.7). In their effort to obtain greater yields, they did not hesitate to adopt risky new technologies such as genetic engineering in crops and animals.

Factory farms generate millions of tons of animal manure, which releases into the air, soil and water massive quantities of powerful chemical pollutants like hydrogen sulfide, methane and ammonia. Those compounds lead to irreversible air pollution whose magnitude exceeds the pollution generated by car emissions. [3] Furthermore, the waste generated in these farms poses high public health risks in the form of deadly biological pathogens such as E. Coli 0157, Salmonella, Campylobacter jejun, Clostridium difficile and Listeria.

Last but not least, the industrial method of raising cattle and hogs is a major cause of water loss. Fresh water, the most important and increasingly scarce vital resource for human survival is thus wasted on cleaning buildings and in the waste management systems. In the meantime potable water availability is becoming a critical issue, particularly in the drier regions of the south and southwest US.

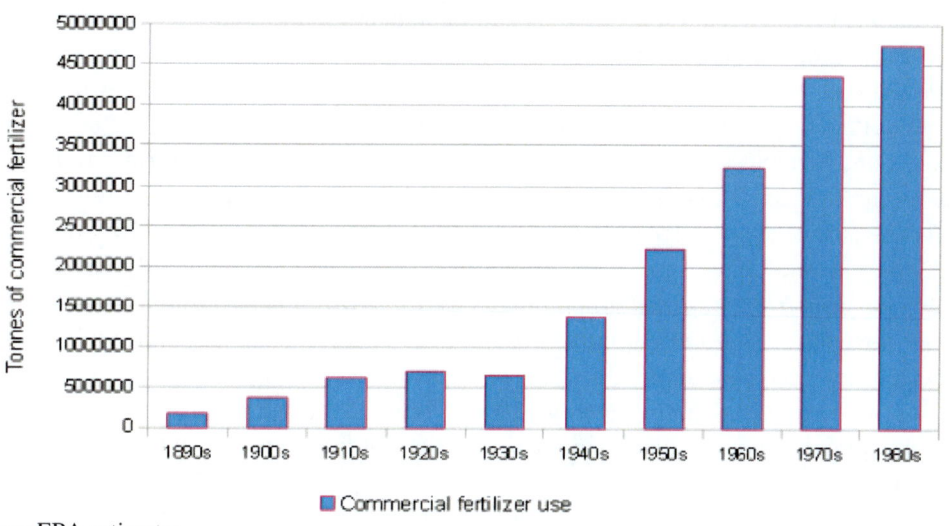

Commercial Fertilizer Use in the US Agriculture
Evolution over 100 years

Source: EPA estimates

Figure 6.6. Commercial Fertilizer Use in the US agriculture – evolution over 100 years.

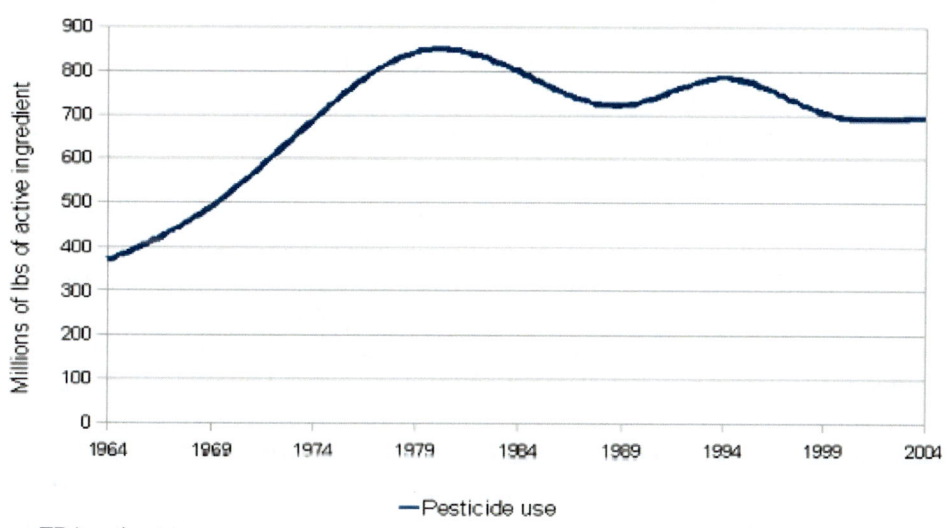

Conventional Pesticide Use in the US Agriculture
Evolution in the period 1964 - 2004

Source: EPA estimates.

Figure 6.7. Conventional pesticide use in the US agriculture evolution over 40 years.

A recent report from the Cooperative Institute for Research in Environmental Sciences at the University of Colorado-Boulder [4] showed that nearly one in 10 watersheds in the U.S. is "stressed," with demand for water exceeding natural supply. They also consider this trend as likely to become the new norm. Major American cities like Washington D.C., Atlanta, Salt Lake City, San Antonio, and even sooner Los Angeles, Houston and San Francisco risk to run out of drinking water supply by 2050 due to the current unsustainable water demand in these cities and neighboring agricultural regions. Clearly the lack of water for drinking means also a lack of water for agricultural needs, thus putting in question the viability of farming in such important farming regions like Southern California.

In addition, the industrial animal farm model utilizes feed, which is grown in monocultures, often far away from the facility. Enormous quantities of both water, chemical fertilizers and herbicides are used in the production of this feed, causing further soil erosion, water resource depletion and pollution.

As the recent report of the Pew Commission on Industrial Farm Animal Production [5] points out *"in the United States, an estimated 173,000 miles of national waterways are impacted by runoff from agricultural sources (Cook, 1998). Animal farming is estimated to account for 55% of soil and sediment erosion, 37% of nationwide pesticide usage, 80% of antibiotic usage, and more than 30% of the total nitrogen and phosphorus loading to national drinking water resources (Steinfeld et al., 2006)."* Naturally, these external costs of water, air and soil pollution are not factored into the calculations of the net profits of the big stars of US industrial farming.

Another serious issue related to the US agricultural model is its abuse of pharmaceuticals in industrial animal farming. Ever since the FDA approval the use of antibiotics in food animal production in 1951, there has been mounting evidence of a close relationship between antimicrobial use in animal husbandry and the increase in bacterial resistance in humans. This fact has already prompted negative reviews of agricultural practices by scientific authorities in a number of countries including many warnings in the US itself. Most recently, in April of 2012 the FDA outlined plans to phase out non-medical uses of more than 200 antibiotics in animals over three years. The voluntary plan requires cooperation by drug makers and farmers [6].

Another source of controversy has been the decades-long use of synthetic hormones in meat and dairy. Some of them, such as diethylstilbestrol (DES), were applied to nearly all beef cattle in the 1950s and 1960s; however, they have been phased out of use in agriculture over the protests of ranchers due to proved harmful effects on humans.

It is also well known that breast cancer risk increases with higher lifetime exposure to estrogen. Still, US animal husbandry is one of the main users of synthetic estrogens, which, via meat and dairy products, are consumed on a daily basis by American women, entering and affecting their body metabolism. Therefore, it is not at all surprising that since the mid-1970s the rate of aggressive metastatic breast cancer in young women under 40 years of age has been increasing in the US at a rate of about 2% per year and shows no signs of abating — a difference too large to be a chance result [7].

In the area of crop production, the situation has not been any better. The drive to profit in the area of crop farming has not only, as mentioned earlier, led to the abuse of chemicals ruining the soil and water, but also resulted in the adoption of genetically engineered plant varieties. The hailed introduction by major GMO corporations of pesticide and herbicide-resistant GMO crops such as corn, soya, colza and cotton caused in return the appearance of pesticide-resistant super bugs and herbicide-resistant super weeds (see Figure 6.8 and 6.9).

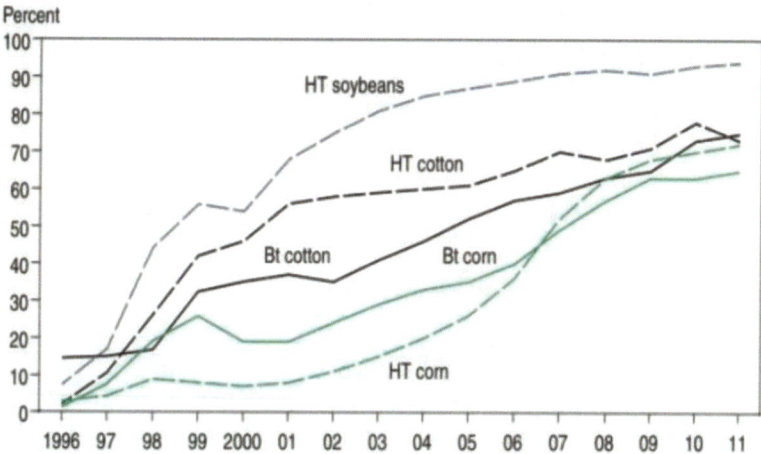

Source: BigPictureAgriculture.com [8].

Figure 6.8. Adoption of genetically engineered crops in the US, 1996-2011.

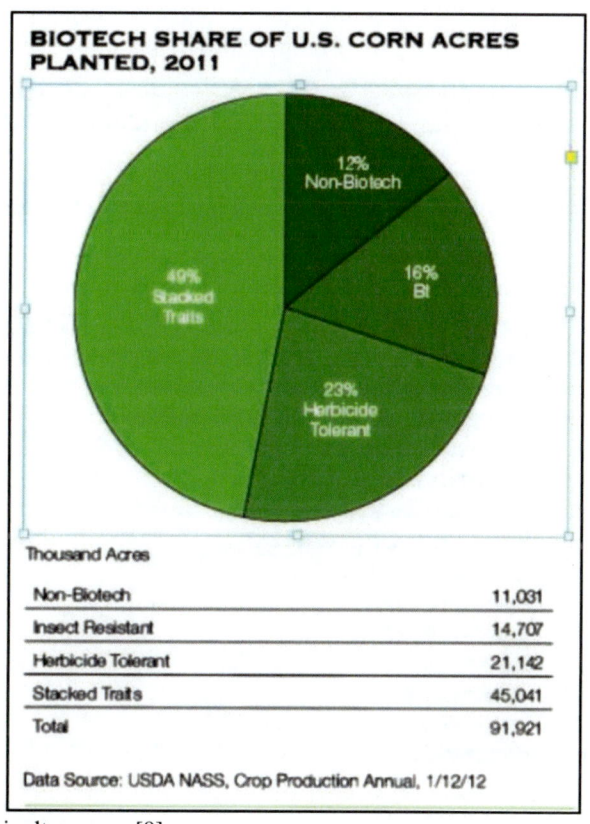

Source: BigPictureAgriculture.com [9].

Figure 6.9. Biotech share of the US corn acres planted in 2011.

According to the specialized scientific website, WeedScience.org, herbicide-resistant weeds have been reported in 80 crops in 63 countries, and it stands out that the greatest number of super weeds is associated with crop varieties like corn, rice and soybeans genetically engineered to withstand herbicides (see Figure 6.10 and 6.11).

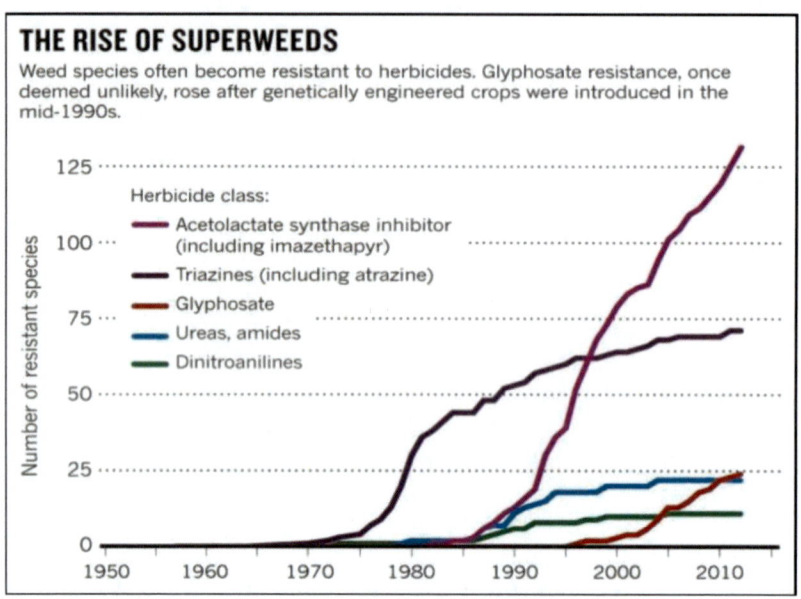

Source: WeedScience.org

Figure 6.10. The rise of super-weeds resistant to herbicides: 1950 to 2010.

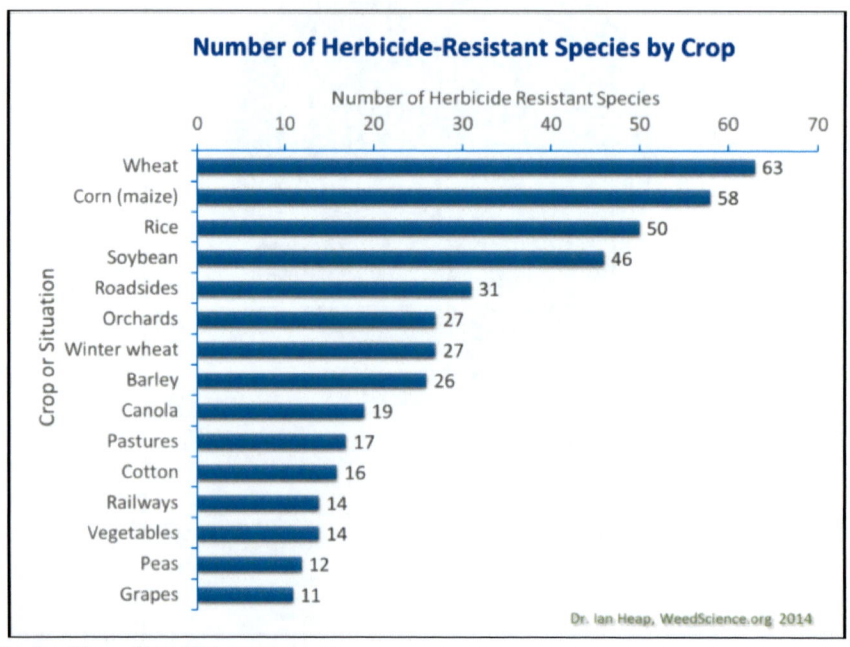

Source: Dr. Ian Heap, WeedScience.org

Figure 6.11. Number or herbicide-resistant species by crop.

By now it is already clear that the only solution chemical corporations can propose to farmers in response to this increasingly dangerous situation will come in the form of even stronger and more environmentally harmful chemical cocktails and GMO concoctions. As the eternal logic of action and reaction demands, scientists and farmers will soon be witnesses to the appearance of yet more resistant varieties of bugs and weeds.

In this contest of *human versus nature*, we are dealing with a typical "win-lose" game situation, where there can only be one winner – the chemical corporations which take increasing profits from their super sales, while the losers are many and include farmers, public authorities, taxpayers, and last but not least – Nature itself.

The U.S. Politics of Losses

Corn/maize production plays a major role in the economy of the United States. The US ranks first in the world in corn production, and 20% of its annual yield is exported. Eighty eight (88%) percent of the US crop is genetically engineered.

The major uses of corn are feed for industrial animal farms (about 44%) and ethanol (27%). *The third most important corn use is human consumption which represents 20% of the total production* and includes the production of High Fructose Corn Syrup, sweeteners, starch, alcoholic beverages, cereals and dairy. Furthermore, such products are critically important in the on-going discussion of the present obesity and diabetics epidemic in the US (see Figure 6.12).

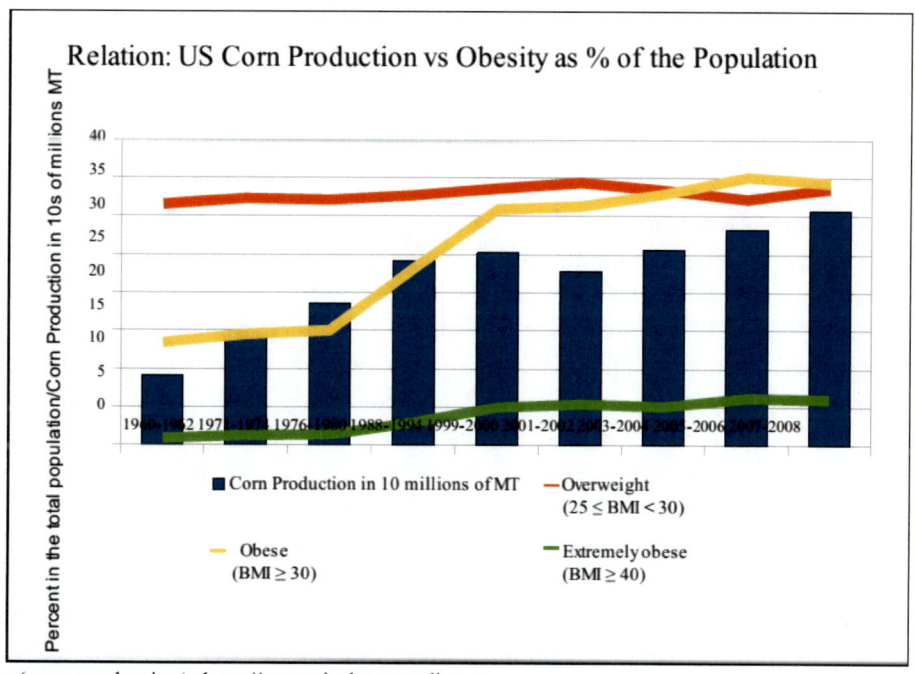

Source (corn production): http://www.indexmundi.com
Source (Obesity): CDC/NCHS, National Health and Nutrition Examination.

Figure 6.12. Relationship between corn production and obesity epidemics in the US in %.

And while the most recent (November 2013) Gallup-Healthways study shows clearly that the majority of the US population is, at best, suffering from being overweight (35.5%), with obese and very obese individuals representing over 27% of Americans, corn, a key factor in causing the epidemic, still remains the most subsidized crop by the US government (never mind the free market economy talk) (Figure 6.13). The Federal Crop Insurance Corporation has spent in the fiscal year of 2012 over 15.8 billion insuring farmers.

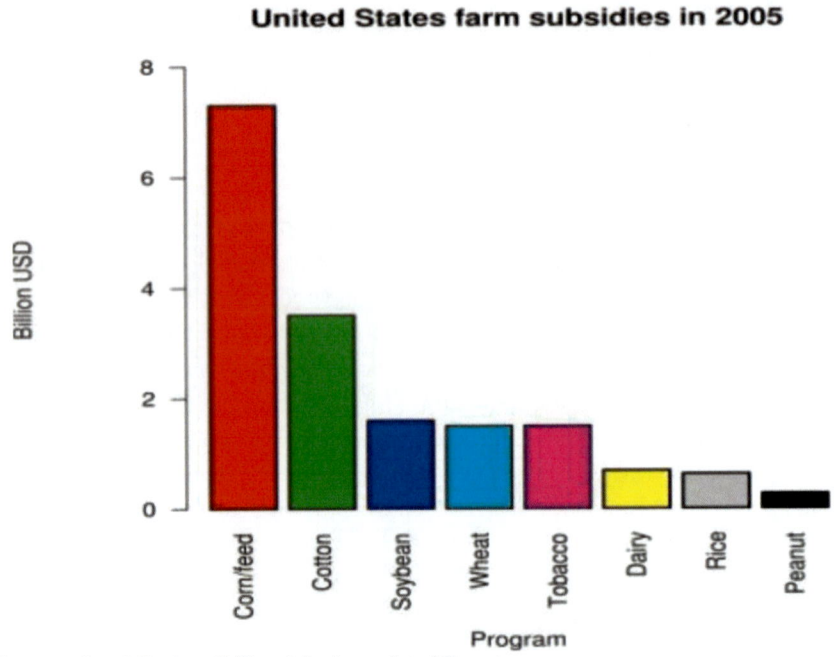

United States farm subsidies in 2005

Source: Congressional Budget Office (via Associated Press)

Figure 6.13. US farm subsidies in 2005 in billions of US dollars.

The subsidies go primarily to a handful of large operators with no conservation strings attached to protect water and soil, no means testing, and no payment limit on how much a farm business can collect. In 2011, 3.9 percent of all growers covered by insurance policies received 32.6 percent of the premium subsidies. The other winners include insurance companies who are handling the program in exchange for healthy profits.

The subsidy-obesity relationship was recently confirmed by a new study [10] in the America Journal of Preventive Medicine which highlights: "how agricultural subsidies that favor corn, soy and grains are fueling the obesity epidemic, putting small farms out of business and discouraging sustainable, bio-diverse farming.

It furthermore states that farm subsidies are no longer based on need; mega-farms receive an annual fixed cash payment based upon the number of acres on the farm, which are given whether they need them or not, no strings attached. Large corporate farms receive the majority of farm subsidies while the bulk of small farmers receive little or none.

Yet the farm subsidies are but a drop in the US taxpayer's pond of tears. Obesity and its accompanying illnesses cost American society as high as $147 billion per year, according to a new study [11] by researchers at RTI International, the Agency for Healthcare Research and

Quality, and the U.S. Centers for Disease Control & Prevention. Annual medical expenditures attributable to obesity have doubled in less than a decade (see Figure 6.14).

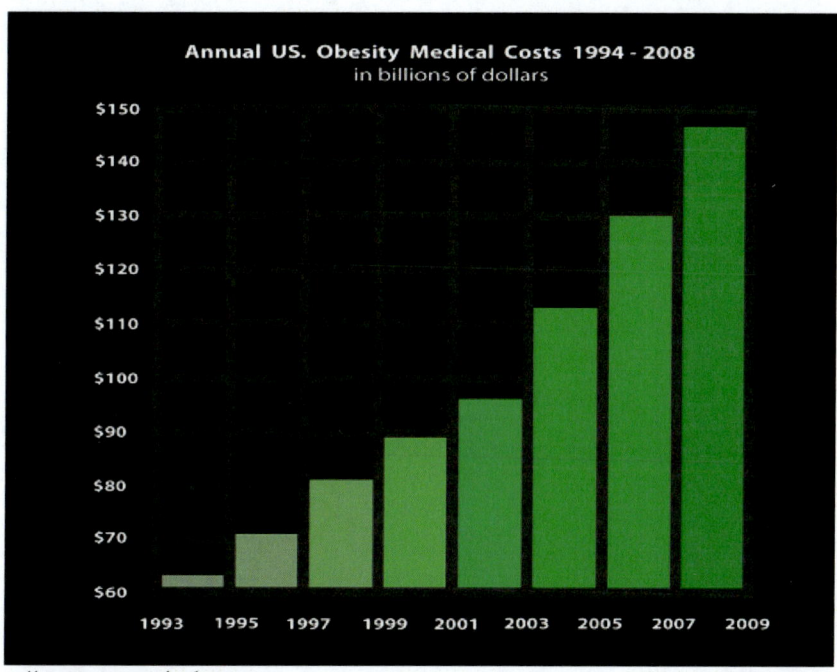

Source http://www.mozartinshape.org

Figure 6.14. Annual US obesity medical costs 1994 – 2008 (in billions of US dollars).

The agricultural model in the US is one of the best textbook examples of a system that profits a handful at expense of many. As we see from the above discussion, its negative externalities range from air, water and soil pollution to very costly damages in the area of the public health sector.

Last but not least, there are also social and cultural damages to the rural communities. With the disappearing farms, that which also vanished was the whole centuries-long system of social values and cultural traditions. The decrease in the number of farms left behind many abandoned farmhouses. Entire villages were emptied. Such desertification of the countryside in the direction, initially, of industrialized cities led to a permanent weakening of social and family bonds. The farmer's bond to the land was to him a foundation which he and his family could rely on during the better but also the worst of times. It was a guarantee of survival in the hardest periods. The earth could always feed a farmer and his family. His farm gave the farmer a sense of independence and pride.

Rural immigrants who moved to the cities lost this base. What did they gain in exchange? Initially, it was a prospect of better earnings and a higher quality of life with asphalted roads, sewage systems, and a modern house in one of the sprawling sub-urban neighborhoods of Detroit or another industrialized city like it. And while industry constituted an important part of the US gross domestic product at 27 percent in 1950 and the rate of industrial employment was high at nearly 34% of the total labor, the American Dream and the American Middle Class were strong and flourishing.

From the early 1970s with the decline of manufacturing, the American Dream began to crumble, notwithstanding the nominal GDP growth. The share of industrial production in terms of GDP and its share of employment decreased by a factor of 3 to 11% of GDP in 2009 and 11% of the total employment force (see Figure 6.15).

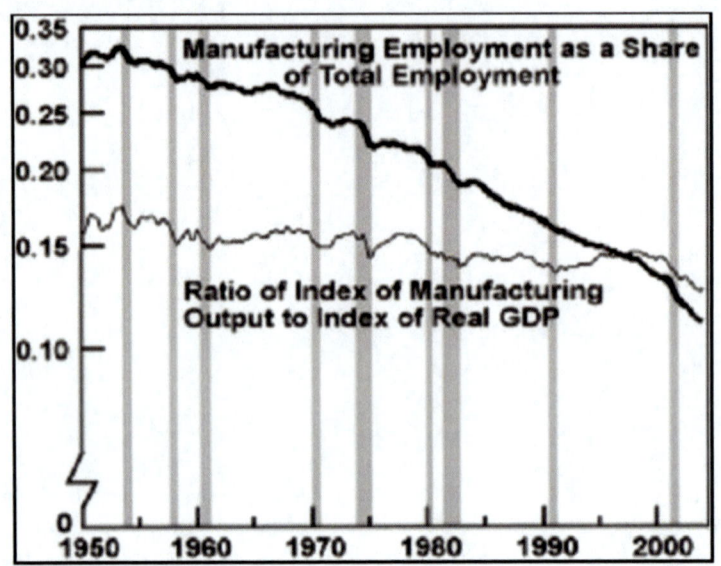

Sources: Congressional Budget Office; Department of Labor, Bureau of Labor Statistics; Department of Commerce, Bureau of Economic Analysis.

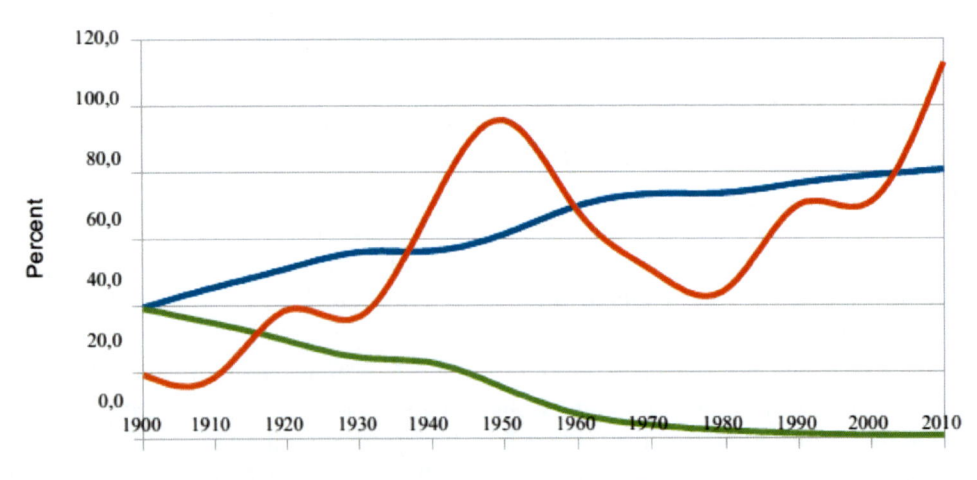

Figure 6.15. Manufacturing decline in the U.S. on a logarithmic scale.

Source (population): U.S. Census Bureau, decennial census publications/
Source (US Public Debt): http://www.usgovernmentdebt.us

Figure 6.16. Urbanization of USA versus s its Gross Public Debt/

According to a survey by the Associated Press, today four out of five U.S. adults struggle with joblessness, near-poverty, or reliance on welfare for at least part of their lives. [12] As of January 2014, 17% of men in the US in the prime working age (age 25 to 54), a total of 10.4 million, remain without work as opposed to just 6% in the early 1970s.

Today the US has the greatest gross public debt, the highest income inequality rate of western countries (0.468 in 2009) and the weakest social safety net. Half of the U.S. population lives in poverty or is low-income, according to U.S. census data [13].

There is growing malaise in American society that the very values on which the country was built have been inevitably lost. One day this malaise, compounded by the multitude of environmental problems, and most acutely by the lack of potable water, will grow into very serious social discontent and destabilize the political system of the US. This shall be the longest-running effect of the past, excessive urbanization of the country and its politics of unequal, unsustainable development (see Figure 6.16).

CHINA'S URBAN VS RURAL DEVELOPMENT
IS CHINA FOLLOWING THE WRONG PATH OF US AGRICULTURE?

Agriculture as the Defining Element for Chinese Civilization

For thousands of years, since the 8th millennium BC, China's social, cultural and economic activities have revolved around agriculture. Excavations at Kuahuqiao, the earliest known Neolithic site in eastern China, have documented rice cultivation as early as 7,700 years ago [14].

The agricultural tradition is very present in the Chinese mythology. Anyone learning Chinese Mandarin can easily note its impact on the language development. Farming-related concepts like rice, harvest or domestic animals are omnipresent in the character formation. For example, a grain of rice 米 (mǐ) is used today as the fundamental length measurement unit representing one meter. The Chinese character for family home 家 (jiā) which first appeared over 3,000 years ago on Shang Dynasty bronzes is a drawing that depicts a house with a pig inside it, proof that animal husbandry at that time was not only already well developed but also fundamental for the Chinese. As pigs were kept indoors with their owners, drawing a pig under a roof meant that it was a place where people also lived; that's why "a house with a pig in it" could be used to write a character that meant "a place where people live."

The role of rural agricultural society for Chinese civilizational identity is, therefore, critical and must not be understated. Therefore any process leading to a change in this traditional balance will be incomparable in importance to the one which occurred in the US, a country with a history of civilization spanning over only two centuries.

Urbanization in China

The beginning of the economic transformation of China in 1978 by Deng Xiao Ping has set the stage for a previously unseen rate of urbanization of the country. Still in 1980, two years after the Four Modernizations campaign's take off, *the rural population of China comprised 81% of the total 981 million inhabitants*. Twenty four years after the onset of the reforms, *the rural population of the country decreased nearly by half, to 48% of the total* population established in 2012 as 1.36 billion inhabitants. Today, we can already say that *the majority of the Chinese live in urbanized areas which represent about 3% of the total land area* in the country.

From the first special economic zones like Shenzhen and Guangzhou, initially located in the southern province of Guangdong close to Hong Kong and Macao, the urbanizing trend spread rapidly to other primary "national central cities" like Beijing and Shanghai.

Since the beginning of this millennium, the urbanization process has already affected China's other national central cities like Chongqing and Tianjin as well as several provincial capitals like Chengdu, Wuhan, Xi'an, Nanjing and Shenyang which by now have all become megalopolises in their own right with populations bordering on 10 million inhabitants. The urbanization trend has equally embraced the so-called *third-tier* towns like Ningbo, Fuzhou, Wuxi and Harbin.

The urbanization that took almost a century in the West has occurred in less than thirty years in China. In 1979, Shenzhen was still a poor fishing village with some 20,000 inhabitants. In 2009, it had a population of 9 million.

Altogether by the year 2013 when compared to 1980, notwithstanding the total population growth by nearly 380 million people, the rural areas in China registered a net population loss of 142 million. That means that within only three decades, the urbanization process has engulfed nearly half of the present population of China.

This figure strikes in sharp contrast even to the scale of US urbanization, where during its most aggressive decades of the 1950s through the 1970s the net increase in the country's population was "only" 93 million inhabitants, and where the rural areas actually registered population growth by about 1 million people.

This means that over a comparable period of three decades and on comparable land area (3% vs. 2% respectively) the Chinese cities in their process of development had to accommodate a six-time greater urban population than the American towns. No wonder, then, that the *chengzhenhua* process has had a wringing impact on the Chinese social and cultural identity as well as the environment in which it evolves.

Air Pollution in China as Result of Rapid Urbanization

Due to the fact that the greater part of China suffers from cold winters, a key issue is providing city inhabitants with suitable heating during cold seasons, as well as water and electricity all year long. Furthermore, just as it had been the case in the US, the urbanization process in China is connected to industrialization and the growth of services, both of which involve high energy consumption. Thus, in line with being the record breaker in the urbanization rate, China in 2011 also became the world's largest power generator (see Figure 6.17).

The main source of energy production in China still comes from highly-polluting coal (69%). China is the world's top coal producer, consumer, and importer, and accounted for about half of global coal consumption, an important factor in world energy-related carbon dioxide emissions (see Figure 6.18).

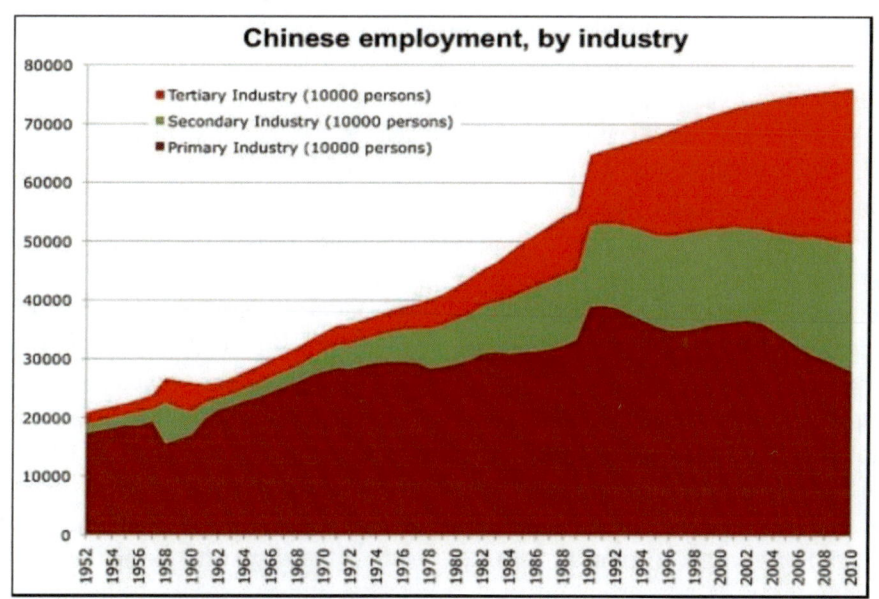

Source: U.S Energy Information Administration.

Figure 6.17. Chinese employment by industry.

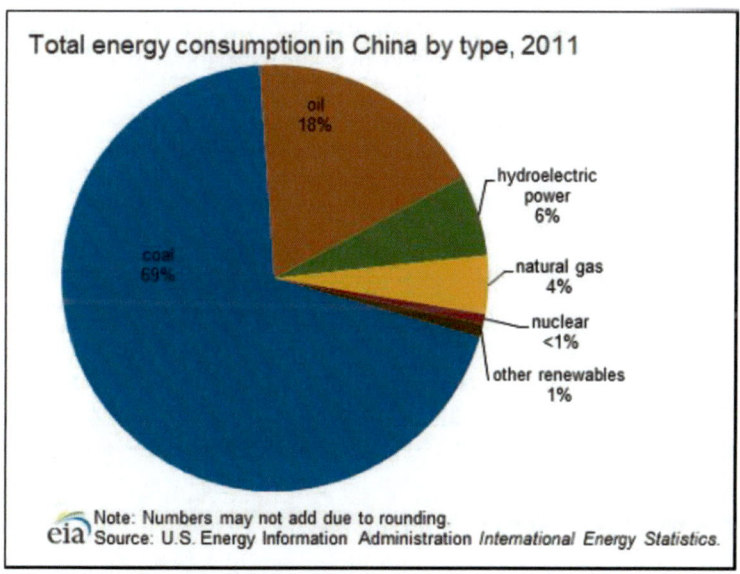

Source: U.S Energy Information Administration.

Figure 6.18. Total energy consumption in China by type, 2011.

Furthermore, growing urbanization means greater use of cars and public transportation. The number of vehicles in China went from 1.78 million in 1980 to over 78 million in 2010 (that is 58 cars per 1000 inhabitants vs. the present US level of 797 cars per 1000 inhabitants.) Even at just one fourteenth of the US car use level, China is already the world's second-largest oil consumer behind the United States, and in 2010 it became the largest global energy consumer.

The above elements contribute to the fact that air pollution in the biggest Chinese megalopolises has become the daily bread to news agencies, and the economic and human health losses inflicted by it are tremendous.

In the 1980s, China's particulate-matter concentrations were at least 10 to 16 times higher than the World Health Organization's annual guidelines. Even after significant improvements by 2005, the concentrations were still five times higher than what is considered safe. According to World Health Organization estimates from 2007, these sky rocketing levels of pollution in China lead each year to 656,000 premature deaths from ailments caused by indoor and outdoor air pollution.

The study *"Evidence on the impact of sustained exposure to air pollution on life expectancy from China's Huai River policy"* [15], published in 2013 by a group of Chinese and international scientists reveals that the Chinese system of heating, which greatly increases total suspended particulates air pollution, is causing the 500 million residents of Northern China to lose more than a combined 2.5 billion years of life in terms of average life-expectancy. In an experiment where the north of the Huai River boundary was heated by coal during winter, particulate pollution was 55 percent higher, and residents had a life expectancy 5.5 years shorter than their compatriots in the south of the river who did not have access to coal based heat.

Another study by MIT scientists, "China's pollution puts a dent in its economy", [16] shows that, notwithstanding China's progress in cleaning up the air pollution, its economic impact has risen dramatically. Quantifying costs from both lost labor and the increased need for health care while looking at pollution's long-term effect on health, and not just its immediate costs, the study found that that ozone and particulate matter have substantially impacted the Chinese economy over the past 30 years.

According to those estimates, in 2005 alone air pollution cost the Chinese economy $112 billion as compared to $22 billion in such damages in 1975. The *rapid urbanization in conjunction with population growth and higher incomes were the chief reasons* for the increase in pollution's costs.

Attempting to relieve the pressure on the major agglomerations, at the beginning of 2012, China's State Council issued a notice to relax rules on *hukou* – residency permits. The notice encourages rural residents to settle down in small towns, not just big cities that are already overcrowded.

Thus to summarize, although when compared in terms of percent to the situation in the US (see Figure 6.19), there theoretically still seems to be room for further urbanization of China. One now must ask the question: how far and in what way, if at all, should such a process be continued.

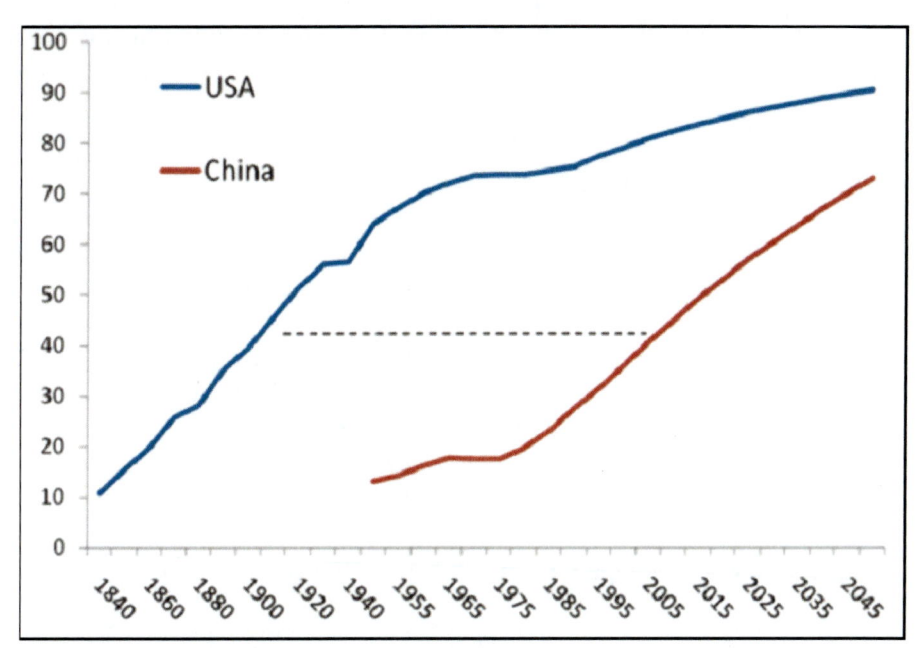

Source: http://www.newgeography.com

Figure 6.19. Urban Population Growth: China vs US.

Erosion of the Cultural and Social Foundations in China

The abrupt pace of Chinese urbanization is contributing at the loss of its precious, cultural heritage build by past generations over five thousand years. This process mirrors the earlier described US village desertification of the mid 20th century; however, in China it is happening at an accelerated rate, and its consequences due to the particularities of the Chinese cultural fabric are much deeper and devastating.

According to research by Tianjin University [17] in 2000, China had 3.7 million villages. By 2010, that figure had dropped to 2.6 million: a loss of about 300 villages a day. Because of the clan structure specific to Chinese society, each village has developed over centuries its own micro-culture with its own traditions in music and dance, ritual celebrations, martial arts, cuisines and theater. With its disappearance they are gone forever. Out of 9,700 examples of nationwide "intangible cultural heritage" cataloged by the Chinese government, about 80 percent are rural [18].

Precious knowledge like, for example, wood printing is at risk of vanishing. Demolition of villages and migration of entire communities to large cities irreversibly results in a breaking of social bonds, including bonds between close family members. Without the physical proximity and the village lifestyle, people scatter. Society becomes atomized and traditions are no longer passed from one generation to another leading to cultural impoverishment of the country. The cultural fabric of the rural US is insignificant when compared to the Chinese. China's cultural losses due to urbanization will be of much greater caliber.

Without a thoughtful strategy of preservation of this national heritage axed on "in situ" development of rural communities and not on their destruction, any government-sponsored programs to protect these traditions will be as insubstantial as an attempt to clog a waterfall with cotton balls.

Farms and Farmers: China versus USA

Even today, agriculture is still a fundamental activity in China, employing about 340 million people: that is about one third of the labor force. China ranks first in worldwide farm output, primarily producing rice, wheat, potatoes, sorghum, peanuts, tea, millet, barley, cotton, oilseed, pork, and fish [19]. The agricultural land in China represents about 57.6% of the total country area, only 25.4% of which is arable land. The number of farmers in China for the year 2013 is estimated at about 338 million. They labor on about 200 million tiny farms. Thus on average *each farmer in China disposes of circa 1.64 ha* of farming land, *10 times less* than his American counterpart (see the Table 6.1. below.)

Table 6.1. The comparison of agriculture in China with the U.S.

Agricultural Characteristic	China	US
Total agricultural land in ha in which:	553 million	479 million
Arable land in ha	141 million	216 million
Permanent crops in ha	12 million	97 million
Meadows in ha	400 million	254 million
Farming population (2013 est.)	338 million	3 million
Agricultural land in ha/farmer in which:	1,64	159
Arable land in ha/farmer	0,42	72
Permanent crops in ha/farmer	0,03	33
Meadows in ha	1,18	84

Crop Production and Fertilizer use in CHINA

Since the beginning of the reforms, China, faced with its rapidly growing population, strove to maintain its food self-sufficiency and increase crop yields. In doing so, just as the US had done before it, China embraced chemical fertilizers. Today, *China is the world's largest consumer of inorganic nitrogen fertilizers*, accounting for about one third of total global consumption. *Fertilizer use increased by factor of 4.5* from 85 kg per ha in 1980 to 350 kg per ha in 2010, *while the crop yield grew only by a factor of 2* (see Figure 6.20).

For comparison, in the US, the chemical fertilizer use level in 2010 was three times lower at 120.5 kg/ha, while the corresponding crop yield was by the factor of 1.22 higher than in China.

Only part of this low efficiency can be explained by the increased production of fruits and vegetables (40% between 2000 and 2010) and the lower quality of the Chinese fertilizer product. The other reason lays simply in the overuse of nitrogen fertilizer. Similarly to vitamin "C" which can only be absorbed by a human body in certain amount per day, so does nitrogen fertilizer, and past certain levels, it no longer adds to the crop's efficiency.

Specialists consider that application of fertilizers for grain crops in China could be easily reduced by 20-30% while still maintaining or increasing yields. Naturally, excessive fertilizer use leads inevitably to very important water and soil pollution. And so the levels of farming related methane and nitrous oxide emissions in China in 2010 were higher by respectively factors of 3 and 2.3 than the US levels.

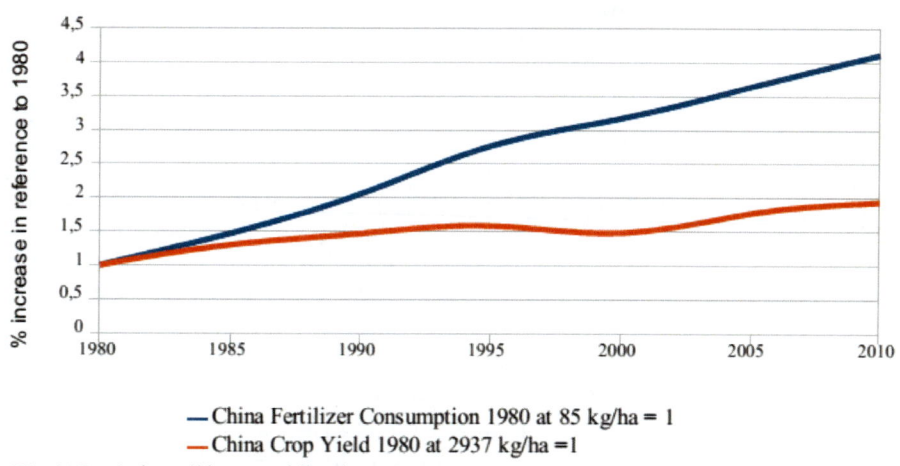

Fertilizer Use vs Crop Yield in China
In relation to the reference year 1980

— China Fertilizer Consumption 1980 at 85 kg/ha = 1
— China Crop Yield 1980 at 2937 kg/ha = 1

Source: World Bank, http://data.worldbank.org/

Figure 6.20. Fertilizer use vs. crop yield in China (in relation to the reference year 1980).

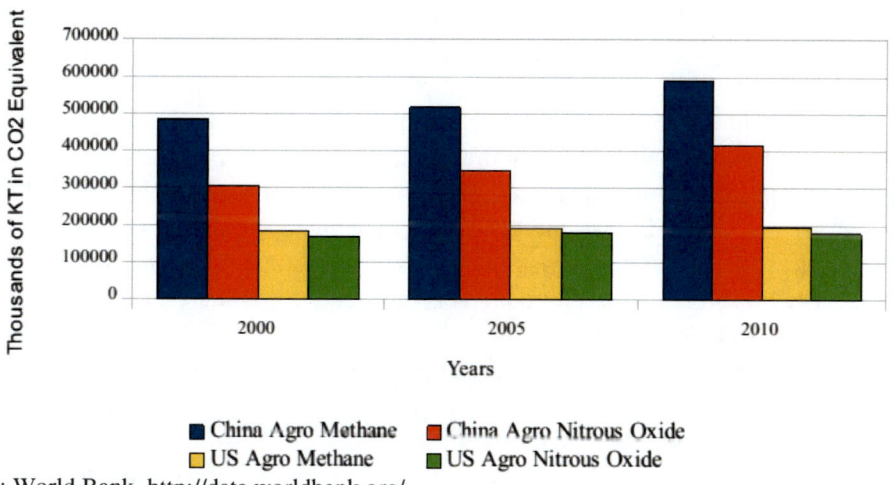

Agro Pollution Growth in China and USA
Methane and Nitrous Oxide Emissions due to Farming

■ China Agro Methane   ■ China Agro Nitrous Oxide
□ US Agro Methane   ■ US Agro Nitrous Oxide

Source: World Bank, http://data.worldbank.org/

Figure 6.21. Agricultural pollution growth in China and the US (methane and nitrous oxide emissions due to farming).

Even at the use rate of fertilizer stipulated by Chinese experts, the chemical fertilizer level would still be much higher than in the US where, as we know from the previous discussion of the US agricultural model, its application has led to massive water pollution, and in consequence to water shortages which threatens the long term viability of US farming (see Figure 6.21).

Meat Production and Animal Husbandry

In the area of animal husbandry, China's favorite meat is pork (beef production demands land space availability which China cannot afford). At present about a half of the world's pigs, approximately 476 million, are raised in China.

Traditionally, hog production in China has been conducted by backyard family farms. However, following the example of the United States, China's growing demand for pork has led it to adopt U.S. style factory farms. In September 2013 the Chinese company Shuanghui International, owner of China's largest meat processor, announced the acquisition of U.S. meat giant Smithfield Foods Inc., the world's leading pork producer and one of the chief culprits of animal farm related water pollution in the US.

Considering the importance of pork in the Chinese diet and its implications for national food security, the Chinese Government has adopted an aggressive policy stance since 2007 with the intention, in its view, to modernize hog production units through vertical integration and scaling up, so as to control quality and reduce direct costs.

In 2007, funding for industrial pig farming in major hog-producing counties was introduced and in the period from 2007 to 2012, the number of major hog-producing counties benefiting from this support doubled from 253 to 536, while the total amount of support dispensed tripled from CNY1.5 billion to CNY5.4 billion. In addition, the government began to offer specific grants for larger hog operations. The total value of grants dispensed amounted to CNY15 billion for the period 2007-2012.

This public policy, not surprisingly, has led to the rapid decline of backyard producers. The share of specialized household production has risen rapidly while large-scale integrated industrial units have also experienced more moderate growth. The share of hogs slaughtered on farms with less than 40 pigs declined by a factor of 2 from 73% in 2002 to 34% in 2010. According to Kevin Chen, Senior Research Fellow and China Program Leader for the International Food Policy Research Institute in Beijing, China, in a randomized survey from Zizhong County in Sichuan Province [20], it was reported that almost 32% of smallholders exited from pig production in just one year due to continuing rural-urban migration, rising wage costs, price volatility and high risk in the hog business due to disease outbreaks (Chen et al. 2012). The Ministry of Agriculture predicts this trend to continue, and that it will be led by large pork production companies in China.

All of this is happening at the same time as pig farming costs continue to grow in China, especially since 2006, due to the rising costs of feed and labor. As a result, the profitability of the hog industry has decreased, and average hog prices in China have risen considerably higher than those in the United States for the first time, triggering large imports of pork into China. This has raised serious concerns about 'pork security' and the future of the hog industry in China. Just as is the case in the US, the chief factor which currently affects the profitability of hog production is energy prices, which affect the cost of feed, itself representing more than 50 per cent of pig production costs. Clearly, as discussed previously, one may expect that water availability will soon become the next critical issue. Furthermore, epidemics, which are the natural consequence of densely packed animal farming, have led to further cost increases associated with losses and animal deaths. As the example of the US shows, those unpleasant phenomena will continue in the foreseeable future, putting in question the long-term viability of the food security policy in China. In conclusion, it appears clear that also in this field China is unfortunately falling into the false efficiency trap of industrialized animal husbandry. In addition to the dangers of pollution, which China simply cannot afford due to its limited potable water and soil resources, the increased intake of meat by the Chinese already results in diet related health problems which will be discussed later.

GMO in China

In search of greater efficiency in food production, China's agricultural authorities have pushed for the use of GMO (Genetically Modified Organism) technologies in hopes of improving the seed sector. According to media reports, the country's national science and strategy lists the development of pest and disease-resistant GMO crops as a key project. [21] In November 2009, the agricultural ministry issued bio-safety certificates to two strains of pest-resistant GMO rice and one variety phytase corn, approving them for use on experimental plots. In June 2013, notwithstanding the public fear of GMO technology, Chinese agricultural authorities approved imports of three new genetically modified soy bean varieties, including two produced by U.S. seed giant Monsanto and one by German chemical producer BASF. China has been importing genetically modified soybeans since 1997, and also allows the import of some varieties of genetically modified corn, both subject to strict controls. At present, imported genetically modified corn and soy are only approved for processing into soyoil, soymeal and animal feed, not for direct human consumption, and commercial planting of GMO crops is still strictly prohibited.

Still there is mounting pressure by GMO producers on the Chinese Ministry of Agriculture to go further and allow GMO seeds for planting in China. Luckily, the Chinese public and part of the authorities are not easy to be duped. There is strong opposition to GMO technology on account of its potentially harmful long-term effects on human health and the environment as well as the issue of national security. It is particularly this last point that needs to be developed, for it is often overlooked. The Chinese government should have a closer look at its foreign corporate GMO angels and evaluate their arguments by looking into their past. Just as one would be careful about entrusting the keys to one's safe with millions of dollars in it to an individual that not once, not twice but thrice had been sentenced for a bank robbery, in the same way one should mistrust assurances which come from the likes of Monsanto. When deciding on GMO technologies that bring along with them irreversible changes, it is wise to look at the results of applying other technologies manufactured and commercialized as safe for public health by the leading GMO seed manufacturer, Monsanto. Those technologies include, for example, DDT, an insecticide banned in the US in 1973 after three decades of use due to its proven toxic effect on environment and human reproductive system; there is also Monsanto's highly toxic PCBs shown to cause liver damage and poor cognitive development in children, at last banned by the United States Congress in 1979 after 50 years of wide use in a variety of products from coolants to surgical implants!

GMO technology, though, is not only about environmental and human health protection. First and foremost it is about controlling access to the basic human necessity of food. This control is executed through patents and secret scientific knowledge owned by a handful of large multinationals, whose only interest in humanity is the profit obtained from selling their products. The Chinese government should know it by heart: those who will have the key to the grain barn in China will be those who will wield the true power. Being afraid of corporations cutting off the Chinese grain supply is a valid and extremely timely concern now that modern genetically engineered *suicide seeds* that produce sterile seeds with the so-called *terminator technology1 not only are ready to use, but, moreover, are in the hands of only one corporation – Monsanto – and the United States government.*

Agro Development versus Diet Related Public Health Issues in China

Just as is the case in the United States, urbanization, improper agricultural public policy and higher salaries in China have led to major changes in the Chinese people's diet, leading to its "Westernization". Acting against their best interests, the Chinese have increased by more than half their intake of high-calorie, high-fat, and high-sodium foodstuffs such as sugar, oil, meat and eggs, while reducing by nearly one half their traditional consumption of vegetables and grains (see Figure 6.22 and 6.23).

Food Consumption Trends in Urban China

Relative to the reference year 1982 = 1

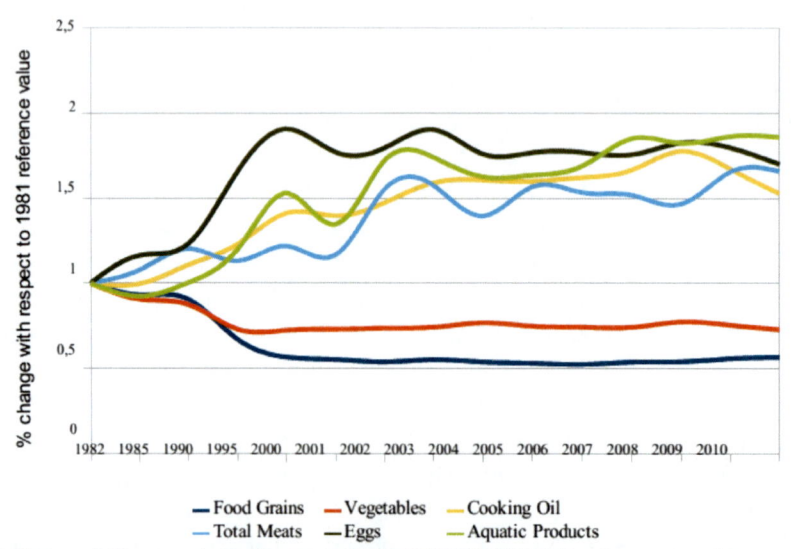

Source: http://www.daff.gov.au/ data/assets/pdf_file/0006/2259123/food-consumption-trends-in-china-v2.pdf retrieved February 15th 2014

Figure 6.22. Food consumption trends in China (reference year 1982 = 1); 1 Scientifically called GURT for genetic use restriction technology 2 Delta & Pine Land Company (D&PL, now owned by Monsanto) and the United States Department of Agriculture (USDA).

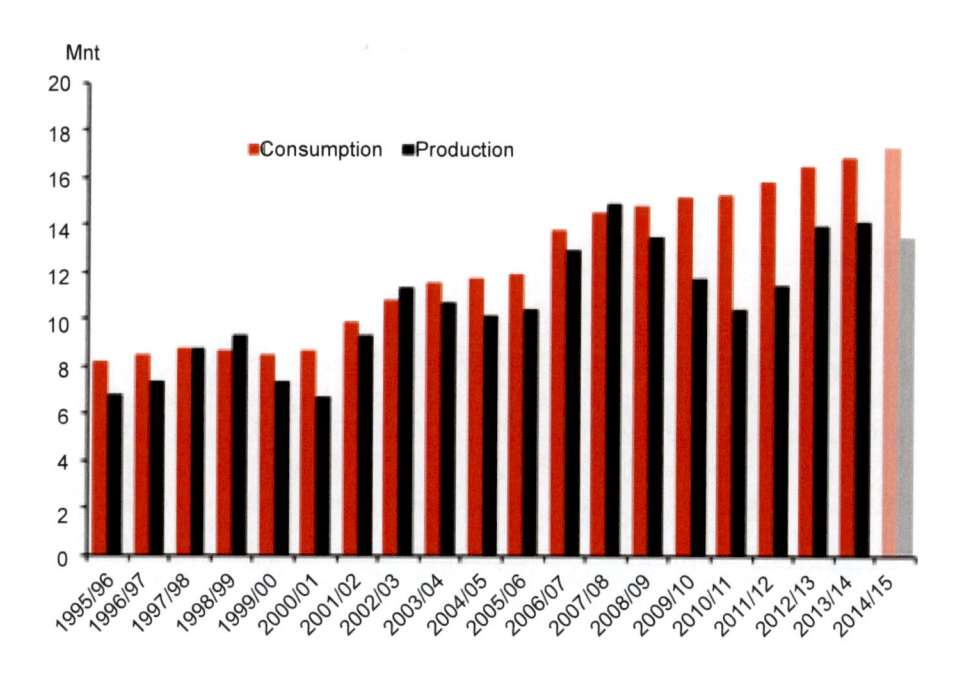

Source: LMC, Kingsman, Macquaries Research, February 2014.

Figure 6.23. China sugar production vs. consumption 1992 to 2012 in millions of metric tonnes.

As could be expected, the negative consequences of this dietary switch became soon visible to the point of being extremely worrisome. The average BMI of the population has soared. The genetic make-up of the Chinese makes them more prone to diabetes at much lower BMI indexes then it is the case with Caucasians. As a consequence of the Chinese growing overweight, the country's health experts are talking already about a diabetes epidemic.

According to the most recent JAMA journal [22], in 2013 about 11.6% of Chinese adults (114 million people) already suffer from diabetes as opposed to 1% in 1980. This means that globally almost one in three people with diabetes live in China, and the rate at which the epidemic is spreading in China is unparalleled elsewhere. According to scientific estimates, half of adults in China are today in a pre-diabetic state, and what is particularly dramatic is the fact that diabetes disproportionately falls on young and middle aged adults, that is on the working age population.

According to Dr. Ji Linong, a leading Chinese expert on diabetics, each year, six to seven percent of those with pre-diabetes - amounting to approximately 30 million - will be added to the diabetes population estimate [23].

China's diabetes-related medical costs were estimated at $26 billion in 2010 alone. According to the International Diabetes Federation, diabetes treatment accounts for about 13 percent of medical expenditures in China. [24] This rising trend has strained health services and helped fuel growth in drug sales of 20% a year. Costs are expected to skyrocket in the next 10 to 20 years as millions of sufferers seek treatment and care for related ailments such as kidney failure, stroke and blindness. China will have lost $558 billion of national income to diabetes and heart disease between 2005 and 2015, the World Health Organization and World Economic Forum said in a 2008 report [25].

CONCLUSION

- It is no longer possible for China to follow the American urbanization model

Since 1980, as a result of the industrialization and urbanization of China, its agricultural sector lost approximately 196 million jobs. Should China wish to follow the American agricultural model and end up with about 1% labor force in agriculture, assuming no further population growth, the country would have to accommodate in its industry and service sectors another 324 million people (slightly more than the entire US population as of 2013). It would have to base its entire food production on the remaining 13.6 million farmers. That seems entirely impossible due to sustainability barriers; thus, other solutions for the development of the urban-rural balance must be found.

- China's agricultural model must take in account the country's natural resource limitations

As discussed above, the agricultural development model adopted by the Chinese government, though certainly with the best intentions to feed the growing population, is not optimal for China in view of the country's natural resource limitations, first and foremost in potable water and energy.

Currently, the Chinese water use per capita is still at only one third of the volume used by the Americans. Taking in account the fact that China's freshwater availability per capita is at one third of that in the US while its pollution is already at twice the US level, the actual potable water availability ratio per capita between China and US is 1 to 6. Should the Chinese want to arrive at the American per capita use of their scarce water resources by multiplying their per capita use by three, after a few years there simply would be no water left.

Alternative ways of "producing" freshwater via, for example, desalinization require tremendous amounts of energy resources which China also does not possess. Thus *the best solution for the Chinese is to save and recycle their available water* maintaining its availability levels at their maximum.

- The Chinese Government needs to "green up" its system of subsidies to economy, science and technology

This demands from the Chinese government that they envisage and immediately put in execution *a whole new strategy* with respect to the agricultural (as well as industrial and urban development) sectors, wherein *water preservation would become the top priority*. That would also mean *reducing subsidies to water polluting animal and crop farms*. A good example to follow here would be the most recent "greening" of the European Union Common Agricultural Policy (voted in 2013) which provides for decreases in subsidies to farmers who do not fulfill environmentally friendly compliances. Research should be guided to water preserving techniques like for example root irrigation, organic fertilizers and methods of crop rotation. The Chinese agricultural model should *stay away from such doubtfully "great" ideas like GMOs* for a variety of reasons: from environmental and public health to last but not least, national security.

On the contrary, *China should invest in high tech but environmentally sustainable farming and distribution.* It should strive to specialize in these fields and become the world champion of "green" foodstuffs for which the global market is growing (by more than 25% since the start of the global economic crisis between 2008 and 2011.) [26] It needs to concentrate on family and NOT on corporate farming promotion. Economies of scale can be found in other ways, for example through voluntary collective farm associations (promoted by the authorities through adequate tax and subsidy instruments) along the models found in France or Denmark. The country should follow as closely as possible the green food distribution model: local production sold in local markets. It is worth noting that this model, and in general ecological farming, are more and more popular also in the US, especially that the newest studies have revealed that organic farms are only 10 to 20% less productive than conventional plots over a 21-year period, while their social and environmental costs incomparably smaller [27].

- The Chinese Government needs to develop healthy food products in order to address its looming diabetes epidemics

It is equally clear that China's money safe will also not be deep enough to treat the whole population of diabetics. If everyone is diabetic then who is left to work? This looming danger must be immediately addressed by the Chinese authorities in an all-encompassing fashion with a particular emphasis on agricultural policies (shifting subsidies to healthy food production with small ecological footprints), educational and public communication policies (targeted education to increase diet vs health awareness and right attitudes toward sport) and finally, tax policies (increasing taxes on unhealthy foodstuffs, decreasing on the healthy ones).

In the final conclusion, China has the right combination of hands and brains that should allow it to tackle the above described problems which pose natural limits to its development and, in fact, to its 5,000 thousand year old civilization. *What it needs now more than anything is the political will to make necessary strategic changes.* The Chinese political leaders must remember at all times that without freshwater the Chinese will not only be unable to satisfy thirst but there will be no home grown food as well. So that *without addressing the water crisis, very soon the Great Chinese Dream may become the Great Chinese Nightmare.*

REFERENCES

[1] Jared M. Diamond, (2005), *Collapse: how civilizations choose to fail or succeed*, New York: Viking Press.
[2] http://www.nationmaster.com/compare/China/United-States/Environment, retrieved February 6th 2014.

[3]   http://www.examiner.com/article/factory-farms-are-major-contributors-to-greenhouse-gasses-climate-change, retrieved February 6th 2014.
[4]   K. Averyt, J. Meldrum, P. Caldwell, G. Sun, S. McNulty, A. Huber-Lee and N. Madden, (2013), *Sectoral contributions to surface water stress in the coterminous United States,* Philadelphia: IOP Publishing.
[5]   http://www.ncifap.org/_images/PCIFAPSmry.pdf, retrieved February 6th 2014.
[6]   http://www.propublica.org/special/a-history-of-fda-inaction-on-animal-antibiotics, retrieved February 6th 2014.
[7]   http://articles.latimes.com/2013/feb/26/science/la-sci-breast-cancer-younger-women-20130227, retrieved February 5th, 2014.
[8]   http://www.bigpictureagriculture.com/2012/10/an-evaluation-of-benbrooks-pesticide-use-study-super-weeds.html, retrieved February 5th 2014.
[9]   http://www.ajpmonline.org/webfiles/images/journals/amepre/3834-stamped-070913.pdf, retrieved February 7th 2014.
[10] Eric A. Finkelstein, Justin G. Trogdon, Joel W. Cohen and William Dietz, *Annual Medical Spending Attributable To Obesity: Payer-And Service-Specific Estimates*, http://content.healthaffairs.org/content/28/5/w822.short, retrieved February 7th 2014.
[11] Yen, Hope, *80 Percent Of U.S. Adults Face Near-Poverty, Unemployment: Survey.* The Huffington Post, 28 July 2013, retrieved February 8th , 2014.
[12] *U.S. Poverty: Census Finds Nearly Half Of Americans Are Poor Or Low-Income,* The Huffington Post, December 15th 2011, retrieved February 8th 2014.
[13] Zong, Y., Chen, Z., Innes, JB., Chen, C., Wang, Z., Wang, H., (2007), *Fire and flood management of coastal swamp enabled first rice paddy cultivation in east China, Nature* 449 (7161): 459–62.
[14] http://www.pnas.org/content/early/2013/07/03/1300018110.abstract, retrieved February 10th 2014.
[15] http://web.mit.edu/newsoffice/2012/global-change-china-air-economy-0213.html, retrieved February 10th, 2014.
[16] Ian Johnson, *Chinese culture fades with empty villages,* New York Times, February 1st 2014.
[17] idem.
[18] Encyclopedia of Modern China, Vol. 1A–E, (2009), Farmington Hills, Michigan: Charles Scribner's Sons, a part of Gale, Cengage Learning.
[19] http://www.thepigsite.com/articles/4262/hog-farming-in-transition-the-case-of-china, retrieved February 17th 2014.
[20] http://blogs.wsj.com/chinarealtime/2013/07/08/china-grapples-with-genetically-modified-foods/, retrieved February 17th 2014.
[21] http://jama.jamanetwork.com/article.aspx?articleid=1734701, retrieved February 18th 2014.
[22] http://www.theatlantic.com/china/archive/2013/09/chinas-looming-diabetes-epidemic/279670/, retrieved February 18th 2014.
[23] http://www.bloomberg.com/news/2010-11-14/china-s-annual-26-billion-diabetes-bill-to-skyrocket-researchers-report.html, retrieved February 18th 2014.
[24] http://www.weforum.org/pdf/Wellness/WHOWEF_report.pdf, retrieved February 18th 2014.

http://www.thepoultrysite.com/poultrynews/29890/global-organic-food-market-growing, retrieved February 18th 2014.

[6] https://www.fibl.org/fileadmin/documents/shop/1500-climate-change.pdf, retrieved February 18th 2014.

End Notes

1. Jared M. Diamond, (2005), Collapse: how civilizations choose to fail or succeed, Viking Press.
2. http://www.nationmaster.com/compare/China/United-States/Environment Industrial organic pollutants per available freshwater Units: Metric Tons of BOD Emissions per Cubic Km of Water Units: Emissions of organic water pollutants are measured by biochemical oxygen demand, which refers to the amount of oxygen that bacteria in water will consume in breaking down waste. This is a standard water-treatment test for the presence of organic pollutants. The data from the World Bank, which represented BOD emissions (kilograms per day) were normalized by the combination of water availability per capita and water inflow availability per capita from the WaterGap2.1 model. In calculating the ESI, the base-10 logarithm of this variable was used. Source World Bank, World Development Indicators 2001, Washington, DC: World Bank, 2001 (for BOD emissions)and Center for Environmental Systems Research, University of Kassel, Water Gap 2.1, 2000 (for data on water quantity). Via.ciesin.org
3. http://www.examiner.com/article/factory-farms-are-major-contributors-to-greenhouse-gasses-climate-change There are nearly 10 billion land animals raised each year in the United States for meat, milk, and eggs. In the world there are 65 billion. A large and growing percentage of these animals are confined in 18.800 CAFO's in the U.S. Typical factory farms intensively restrict animals in large, overcrowded, and barren sheds, denying them the ability to engage in most of their natural behavior. These sheds necessitate the heavy use of antibiotics, which are another problem. The USDA estimates these animals produce 335 million tons of manure a year. Much of this runs off into streams, or is stored for long periods of time in tanks or lagoons. This animal waste produces 400 different gasses and a lot of each. Hydrogen sulfide, methane, ammonia, nitrous oxide, and carbon dioxide are the major hazardous gases produced by decomposing manure. The EPA estimates that methane emissions from manure increased by 26% in the United States between 1990 and 2004, due primarily to larger, more concentrated dairy cow and swine facilities. North Carolina's hog industry alone produces about 300 tons of ammonia each day. According to the Food and Agriculture Organization of the United Nations (FAO), the confined animal sector alone is responsible for 18% of all greenhouse gas (GHG) emissions, measured in carbon-dioxide equivalent in the world. According to the FAO, the farm animal sector annually accounts for: 9% of human-induced emissions of carbon dioxide (CO_2)• 37% of emissions of methane (CH_4), which has more than 20 times the global warming potential (GWP) of CO_2 and • 65% of emissions of nitrous oxide (N_2O), which has nearly 300 times the GWP of CO_2. Manure is not the only culprit from factory animal farming. Today's animals do not forage and graze the way nature intended. They are fed high energy feed. Growing that feed requires fertilizer and that fertilizer accounts for 41 million tons of CO_2 per year—on top of the CO_2 from the manure. Transporting the fertilizer to the centralized factory feed lots also has a huge carbon foot print. Unlike the open pastures or unheated barns and chicken coops of old, today's CFO's have huge inefficient sheds that require heating, cooling, and ventilation. This generates another 90 million tons of CO_2 a year. Lastly slaughtering and packaging of animal products adds tens of millions of tons of CO_2 a year on top of the rest. Methane is the big culprit since it is heavier and traps more heat in the atmosphere. Animal CFO's generate between 35%-40% of all methane released into the atmosphere. Putting that in simpler terms, factory animal farms produce more greenhouse gas than the entire transportation system of the country. CFO's produce more GHG's than most cities. Traditional animal farming would also produce gasses. However, on a traditional farm, there are fewer animals in one spot, and much of their foods would come from on-site sources like grass and grains. The naturally occurring gasses from their waste would be absorbed in large part by trees and shrubs surrounding the farms. It is not concentrated like in a CFO. In other words, nature would clean the air turning the carbon gas into oxygen.
4. Sectorial contributions to surface water stress in the coterminous United States K Averyt1, J Meldrum1, P Caldwell2, G Sun2, S McNulty2, A Huber-Lee3 and N Madden4© 2013 IOP Publishing Ltd 17 September 2013 http://iopscience.iop.org/1748-9326/8/3/035046/article?fromSearchPage=true

5. PCIFAP is a project of The Pew Charitable Trusts and the Johns Hopkins Bloomberg School of Health http://www.ncifap.org/_images/PCIFAPSmry.pdf
6. http://www.propublica.org/special/a-history-of-fda-inaction-on-animal-antibiotics: - 1951 The F approves the first antibiotics for use in animal feed based on studies showing it helps chickens, pigs and livestock put on extra weight. -1969 A committee of government experts in the U.K. concludes that the use of antibiotics in animals has contributed to antibiotic resistance in humans. - 1970 A U.S. task force, including scientists from the FDA and other agencies, recommends some antibiotics used in humans be banned from use in animals. - 1977 The FDA proposes a ban on the use of penicillin and tetracycline in animal feed, unless drugmakers can show the practice is not a danger to humans. The proposal is opposed by farmers, drugmakers and some federal lawmakers. Members of Congress order the FDA to do additional research. - 1980 An FDA-commissioned report by the National Academy of Sciences finds little scientific data on antibiotic resistance caused by feeding the drugs to animals. However, the group says that the lack of data is not "proof that the hazards do not exist." - 1997 The World Health Organization recommends antibiotics used in humans should not be used to promote growth in animals. - 1999 The European Union issues a ban on using popular human antibiotics in animals for growth promotion due to risks to humans. - 2003 The U.S. Institute of Medicine issues a report on the rise in dangerous bacteria, or superbugs. The group's recommendations include banning use of antibiotics for growth promotion in animals. - January 2012 The FDA orders limits on cephalosporin antibiotics given to animals. The drugs are used to treat pneumonia and other diseases in humans. - April of 2012 FDA outlines plans to phase out non-medical uses of more than 200 antibiotics in animals over three years. The voluntary plan requires cooperation by drugmakers and farmers.
7. http://articles.latimes.com/2013/feb/26/science/la-sci-breast-cancer-younger-women-20130227
8. http://www.bigpictureagriculture.com/2012/10/an-evaluation-of-benbrooks-pesticide-use-study-super-weeds.html
9. http://www.bigpictureagriculture.com/2012/10/an-evaluation-of-benbrooks-pesticide-use-study-super-weeds.html
10. American Journal of Preventive Medicine September 2013, Vol. 45, No. 3 Medical News Today July 9, 2013
11. Annual Medical Spending Attributable To Obesity: Payer-And Service-Specific Estimates, Eric A. Finkelstein, Justin G. Trogdon, Joel W. Cohen and William Dietz http://content.healthaffairs.org/content/28/5/w822.short
12. Yen, Hope (28 uly 2013). 80 Percent Of U.S. Adults Face Near-Poverty, Unemployment: Survey. The Huffington Post. Retrieved July 28, 2013.
13. "U.S. Poverty: Census Finds Nearly Half Of Americans Are Poor Or Low-Income". The Huffington Post. December 15, 2011. Retrieved June 5, 2013.
14. Zong, Y; Chen, Z; Innes, JB; Chen, C; Wang, Z; Wang, H (2007). "Fire and flood management of coastal swamp enabled first rice paddy cultivation in east China". Nature 449 (7161): 459–62. doi:10.1038/nature06135. PMID 17898767.
15. http://www.pnas.org/content/early/2013/07/03/1300018110.abstract
16. China's pollution puts a dent in its economy, Vicki Ekstrom, Joint Program on the Science and Policy of Global Change, February 13, 2012, http://web.mit.edu/newsoffice/2012/global-change-china-air-economy-0213.html
17. As reported in the New York Times article of February 1st 2014 By: Ian Johnson Chinese culture fades with empty villages
18. idem
19. Encyclopedia of Modern China, Vol. 1A–E, (2009), Charles Scribner's Sons, a part of Gale, Cengage Learning
20. http://www.thepigsite.com/articles/4262/hog-farming-in-transition-the-case-of-china
21. http://blogs.wsj.com/chinarealtime/2013/07/08/china-grapples-with-genetically-modified-foods/
22. http://jama.jamanetwork.com/article.aspx?articleid=1734701
23. http://www.theatlantic.com/china/archive/2013/09/chinas-looming-diabetes-epidemic/279670/
24. http://www.bloomberg.com/news/2010-11-14/china-s-annual-26-billion-diabetes-bill-to-skyrocket-researchers-report.html
25. http://www.weforum.org/pdf/Wellness/WHOWEF_report.pdf
26. http://www.thepoultrysite.com/poultrynews/29890/global-organic-food-market-growing
27. https://www.fibl.org/fileadmin/documents/shop/1500-climate-change.pdf

Part IV. Globalizing Chinese Civilization

In: Chinese Civilization in the 21st Century
Editors: Andrew Targowski and Bernard Han

ISBN: 978-1-63321-960-1
© 2014 Nova Science Publishers, Inc.

Chapter 7

THE MYTHS AND REALITIES OF THE CLASH OF WESTERN AND CHINESE CIVILIZATIONS IN THE 21ST CENTURY

Andrew Targowski[*]
Western Michigan University, US
President Emeritus of the International Society for the Comparative
Study of Civilizations (2007-2013)

ABSTRACT

The *purpose* of this investigation is to define the central issues of the current and future relations between the Western and Chinese Civilizations through the evaluation of the myths and realities of these relations. The *methodology* is based on an interdisciplinary big-picture view of the world scene, driven by the global economy and civilization with an attempt to compare both civilizations according to key criteria. Among the *findings* are: Today China has become a "robot" of the West by producing goods with its cheap labor force. Due to its old culture and ability to invent important civilizational tools, China is becoming an independent developer of its own economic power, and it is very probable that it will surpass its master sooner or later. Due to its transformation to a Global Civilization, Western Civilization has lost its Christian values and adopted new ones based on business. This has led to a huge wealth bifurcation between the "1%" and "99%" which affects the grand strategy of the U.S. and E.U. and diminishes their ability to self-correct. It is probable that the economic success of China will lead to a clash between civilizations, both grasping for access to the strategic resources. Therefore the mid-term future projection of a population of 9-11 billion (by 2050) is rather bleak. *Practical implication*: both societies should elaborate the path to the development of wise civilization driven by a new political system, *ecoism*. *Social implication:* It is probable that if the "1%" won't self-correct its misbehavior, a social revolution by the "99%" cannot be excluded from the current calendar of Western Civilization. *Originality:* This investigation, by providing the interdisciplinary and

---
[*] andrew.targowski@wmich.edu

civilizational approach, expands the scope of the traditional approach to this issue, which is mostly economics- or political science-oriented.

INTRODUCTION[1]

The main purpose of this investigation is to evaluate the question: is there a clash between the Western and Chinese civilizations, and what is the myth and reality of this clash? The spectacular economic development of the Chinese and the concurrent decline of Western Civilization provoke many predictions of the near-future world order. So far it seems that the West cooperates with China quite well, since through the outsourcing of Western manufacturing, China can employ its large labor force, and the Western financial elite benefit tremendously in business due to cheap labor. However, the question is how long can that kind of cooperation last? This triggered the financial crisis of 2008-2011, due to the shrinking middle class in the West, and furthermore, increasing numbers of employed Chinese workers can buy more and will need to consume more strategic resources, which are available in limited volumes on the earth. Will the current cooperation be replaced by a clash for resources? These kinds of questions will be investigated in this chapter. The wisdom-oriented abilities of both civilizations will also be evaluated to see which one has better chances to survive a shortage of strategic resources.

The methodology of this investigation is based on the interdisciplinary big-picture view of the world scene, driven by a global economy and civilization, with an attempt to compare both civilizations according to key criteria. A set of conclusions will be provided at the end of this paper, with practical and social implications for eventual implementation.

GLOBALIZATION'S IMPACT UPON THE WESTERN AND CHINESE CIVILIZATIONS IN THE 21ST CENTURY

The development of the modern world began after the fall of Byzantium (1453) and the discovery of America (1492), that is, at the end of the 15th century. In each century since, usually one country has dominated the world. In the 16th century Portugal dominated, in the 17th century Spain was the hegemon, in the 18th century Great Britain was the leader. At the beginning of the 19th century, the hegemon was France, which was later replaced by Great Britain. In the 20th century Great Britain, Germany, the United States, and to a certain degree Russia competed for the main role in world politics. In the 21st century the U.S.'s domination is fading, and many predict it will be replaced by China.

In the last 500 years, different targets and issues were at stake in world politics. For example, Portugal, Spain, and Great Britain were conquering new territories, with good results. Once the world became richer in the 19th century due to the gains of the Industrial Revolution clashing ideologies were at stake. The English Revolution (1688-89) built the foundation for the parliamentary system, the American Revolution (1775-1783) provided the concept of modern democracy, and the French Revolution (1789-1799) created citizenship in

---

[1] Author is grateful to Professors Hun, Rienzo and Tarn from Western Michigan University (USA) for providing improving suggestions to this investigation.

France. The Industrial Revolution (1760-1850-1960) contributed the factory system and industrially manufactured products, financed by capital. It led to accelerated wealth creation and rising inequality among society's members. Eventually to solve rising dissatisfaction and poverty, differing ideologies regarding the further development of civilization were at stake. None of those ideologies—Capitalism, Socialism, and later Communism and Nazism—could solve the societal problems. Eventually these ideologies led to the Mexican Revolution (1910), Bolshevik Revolution (1917), Spanish Revolution (1936), World War II, the Cold War (1945-1991), and to the very successful Scientific-Technological Revolution (1945-), Information Wave (1980-), Global Civilization (21st century), and Virtual Civilization (21st century).

After the fall of the Soviet Union and the end of the Cold War (1989-1991) in Europe, the Information Wave accelerated its activities in Western Civilization, triggering the fourth Globalization Wave.[2] Very soon this revolution embraced the whole world. Its effect has been the development of the global economy, controlled by global financiers. They developed global corporations, which are outsourcing manufacturing to Asia, particularly to China, where the cost of labor is low and the market is the largest in the world. Eventually it led to the rise of Global Civilization in the 21st century.

Supposedly, what is good for the global corporations is good for their maternal countries. With the help of lobbyists, global corporations control governments in Western Civilization, which supports outsourcing its own industrial base, since this leads to better business that can create more jobs. Although this may be true, those jobs are created outside of Western Civilization. The economic crisis in 2008-2013 in the U.S. and E.U. proves that turbo-capitalism is leading to the decline of Western Civilization and the rise of China. Now Chinese Civilization (China and diaspora) is awakening, full of energy to collect the benefits of the West's mistakes. Chinese Civilization does not want to fully westernize (however the younger generation is more open to westernization) since it appreciates its own values and principles that have developed over the last 5000 years.

In 2011 the Chinese economy took second place in the World, after the American and before the Japanese and German economies.[3] This supports arguments made by many authors and politicians that very soon China will move to first place, before the U.S., in the second part of the 21st century. According to the Economist,[4] in 2011 the GDP of the U.S. was still two times bigger than China's (in market prices) and only 25 percent bigger in basket prices (*PPP*[5]). If the current rate of economic development continues, China's economy will reach the same level as the U.S. in 2016 (*PPP*) and 2018 (market).

The Chinese economy looks even better if it is compared in certain categories to the U.S.'s. For example, in 2011 in production of steel, China was producing 6.6 times more than the U.S. The production of goods was 1.1 times bigger, the sale of cars was 1.2 times bigger, export was 1.3 times bigger, 3.3 times more mobile phones were in use, investments were 1.4 times bigger, and energy consumption was 1.1 times bigger. This data should not mislead, since it is the result of the West's strategy to move production to China! If the American

---

[2] The first Globalization Wave (GW I) took place at the end of the 15th century (Discovery of America), GW II in 1837 (British Empire), GW III in 1945, GW IV in 1990.
[3] Nominal GDP list of countries for the year 2010. World Economic Outlook Database September 2011, International Monetary Fund. Accessed on September 26, 2011.
[4] December 31, 2011, p. 61.
[5] PPP – purchasing parity price.

economy is two times bigger and the population is four times smaller, the GDP per capita is still eight times bigger in the U.S. This is the subject of many negative comments about China. However, in time, consumption in China should rise and could reach the American level in 2033.[6]

This type of forecasting is just a simple extrapolation of data, which can lead to erroneous conclusions. If this prognosis maintains what would actually happen, it would imply that the world has limitless strategic resources and Western Civilization is not able to self-correct its strategies. Since the reservoir of strategic resources is limited, the current spectacular development of Chinese Civilization will bring the world civilization to an end sooner or later. Eventually, China could apply its wisdom and go back the Great Wall, as it did in the 15th century, when the Emperor ordered that the Chinese fleet be destroyed (1433).

In these kinds of considerations one can contemplate whether the Chinese Civilization has an expansive character or whether that is it a myth since China's expansion was triggered by the West; and if China is clever, will it stay within its secure territory? Or, contrary to its history, can China change its character and promote not only economic but also cultural and even military expansion far beyond its borders?

The question is, if the West takes back its outsourced jobs, will China be able to continue its current, spectacular development?

CAN CHINA TRANSFORM FROM ROBOT TO MASTER OF MANUFACTURING AND BE AN ECONOMIC SUPERPOWER?

Most of our impressions about China's super economic power to a certain degree are myths. China became the world's factory when the Internet eliminated the problem of distance. It became evident that outsourcing manufacturing wouldn't be so difficult since e-communication speeds up business. In addition, business could be done cheaper and sometimes faster due to the Chinese ability to work hard and on time. In the past, China did not design products or technological processes, invest in the production infrastructure, or even provide the marketing for products that it manufactured. Furthermore, Westerners taught Chinese workers how to work on given products in given manufacturing settings.

In this way China became a "robot[7]" of Western Civilization and is not an independent economic superpower, at least not yet. It is a myth, not reality, that China became such a strong economy due to its own internal ability. On the other hand, the Chinese are a very talented people, who learn fast from the West and sooner or later will be able to develop their own products and manufacturing facilities. But it is less evident whether they will also be able to be successful enough in developing marketing and selling to compete with the Americans and Europeans. First of all, the Chinese do not copy (as the Japanese used to do) foreign

---

[6] China's Economic Heartland: Chongqing. http://www.theglobalist.com/countryoftheweek/sample.htm (retrieved 1-2-2012).

[7] For example, the Chinese labor working for Apple in Faxconn City lives in company barracks and work 6 days per week and 12 hours per shift, making $17 per day. Faxconn employs nearly 300 guards to direct foot traffic so workers are not crushed in doorways bottlenecks. (The New York Times, January 22, 2012, p. 22). No wonder why the American workers cannot compete with the Asian ones. In order to do so the former should return to the 18/19 centuries' working conditions to satisfy the appetite of the global corporations 200 years later. Is it progress?

solutions, because they co-own them, usually in the range of 50%, through venture-oriented undertakings. Also, they have the ability to absorb (comprehend) foreign solutions, due to China's culture of leaving "room" in its Mindsphere (way of thinking)

In the past, a common stereotype was that the Chinese traditionally lack scientific and technological ability, despite the fact that somehow they stumbled upon paper making, printing, gunpowder, and the mariner's compass. Modern Chinese themselves are sometimes surprised to realize that modern agriculture, shipping, astronomical observatories, decimal mathematics, paper money, umbrellas, wheelbarrows, multi-stage rockets, brandy and whiskey, the game of chess, and much more, all came from China. The sciences of astronomy, physics, chemistry, meteorology, seismology, technology, engineering, and mathematics can trace their early origins to China.

From 600 AD until 1500 AD, China was the world's most technologically advanced society. China was the leading maritime power in the years 1405-1433, when Chinese shipbuilders began to build massive oceangoing junks.[8] Between 1405 and 1433, the emperor of that time (the Yongle Emperor) sent Zheng He out on a series of seven naval expeditions, all designed to control trade and impress other nations (in Africa and India) with the power of the Chinese fleet. The successor emperor (the Hongxi Emperor) promptly cancelled Zheng He's expeditions and proceeded to have much of the Chinese fleet burned or destroyed (in 1433) and went into isolation.[9] Thus ended China's period as the world's greatest naval power. The interesting thing is that under the Hongxi Emperor and his son, the Xuande Emperor, many reforms were put in place that proved to be very popular amongst the people and which led to what is often referred to as one of China's Golden Ages. "Where would China be now had they not 'pulled back' from their maritime explorations and had they continued to spread their influence out amongst the world? That's not to take anything away from where China is at the moment, but it's interesting to ponder whether or not things would have been different," (Stanley Bronstein on July 7, 2009).[10]

Today in the 21st century, the Chinese are gaining self-confidence, knowledge, and skills and are awakening from the opium that the British used to colonize these talented people in the 19th century. This advancement of the Chinese can be proved by the following facts. In 2011 the Chinese built the fastest computer in the world: Tianhe-1A (built at the National Supercomputing Center in Tianjin, China, with a performance at 2.6 petaflop/s).[11] Their accelerated program of technological development culminated in Yang Liwei's successful 2003 flight aboard Shenzhou 5. This achievement made China the third country to independently send spacecrafts into space. Future plans include a permanent space station and crewed expeditions to the Moon and Mars.

All this indicates that China has the ability to surpass the "robot" stage and independently become a developer of science, technology, and production. In 2011 China patented 1.1 times more solutions than the U.S.[12] This means that the Chinese are developing their own intellectual potential which will lead China to independence from the West. China also has a huge internal market to support its own production, if the West slows down importing. China

---

[8] http://www.basicrps.com/chine/histoire/china.htm (retrieved on 1-10-2012)
[9] http://www.sjsu.edu/faculty/watkins/treasurefleets.htm (retrieved on 1-2-2012).
[10] http://stanleybronstein.com/china-was-once-the-worlds-greatest-naval-power-but/ (retrieved on 1-2-2012).
[11] 1 petaflop/sec=10^{15} floating-point operations per second, or = 1,000 trillion operations/sec. In comparison, a hand held calculator makes about 10 oper/s.
[12] The Economist, December 31, 2011, p. 61.

is on the way to becoming a real economic superpower, particularly if Western Civilization continues the suicidal de-industrialization and liquidation of the middle class. If this trend goes on, Western Civilization will continue to provide the marketing and selling for China. On the other hand, it is rather doubtful whether China will accept payment in governmental bonds which will never be paid off.

The paradigm of China as a "robot" brings to attention Isaac Asimov's First Law of Robotics (1942): "A robot may not injure a human or, through inaction, allow a human being to come to harm." It is very evident that the West is pushing the Chinese robot to harm the master. It is no wonder that Western Civilization is declining so rapidly in the 21st century. It is not China's fault but rather the West's lack of wisdom.

The question is whether or not such an economically strong China will try to convert the Global Civilization into a Global-Chinese Civilization (Glob-Chin Civilization)? Nowadays, China is installing 150 Confucius Institutes in the U.S. which will train future teachers of the Chinese language at American schools. Is this a long-term strategy of globalization *a la* China?

CAN THE WEST GIVE UP MANUFACTURING AND LIVE ON BORROWING?

The depth of the economic crisis in 2008-2011 indicates that it is not a classic cyclical recession but rather a new structural crisis. The majority of specialists and politicians agree with respect to the scope and depth of this crisis. But can none of them define a convincing diagnosis of this crisis? In the U.S. a leading opinion is that this crisis was caused by easy credit (mortgages) for houses and an expanding federal government deficit. In Europe, a leading opinion is that the deficit of European governments using the *euro* is so large that it cannot be paid off. In other words, those countries are in a practical sense bankrupted. As a result of these causes, Western Civilization has entered a deep structural crisis. The solution recommended by top European leaders for how to get out of this crisis is to pay off debts. In practice, one must take out more loans to service the old loans.

It is a suicidal strategy. To increase the supply of money in the marketplace, one must increase the amount of money in the hands of consumers by employment. In effect those consumers will go to stores and buy goods which must be produced in higher volumes. However, this production will be increased in Asia, particularly in China, and local consumers (in the U.S. and Europe) won't be engaged in production and won't gain income through employment. The service economy in the U.S. and E.U. is too weak (since it is based on low-paying jobs) to generate more money in the hands of consumers.

The presented diagnosis is simple and obvious. However, none of the important economists, politicians, and publicists has even mentioned the presented diagnosis and solution because the manufacturing lobby spends many millions of dollars to control the "mouths" of leading opinion-makers. So far those in the so-called "1%" make very good money in China, where the labor costs are still low. In effect, the U.S. is deep in pending debts. For example, the federal government is $15 trillion in debt, local governments $5T, individuals $16T, and the accumulative deficit of the foreign exchange is $4.6T, totaling about $40.6T.[13] This constitutes about 70 percent of the world GDP. In order to pay off the debts of 320 million American consumers, about 2.45 billion workers must work for a whole year.[14] Of course this is not feasible. The U.S. cannot pay off its debts; it can only take new loans to pay the annual interest of old loans. The same strategy is applied by the E.U. in countries using the *euro*.

In 2011 the politicians of Western Civilization, whose society is steered by the global financiers, refused to regulate the global economy, because obviously, the present state of the global economy is beneficial for global corporations. On the other hand, those who are negatively impacted, the "99%," launched the "Occupy Wall Street" movement aiming against those "1%" who collect the enormous profits from outsourcing manufacturing to Asia and economically colonizing workers over there. This movement will continue to exist and grow, since the reasons for the crisis will not be removed soon. From a logical point of view, Western Civilization should regulate (through WTO, IMF, WB, G7, and national governments) its activities in the global economy to survive in a very broad, sustainable sense. Perhaps this issue will come out during the 2012 presidential election campaign in the U.S, but up until now, nothing indicates that this will happen. There is no correct diagnosis of the crisis or political will to elaborate such a diagnosis and implement the obvious solution in practice.

The correct strategy is to bring back outsourced jobs and re-industrialize the West again. To do so one must implement tax credits[15] to support insourcing for American products which used to be made abroad and imported to the U.S. Another issue is who should finance the safety net for those American workers whose jobs have been off-shore outsourced, regardless of possible tax credits. Perhaps those corporations which make huge profit on it or just the society? But to avoid any form of protectionism and to support free trade, low tariffs for products made by particular countries, such as China, Germany, Japan, France, and so forth, should be minimal, because the theory of free trade is not built upon the necessary transfer of industrial jobs from the developed to developing countries.

This strategy is simple and natural, but due to the conflicting interests and pressure from elites in the world, it is not implementable today. One must remember that "innovation does not happen in laboratories by researchers. It happens on the factory floor. The process of making stuff helps you experiment and produce new products. If everything is made in China, people there will gain the skills, knowledge and experience to innovate. And the Westerners will be behind."[16]

CHINA'S "HIDDEN" CULTURE: A KEY TO UNDERSTANDING ITS ECONOMIC TRANSFORMATION[17]

Westerners look at the Chinese from the Western point of view, neglecting the 5000 year-long phenomenon of this very long lasting nation. It may not be appropriate to equate China's

---

[13] http://www.usdebtclock.org/ (Retrieved on 1-10-2012)
[14] It is assumed that 50% of populations belong to the labor force (7 B x 0.5 x 0.75=2.45 B).
[15] On January 24, 2012 President Obama suggested this kind of credit in his State of the Union.
[16] F.Zaharia. The Case for Making It in the USA. *TIME*, February 6, 2012, p. 19.
[17] This section is based on Professor Bernard Han's advice to this author, who is grateful to him for so honestly sharing his knowledge about the hidden Chinese culture.

economic accomplishments with that of Western Civilization's. Until about 30 years ago, Chinese civilization had not progressed much over the past 200 years. Its economic accomplishment in the past 30 years is simply a duplication of that of Western Civilization (clothing, social behavioral changes, material consumption, etc.). However, the Chinese do have a deeply-rooted "hidden" culture which is not well understood by Westerners. Our writings are primarily focused on the "economic impacts" and "changes" due to the globalization and outsourcing caused by the availability of Internet. They cannot fully explain the intrinsic differences between Chinese people and those in the West. The following are a few culture-wide factors which shall be addressed to emphasize the ability of the Chinese culture to pursue its role in world economics:

a) Strong family values: Most Chinese people prefer not to reveal individual political interests until the whole society has a big problem. In other words, they can tolerate "less democracy" for more national stability, and this is the reason they accept "modified" communism without going against the communist leaders.

b) Hoarding of wealth: Similar to the Japanese, Chinese people do not spend all the money they earn. They care about holding long-term property such as land and gold, which makes their economy less sensitive to the outside world. I.e., the global crisis has less effect on the internal economy in China since most people manage their finances very well, even though they do not have the same life quality or living standards as the West.

c) Emphasis on education: Most parents will put education as the first priority for their children. In other words, they can let go of personal life quality or enjoyment if there is opportunity to upgrade their social status (or position) and knowledge. The Chinese value knowledge and social status more than anything else. They consider merchants the worst class in society. This is the big difference between the East and the West.

In fact, the above three factors are commonly shared by the Jewish culture. This could be the reason that Jews were assimilated by the Chinese 1200 years ago.[18] It also explains why the Chinese are as successful as Jews in commerce and education in the U.S. and beyond.

Most people in China understand that their political system is not good, but they keep silent since the Communist party is lopsided and there is no way to avoid persecution if one goes against the system. But, if the Chinese government continues to allow more economic freedom or make improvements in living standards for the general public, then there will be no "Problem or Revolution" at all. Nevertheless, we cannot underestimate the potential danger embedded in these two factors since the Chinese leaders have to be willing to let go some of their given advantages, curb their corruptions, and maintain a pseudo-democracy to be considered as partners with Westerners?

According to the Chinese's understanding of the 2008-2011 deep economic recession, its roots are not in outsourcing of Western jobs but come from the following factors:

---

[18] see http://en.wikipedia.org/wiki/Kaifeng_Jews.

a) Capitalists' selfishness: Most rich people (1%) do not care about others (99%) but only about their own benefits. This is very true in the United States and possibly true in the E.U.
b) Overemphasized individual rights: Everyone is equal, and this can be applied to people with different value systems, different religions, different life styles, and different morality. No wonder there are no understandable standards of living in the society. Everyone is equal, and it turns out everyone is great and everyone is equally distracted and confused.
c) The inability to conduct self-examination: As shown in Table 1, the poorest country in the whole world is India (not China). However, both India and China are really poor compared to the Western countries. Using the figures presented in Table 1, the U.S. owns 23 times more wealth per person compared to China, and 52 times more wealth per person than in India. All these numbers indicate that one of the real problems in the West is overspending and over-enjoyment of personal life.

If the above factors do not change, the hope for self-correction in the West is very slim. The Chinese collaborate with Westerners from the position of a wiser partner (5,000 years old) who has patience and hope to gain power step by step.

DO WE FACE A CONTEST FOR SUPREMACY OR FOR CIVILIZATION SURVIVAL?

A China that has been resurrected by globalization in the 21st century has become the subject of fascination for intellectuals from the West. They are in a race to publish the most impressive book. Just a few examples illustrate this race: *A Contest for Supremacy, China, America, and the Struggle for Mastery In Asia*, by Aaron L. Friedberg (2011), *China Shakes the World*, by James Kynge (2006), *China on the Brink*, by Callum Henderson (1999), *When China Rules the World*, by Martin Jacques (2009), and *The Quest*, by Daniel Yergin (2011), among others. In these titles there is more myth than reality.

The West has always had well-defined enemies. In particular, the U.S. has always known which country is its enemy. The first enemy was Great Britain, later Germany and Japan, followed by USSR (until 1991 and after 2014). Today the enemy is China. This is an unintended enemy which was created because it is convenient for the U.S. to have an enemy besides terrorists.

China should be a good enemy since it is not a democracy, just ruled by a communistic party in an authoritarian manner (Walter and Howie, 2011). However, China does not want to propagate Communism elsewhere. Contrary to the communistic dogmas, this country has been implementing a managed-marketed economy (a new type of capitalism[19] or a modified

---

[19] China, in terms of its economic systems, "makes 3 steps forward and 2 steps backward." In fact Chinese leadership is afraid of dividing the country into two parts: those who "have" and "do not have." In 2011-2012 China is "crock- downing on capitalism" (R. Foroohar, The Curious Capitalist. *TIME*, January 16, 2012, p.22). The government has intensified Internet controls, limited free speech and human rights in order to prevent a potential Chinese Spring or Summer. When Deng Xiaoping restored his authority in 1978 and said that "to be wealthy is not a sin," the Chinese economy begun growing and flourish. Many officials use this new policy to make unexpected and huge profits. The state monopolies have fallen into the hands of small groups of party

Communism or Socialism with Chinese character), which energizes individuals at the bottom of the hierarchical society. On the other hand this system as the *Chinese model* has inherited a conflict between Communism and Capitalism. Furthermore, China does not want a war with the West, since it is winning without fighting because it is successfully following the rule of its great sage Sun Tzu (544-496 B.C.). However, "an increasingly powerful China is likely to try to push the U.S. out of Asia, much the way the U.S. pushed European powers out of the Western Hemisphere," (Mearsheimer 2001).

The Shi Lang, an aircraft carrier, (purchased as the Varyag, a Kuznetsov-class carrier from Ukraine, refurbished, and is set to service) is intended to show the world that China is a first-class naval power. This suggests China is changing its strategic thinking, which was concentrated on crossing the sea to do battle on land and looking to encircle Taiwan by adroitly deploying forces off Taiwan's east coast. In theory, a Chinese carrier-led naval task force could be used to deny the U.S. the ability to come to Taiwan's rescue.[20] The integration of Taiwan with middle-land China is considered by China as an "internal issue."

Because Western Civilization is intensively supporting its own development by the transformation to a Global Civilization, China has only to comply with this push and continue its own unprecedented development. According to popular estimations, China's economy should reach the level of the American economy in 2027, but it will be two times bigger in 2050 (Jacques, 2009). The question is, won't such a China that feels so strong want to disseminate its "winning" culture around the world? This author thinks the following way. If this happens, it will mean that China has abandoned its famous "middle of the road" politics. It will also mean that China will have entered a period where it will be risking what it has gained during the early 21st century and what it could not achieve in the last 500 years.

The most important questions are, will China be a superpower? And, will there be a civilization clash? The answers are reflected in the following "ifs"[21]:

a) If the Chinese leaders do not deal with corruption or maintain actual political stability, then China will never have a chance to become a superpower.
b) If, ironically, the U.S. helps (or even pushes) China to successfully become a country with a full democracy, then China will definitely become the superpower, assuming that nothing would change in the United States and European Union.
c) If China westernizes, then there will be no clash of "civilization" at all. Rather, there will be conflicts of interests.

The current Western approach to China follows step b, since the West thinks that it is the "best" and every nation/state/civilization should westernize. In this manner, the West is bringing up the future superpower, which will be its strategic competitor or perhaps even an enemy. Despite the wise opposition of Chinese seniors to westernization, the younger generation and the huge Chinese diaspora are westernizing quickly. A good proof of this is the decline of Chinatowns in the United States, which in the past were the hubs of Chinese culture and today are almost empty.

---

apparatchiks who maintain the political status quo for own sake. However, the Party condemns this kind of political corruption.
[20] China's 65,000-ton sec ret. *Bloomberg Businessweek*. January 30-February 5, 2012, p. 65.
[21] These "ifs" were suggested by Professor Bernard Han, who consulted this author on the Chinese culture.

It is obvious that the development of Chinese Civilization according to Western patterns sooner or later will lead to the shaking of the balance of interests rather than to the hegemony of China in the global economy. We are already entering into this state of the world civilization, because it is impossible to maintain the current rate of civilizational development for a population of 7-11 billion people. It is a dream of global corporations to have such a number of potential customers, which is perceived as a good business plan.

Therefore we do not face the race for who will rule the world, but in reality we deal with the race for who will have the best access to the largest sources of energy and other strategic resources which are necessary to maintain our civilization. In this area, China has shown many initiatives and has successfully gained access to sources of oil in Africa, South America, and the Near East.

For example, in 2011 China signed contracts to import 65 percent of the world's reserves of iron ore and 40 percent of copper and aluminum. To secure these supplies, China operates mines from Zambia to Peru, extracts crude oil in Ethiopia, Kazakhstan, and Sudan, and invests in the extraction of natural gas in Australia and Turkey. China even invests in the extraction of coal in North America, since Chinese coal is of low quality. China is the largest importer of soybeans and also corn, which is needed for the rising consumption of meat.[22]

China was self-sufficient in consumption of oil in the 20th century. In the 21st century, China became the second largest consumer of oil after the U.S. By about 2020, China may surpass the U.S. in consuming oil (Yergin, 2011:192). China has 170 cities with populations of one million and several cities with populations of ten million. The rising urbanization of China requires energy. To maintain good social order, China should create 25 million jobs every year.

Today, the economic powers race for access to strategic resources. The most important strategic resource is oil. The question is will such an expanding global economy lead to a war between the U.S. and China?

FROM CHINA'S RISE TO THE TROUBLED FUTURE OF CIVILIZATION

China and the Business Growth Trap

The nonsense of the strategy of continuous economic growth is illustrated in Table 7.1, which compares the U.S. China, India, and the rest of the world's growth at the rate of the so-called "American Way of Life" in 2011. If the Chinese and Indians would like to live as the Americans do, then the world resources consumed would need to be 309 percent larger than are available now, even assuming that the rest of the world would be satisfied with the same material standards of living as they currently have.

This comparison's conclusion can be supported by the analysis done by Lester Brown (2001:17) who noticed that:

- If the Chinese would like to eat as much beef as the Americans, then they will need 343 million tons of grain a year, an amount equal to the entire U.S. grain harvest.

---

[22] China's Buy List, *TIME,* January 9, 2012, p. 46-47.

- If the Chinese would like to eat as much fish as the Japanese, then they will need to consume 100 million tons of seafood – the entire world fish catch.
- If the Chinese would like to have two cars per household as the Americans do, then they would need 80 million barrels of oil per day, which is about 80 percent of the world production in 2011. Needless to say, the bigger size of parking lots would take 50 percent of the 31 million hectares currently used to produce the country's 132-million-ton harvest of rice, which is the basic food of the Chinese.
- If the Chinese are to be more educated, then the consumption of paper would rise from 35 to 342 kilograms/per person (similar to the Americans), and they would need more paper than the world currently produces.

Table 7.1. What Will Happen if China and India Grow as the U.S. Has?

COUNTRIES	Population (millions) 2011	% of World Resources Used 2011	American Way of Life - % of Resources Used 2011
USA	312	27	27
China	1,348	5	117
India	1,204	2	99
The Rest	4,136	66	66
Total	7,000	100	309

Source: Pocket World in Figures, *The Economist*, 2011, official centers and the Author's estimations.

The business growth trap is very obvious in light of the provided examples. Its threat can be well seen in the big-picture perspective. Unfortunately, current business practices are oriented in small-picture perspectives. Also, political control of business is limited to a very short cycle, which neglects the decline of civilization on the small planet called Earth.

In 1972, an MIT research team led by Dennis Meadows published a book, *Limits to Growth*, predicting that growth on this planet will stop within the next one hundred years. They invoked five major trends of global concern: accelerating industrialization, rapid population growth, widespread malnutrition, depletion of nonrenewable resources, and a deteriorating environment. In the years following the publication of this book, people began to recycle wasted resources and thought more about sustainable growth. After the subsequent 36 years, a sixth trend of global concern must be added: unregulated turbo-capitalism (global economy), which threatens the well-being of Western Civilization.

The Race for Resources and the Death Triangle of Civilization

"The race between population and resources leads to two related problems, the rate at which resources are being used (and used up), and the inequality in the distribution of resources," (Cameron, 1993:404). The first threat can and perhaps will stop civilization sooner or later. The second threat will lead to internal and external wars of civilizations, which eventually will result in a more aggressive civilization at the expense of other civilizations.

Seen from space, Earth exhibits a striking difference from the other planets of the solar system: more than two-thirds of its surface is covered with water. Earth is the only planet in the solar system known to support life. Unlike the other planets, its crust is broken into plates that are in constant motion, borne along by currents of heat below. The Earth has a magnetic field generated by this heat, which is one of the sources of energy which drives civilization. The Earth is among four of the smallest planets in the Solar System. Its resources are finite. From 4000 B.C. through 1800 A.D., our civilization grew three percent per 1,000 years, and the budgeting of strategic resources was not an issue (Maddison, 2001). Since the Industrial Revolution in the 19th century, civilization has been in accelerated growth and in the 21st century, it has entered the "growth trap" period. The growth trap is when accelerated growth is intensified by the growth of population and managerial/global turbo-capitalism, which looks for tremendous growth in executive benefits and replaces voters with lobbyists.

We used to think and act in terms of a local community, nation, region, or even a group of nations. But now we need to take these considerations in a broader – planetary – context if we want to sustain our social life. The planet is so large in relation to every individual but for the population it is becoming smaller and smaller. In the last 200 years the population has grown from 300 million to seven billion and is still growing. We have about 4.7 acres of available footprint but we use 5.4 acres in terms of calculated resources. "We are living beyond our ecological means. The planet is shrinking, because we are running out of resources. We are using the planet with such intensity that it is unable to restore itself," (Steffen, 2008:16).

In terms of the two most important strategic resources of civilization, water and energy, the situation is as follows:

- **Water** – Over 97 percent of the Earth's water is in the oceans and has too much salt for the use of most land plants and animals. Of the 2.5 percent that is fresh water, about two-thirds is locked up in glaciers. This means that slightly less than one percent of the Earth's water is fresh and in liquid form. Irrigation systems are drying up the deltas of such major rivers as the Indus, Nile, Colorado, and some rivers in Europe. The U.N. set a goal to provide 13 gallons of safe water per day (within a few hundred meters of each family) to eight billion people in 2025. This goal is unrealistic, taking into account that according to the World Health Organization, the minimum need is five gallons of treated water a day per person, and it is difficult to provide this amount of water to everybody (Conkin, 2007:66).
- **Energy** – How long will our fossil fuels like oil, gas, and uranium last? Oil reserves should last about 40 years; gas, 51 years; uranium, 30-70 years; and coal, 200 years. Therefore, humans' knowledge and skills must replace these nonrenewable resources with ones that are either man-made (e.g., ethanol) or not subject to depletion (e.g., solar and wind energy). Otherwise, civilization will stop (Targowski, 2009:398).

There are many more threats to civilization, presented in Figure 7.1, which connects three dangerous bombs: the Population Bomb, Ecological Bomb, and Strategic Resources Depletion Bomb (Targowski, 2009:404). The Death Triangle of Civilization will be controlling the global economy sooner than will China, which allegedly will become the largest economic power in 2050, because the rise of China only accelerates the activation of that Triangle. In effect the whole world will enter such a complex, practically suicidal, situation that nobody will be able to manage it.

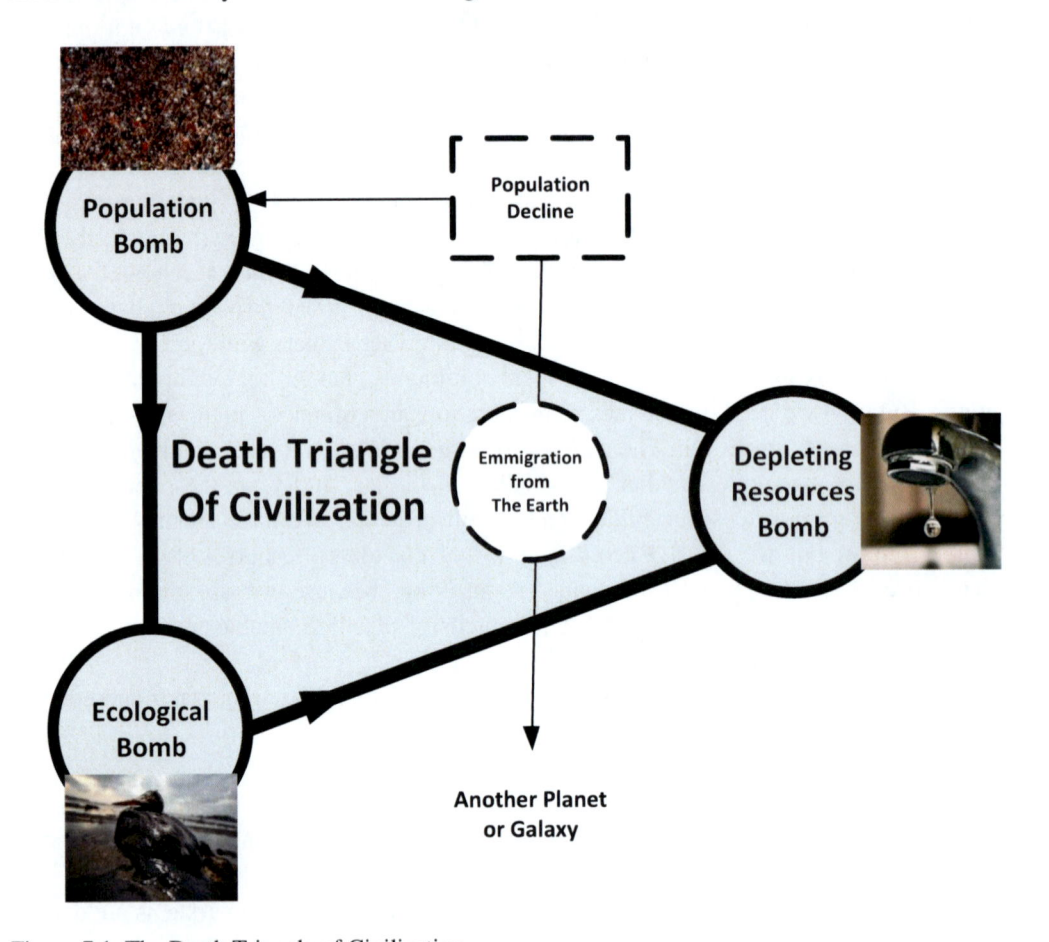

Figure 7.1. The Death Triangle of Civilization.

CAN WESTERN KNOWLEDGE WIN OVER CHINESE WISDOM?

The present situation in the world civilization is not yet a confrontation between the Western and Chinese civilizations because the West still treats China as its "robot." It plans to utilize the cheap Chinese labor force as long as possible and to make a good profit. However, China is slowly getting out from under that subordination and beginning to surpass its master.

Western Civilization, represented by the "1%" with the highest income, brings to mind the last phase of Rome (476 A.D.), which dominated the world for nearly 1200 years. Similarly Western Civilization dominated the world for nearly 1200 years since the rise of the Frank Empire (800 A.D.). Table 7.2 compares the state of Rome I with the U.S. (Rome III).

The comparison of Rome I and Rome III (the U.S.) gives the impression that the U.S. is in bad shape from the civilization point of view. It cannot lead Western Civilization back to its previous prominent state.

Table 7.2. The Comparison of the Roman Empire and the U.S. in Times of Crisis

Criteria	The Roman Empire 5th Century A.D.	The United States The 2000s A.D.
Rulers	Insensitive	Misleading
Politicians	Irrelevant	Self-serving
Elite	Passive	Detached
Military	Dispersed	Stretched-out
Work done by	Slaves & Servants	Computers and illegal immigrants working like slaves Offshore cheap labor
Ideas	Lack of ideas	Lack of ideas
Purpose of life	*Dolce vita*	The fun society
Mindset	Return to country-side and autarchy	Protectionist feelings and besieged
Viewed by others	Falling & attacked and beaten by weaker forces	Falling (Iraq & Afghanistan); attacked by terrorists against whom one cannot decisively win

The West is sure of its ability to create and disseminate knowledge, since it has been doing so very spectacularly for the last 500 years. In the Encyclopedia Britannica about 85 percent of the entries are about contributions made by Western Civilization. Ricardo Duchesne in his book *The Uniqueness of Western Civilization* (2011) asks: what makes the West unique? He explains it is partly the singular emergence of democratic culture, including the capacity for self-criticism from which revisionism itself derives. It is partly the rationalization of so many spheres of life, from science to law. It is partly the culture of innovation and widespread competition. These are all classical explanations for the divergence of the West. What Duchesne adds is an emphasis on the "continuous creativity," as he calls it, of the West, and the argument that the creativity of Western Civilization derives from a longstanding matrix of aristocratic libertarianism. Another unique feature of Europeans was a relatively egalitarian (actually egalitarian-aristocratic) spirit. A king in Europe was usually a first among equals, at least among the aristocrats; at the very least no member of the nobility or aristocracy had to prostrate themselves before kings. This is quite in contrast to despotic cultures almost anywhere else in the world. While some other warrior aristocracies (most notably Japan) had a similar "noblesse oblige" ethos, the egalitarianism was missing.

Of all these factors, the Western Civilization lost the ability for self-correcting by its elites which created very strong economic inequality. Consequently, these two factors triggered the collapse of democratic values and the foundation of civil society. Such a society, while knowledgeable, cannot make good judgments and choices, which used to define its wisdom. Western Civilization developed the belief that knowledge and technology can solve any crisis. In many cases this worked in the past. But when 9-11 billion people populate the Earth in 2050 and would like to live at the level of Westerners at the end of the 20th century, neither knowledge nor technology will solve the coming crisis.

Western society's loss of wisdom cannot compete with China's famous smartness, hard work, and wisdom to survive in very harsh conditions. This is contrary to some expectations that China must westernize[23] like Japan in order to succeed, or that it will only be successful if it copies the American democratic model. In fact China learned much more from the failure of the Soviet Union and its fall in 1991, after seeing Russia's convulsions when transforming into the Western model.

The Chinese Communist Party saw that the Soviet Union was very economically inflexible at the citizen level. This led to its collapse in 1991. On the other hand, post-Soviet Russia lost its grip on the economy and is in permanent turmoil. The lesson learned led China to two main rules: allowing economic freedom at the bottom of society and simultaneously keeping strong control at the top of the state by the authoritarian government. Perhaps this political system may be called modified Communism or Socialism with Chinese Character. Needless to say, this is the future system of governing, in which the world will distribute limited strategic resources by coupons. Then a strong government at the top will be required to supervise a life with limited resources. Perhaps it may even return to the level of Russian life under Leninism-Stalinism (1917-56). It will be a corrupted and ineffective system, of course, but people will be happy just to have something to eat and to keep them warm. Due to this system, China, which used to have a less comfortable civilization than the West, will be better off than the West during the time of the Death Triangle of Civilization's threats. Very probably this Chinese model will be adapted by the West for these critical times of the Triangle.

Table 7.3. The Comparison of Western and Chinese Civilizations

CRITERIA	WESTERN CIVILIZATION	CHINESE CIVILIZATION
State	Nation-states	Civilization-state spread through country and diaspora around the globe
Government	Democracy	Authoritarian Hierarchy
Culture	1200+ years old	5000 years old
Main values	Individualism / Neglect of Seniors	Family / Respect for Seniors
Hardship threshold	Low	High
Focus	Short and Instant	Long and Patient
Strongest knowledge	Scientific and Universal	Conventional and Scientific
Infrastructure	Complex	Simple and Complex
Interest	Extraverted	Introverted
Level of energy needed to support life activities	High	Low to Medium
Character	Arrogant	Submissive
Survival ability	Moderate	High

Source: Author's opinion, and Targowski (2009).

---

[23] Chinese intellectual, Nobel Prize winner Liuy Xiabo wrote that "I now realize that Western Civilization, while can be useful in reforming China in its present stage, cannot save humanity in an overall sense. I must 1). Use Western Civilization as a tool to critique China. 2). Use my own creativity to critique the West." The New York Review of Books, February 9, 2012, p. 53.

This comparison indicates that in the sense of enduring, Chinese civilization has better characteristics than Western Civilization. This is proven by comparing 5000 to 1200 years, which means that the former has lasted four times longer than the latter. It is interesting that while Chinese Civilization is still functioning, Western Civilization is being transforming into Global Civilization. This means that Western Civilization is fading. The West in facing China's challenge does not show any strong vision, strategy, or will to correct its situation.

TOWARD THE WISE CIVILIZATION AND THE REMAKING OF THE MODERN WORLD IN THE 21ST CENTURY

In the 21st century we are facing the empirical facts that neither capitalism (particularly liberal and unregulated), socialism, nor communism is accomplished systems in the long-term. One must predict that a wise civilization (Targowski, 2011:185) will need a new political system in the 21st century which will be called Ecoism (or Eco-Superiority). This means that the ecosystem's long-term sustainability is superior to humankind's well-being in the short-term. This system is based on the following values:

- Eco-Justice, Eco-Freedom, and Eco-democracy

To steer the development and operations of:

- Complementary Spirituality
- Integrated Society
- Deep Economy (Eco-Economy)
- Deep Communication
- Eco-Infrastructure

The values of Eco-Justice, Eco-Freedom, and Eco-Democracy mean that limits in terms of the well-being of the ecosystem must be given greater weight in traditionally perceived justice, freedom, and democracy. It is like in Deep Economy (Eco-Economy), where full economic cost cannot be limited only to business cost, but must include environmental and social costs as well.

Eco-Justice means that any crime and its consequences must also be evaluated from the ecosystem point of view.

Eco-Freedom means that humans are free in their choices and movements as long as they do not destroy the ecosystem. For example, deforestation should be forbidden, and the development of megacities should be controlled from an eco-policy point of view.

Eco-Democracy means that the balance of power must be preserved through free elections and a free press but that politicians and the press cannot act against the ecosystem, as they do today in the form of lobbyists' hidden support for politicians and the media. Consequently, the ecosystem will be *superior* to humans, who among themselves behave democratically but in facing the ecosystem are subordinate to it.

Complementary Spirituality - The level of spirituality and its complexity determines the possibility for a wise civilization. A low level or lack of spirituality in society puts a given civilization at risk. In the world's approximately 100 active major cultures, each one has its own kind of spirituality. To remove potential, if not certain, conflicts among them, one must find a common ground for them. This can be done by sharing selected values of each civilization and make of a set of complementary spiritual values. This will eventually lead to a Universal civilization as the potential wise civilization.

Integrated Society - The society of a wise civilization should be composed of people who are in solidarity with each other and are wise. In the age of globalization, most societies are multi-cultural, wherein each ethnicity has its own agenda and lives in an almost closed environment. To overcome this situation, they have to be able to integrate around a common culture, which will be called a *middle culture*.

Deep Communication - Current civilizations are driven by "shallow communication," particularly in mass media. They are very simplistic in delivering the news, focusing mostly on negative news about current events. The media rarely covers long-term issues within the "deep background," which contains theoretical, global, and universal knowledge/wisdom about discussed issues.

Eco-Infrastructure - Contemporary civilizations have developed many supportive infrastructures (Targowski, 2009:15), which determine the well-being of humans. The most eco-driven infrastructures are urban, transportation, and information. The last two infrastructures created the foundation for the development of the Global civilization by the development of global transportation systems and the Internet. The eco-orientation of this infrastructure should be as follows:

- In the scope of the transportation infrastructure for a wise civilization, particularly for its North American part, one must expand metro transit systems and intercity trains to reduce individual use of cars and save energy. The fuel consumption of cars should be regulated, and cars such as Hummers should not be produced.
- In the scope of the information infrastructure for the wise civilization, one must regulate the development of automation, according to the following laws (Targowski, 2009:273):
    o Law I. Do not develop service systems without human presence.
    o Law II. Do not develop service systems which harm society.
    o Law III. Do not develop service systems which endanger the human race.

Law I protects people against passivity; Law II protects society against structured unemployment; Law III protects the human race against bifurcation into two kinds of species.

Another set of laws for automation in manufacturing is provided by Targowski-Mordak (2011):

o Law I. Do not implement high automation technology before you are sure that the same goal cannot be achieved by other means.
o Law II. Do not implement automation technology with the aim to totally eliminate a human presence in a manufacturing process.
o Law III. Do not develop automation which harms society or endangers the human race.

In effect, the Ecoism (Eco-Superiority) political system satisfies all laws and rules of civilizations and adds new ones to expand human knowledge and wisdom, working for the sake of mankind and its environment.

CONCLUSION

One can draw the following conclusions:

1. The spectacular development of China in the 21st century has been triggered by Western Civilization, which treats this country as its "robot" by economically colonizing its workforce, based upon benefiting from cheap labor. It is a myth that so far China has improved its development mainly through internal factors.
2. China is transforming in the 21st century from "a colonial robot" (low-level labor) into an economic superpower (high-level-labor, following the Japanese paths in the XX century), due to its wise top management, old culture, and increasing intellectual and infrastructural potential which is strengthening its internal developmental. As a result, China could surpass the U.S. in the 21st century in the size of its economy and eventually may become the hegemon of Asia and even the world. In this respect, China's ascendance is not a myth. However, if this premise should become a reality, it is assumed that the West will not be able to practice self-correction anymore, as it used to.
3. Today, it is doubtful whether the West can correct its service economy and return to the industrial or mixed economy because the financial elite still make huge profits through the strategy of outsourcing. This will continue until the "99%" movement transforms into a social revolution. This is the reality of Western Civilization, which after transforming to the Global Civilization has lost its Christian values and work ethics.
4. In the coming 10-15 years, the economic cooperation between the West and China will transform into a conflict over strategic resources and particularly for oil. This may even reach a level of military confrontation, probably first *by proxy*. On the other hand, it is a myth that China is planning a military confrontation to establish a world order *a la* China. China will be content with achieving the status of the leader in Asia and the annexation of Taiwan, which is imminent. It would be a waste of time and resources for the U.S. to try to maintain its leading role in Asia[24], because due to the shrinking of American financial might, this is impossible. The U.S. should keep its leadership in Europe, the Americas, and the Near East. This is a strategy which differs from the strategy offered by Z. Brzezinski (2012). It is too much for the declining U.S. to be a leader in another, faraway part of the world. Furthermore, competition from a richer and wiser China will be too much for the declining strategic abilities of the U.S., which so far are driven mostly by global corporations.

---

[24] Some predicts that within 10 years, three of the world's five largest economies will be in Asia: China, Japan, and India (Time, January 30, 2012, p. 26) but only if Western Western Civilization won't self-correct its economic strategy and the planet will double inventory of its strategic resources..

5. The clash over strategic resources and the well-being of citizens between the Western and Chinese Civilizations will trigger the activation of the Death Triangle of Civilization because a huge population of 7-11 billion people will trigger the fight for mere survival *a la* Darwinism. That clash may be very strong, or it may lead to wise cooperation to avoid the death of civilization. The latter is possible, since people usually behave better in a crisis than in good times. The reality of Western Civilization is such that most of its population, particularly its elites, are too well-off and have lost the instinct for wisdom, despite developing rich knowledge.
6. It should be investigated further what is better from the civilizational point of view to support less efficient Red China or more efficient White China? Which "China" will deplete sooner strategic resources of the planet?
7. The development of a wise civilization is the only right strategy in the 21st century. It is necessary to popularize it in schools, colleges, societies, and politics. It would be good to implement this strategy before our civilization declines too fast and disappears.
8. It is very probable that Western Civilization will not outlive the knowledge which it created. Perhaps Chinese civilization will outlive the Triangle since is better at adapting to adverse conditions.
9. It would not be wrong to learn wisdom from the Chinese civilization and how to use it for the sake of all. Should the West switch from 26 to 3000-5000 characters-oriented alphabet?

REFERENCES

Asimov, I. (1942). *Runround*. New York, NY: Street and Smith Publications.
Brown, L. (2001). *Eco-economy*. New York, NY: W.W. Norton & Company.
Brzezinski, Z. (2012). Balancing the east, upgrading the west. *Foreign Affairs*, January/February 2012, 97-104.
Conkin, P.K. (2007). *The state of the earth*. Lexington, KY: The Kentucky University Press.
Friedberg, A.L. (2011). *A contest for supremacy, China, America, and the struggle for mastery in Asia*. New York, NY: W.W. Norton & Co.
Henderson, C. (1999). *China on the brink*. New York, NY: McGraw Hill.
Jacques, M. (2009). *When China rules the world*. New York, NY: The Penguin Press.
Kynge, J. (2006). *China shakes the world*. New York, NY: Houghton Mifflin Co.
Maddison, A. (2001). *The world economy, a millennial perspective*. Paris, France: OECD.
Meadows, D., et al. (1972). *The limits of growth*. New York, NY: A Signet Book.
Mearsheimer, J.J. (2001). *The tragedy of great power politics*. New York, NY: Norton.
Steffen, A. (2008). *World changing, a user's guide for the 21st century*. New York, NY: Abrams.
Targowski, A. (2009). *Information technology and societal development*. Hershey, PA & New York, NY: IGI Global.
Targowski, A. (2011). *Cognitive informatics and wisdom development*. Hershey, PA & New York, NY: IGI Global.

Targowski, A. & Modrak, V. (2011). Is advanced automation consistent with sustainable economic growth in developed world? *The Proceedings of the International Conference, CENTERIS 2011*, Vilamoura, Portugal, October 2011, Part I, pp. 63-72. Berlin, Germany: Springer-Verlag.

Walter, C.E. & Howie, F.J.T. (2011). *Red capitalism*. Hoboken, NJ: John Wiley & Sons.

Yergin, D. (2011). *The quest*. New York, NY: The Penguin Press.

Yusuf, S. & Nabeshima, K. (2010). *Changing the industrial geography in Asia*. Washington, DC: The World Bank.

In: Chinese Civilization in the 21st Century
Editors: Andrew Targowski and Bernard Han

ISBN: 978-1-63321-960-1
© 2014 Nova Science Publishers, Inc.

Chapter 8

THE CHINESE CIVILIZATION: DRIVING FORCES, IMPLICATIONS AND CHALLENGES IN THE 21ST CENTURY

Bernard Han[*]
Western Michigan University, US

ABSTRACT

The *purpose* of this chapter is to investigate the causes of sustainability of 5000 years of Chinese civilization, and its driving forces, implications, and challenges in the 21st century. The *methodology* used is based on an established three-component model (TCM) with some necessary adjustments to pinpoint unique characteristics associated with the Chinese civilization. Major *findings* include: Chinese civilization has lasted more than 5,000 years; this is primarily due to a) strong tacit values (e.g., education-first) and b) family-based activities (e.g., ancestor worship). While these tacit values and family-based activities may not guarantee a nationwide stable infrastructure (e.g., a rigid governmental), they do help each individual become self-motivated and retain the civilizations that have been developed across multiple dynasties in Chinese history. At present, Chinese civilization faces three major challenges —leadership stability, continuous economic growth, and openness to freedom and democracy. *Practical implications:* Chinese civilization will play an increasing role in the new world order, and its economic growth and stability will deeply impact the global financial market. Moreover, its political stability will be reinforced if there is continued economic growth, which may not be sustainable without an infrastructure change. *Social implication:* Chinese civilization may continue to expand if the current leadership is willing to absorb the pressure generated by Western civilization (e.g., human rights and political openness) and expedite the government reform that reflects the societal needs (e.g., balanced wealth distribution). *Originality:* This study successfully explains the sustainability and resurgence of Chinese civilization and the unique characteristics of Chinese civilization. Furthermore, it also provides possible responses for the West to take to minimize undesirable clashes with the rising Chinese civilization.

---

[*] Corresponding author: Email: Bernard.han@wmich.edu.

INTRODUCTION

The rising Chinese economy over the past 30 years, accompanied by China's active role in the international arena, has created hypes and hopes for many countries in the world, in particular, a few developed ones in Asia such as Singapore, Taiwan, Korea, and Hong Kong (China) (Rawski 2011). In the meantime, many others in the West (e.g., USA, Germany, and Japan, etc.) have started to worry whether China's surge in the world platform will impose undesirable threats to their existing roles in world civilization. In other words, will the emerging Chinese civilization become dominant and replace the existing Western civilization created two hundred years ago after the industrial revolution in England (Coffin et al. 2011)? With a limited history of China and its unproven political maturity (Michelbach, 2011), it will not be easy to predict the future or draw any definite conclusions.

As China marches into the fourth decade of economic growth, it does become a valid concern for many countries in the West to know if China will truly be the next superpower, creating the new world order (Jacques, 2009). If this does become a reality, how will it impact the current world order and human civilizations (Huntington, 1997)? In this chapter, it will not be possible to offer all the answers, in particular, regarding whether China will rule the world (Jacques, 2009). However, our intent is to investigate interpretations of questions such as: "How can a socialist democratic country like China (Stanczyk, 2008) achieve such miraculous economic growth?" Or to be more exact "Why did a weak sleeping giant (Berher, 2010) suddenly wake and create a 'new' civilization that overshadows the West?" A detailed examination, with a proper interpretation, of this world phenomenon will help us obtain answers for many sub-questions such as: "Why did China bypass the global recession in 2008-2009 (Dullien et al., 2010)?" "How did China sustain continuous economic growth in an environment with limited human rights?" and "Will China's emerging civilization be self-sustainable and provide positive impacts on the world civilizations?" While answers for these sub-questions are not provided in this chapter, it does address the implications of and challenges to the emerging Chinese civilization. As part of the research aims, this chapter does provide suggestions to the West to better prepare and develop strategic moves to work with China to pursue the best benefits of mankind and avoid preventable catastrophes resulting from political conflicts or human rivalry (e.g., genocide).

This chapter is organized as follows. The next section details the driving forces behind Chinese civilization and offers some explanations about why it has lasted so long. In fact, once upon a time Chinese civilization reached its climax in the Tang (唐) dynasty, which was 1,500 years ago (Gernet, 1999). To help us understand these driving forces, a revised Three-Element Model (TEM) (Targowski 2009) will be presented before the detailed explanation. The section follows will discuss the implications of the resurgence of Chinese civilization. Our discussion is based upon the author's understanding of the Communist Regime in China and the unique characteristics of Chinese culture. Will these implications fully crystalize in the coming years? This is a highly contingent matter. The next section will address the critical challenges currently encountered by China's Communist Regime. Then, some recommendations will be given for actions that the West should take as a response to the rise of China (Jones, 2007).

Figure 8.1. A Three-Component Model (TCM) to Express Chinese Civilization.

WHY DOES CHINESE CIVILIZATION LAST SO LONG?

Is it an illusion that Chinese civilization is regaining its world power? This is not likely (Jacques, 2009). It is amazing that China has 5000 years of civilization, which has never been discontinued even when China was conquered and temporarily lost its political power to two foreign races – the Mongols led by Genghis Khan (成吉思汗) and the Manchurians led by Dorgon (多爾袞). The former created the Mongol Empire that covered both Asia and Europe and then withdrew to a neighboring country in the northern China, and the latter was fully assimilated into China as one of the fifty-five ethnic minorities (Poston and Shu, 1987).

Why has Chinese civilization lasted so long without being destroyed? Will it recapture its power and become the new world leader? Answers to these questions may be multiple. In this chapter, a thorough interpretation is provided based on the author's ethnic background and his in-depth understanding of Chinese civilization. Also, a graph model, similar to the one created by Targowski (2009), is used to point out the driving forces behind Chinese culture. These driving forces (detailed later) are identified as critical factors essential to the sustainability of Chinese civilization.

To assist us in understanding the ramifications of these factors in Chinese civilization, a three-component model (TCM) is presented in Figure 8.1 to characterize Chinese civilization. Note that the TCM model resembles the three-element model (TEM) proposed by Targowski (2009) except some modifications are made to highlight the unique characteristics of Chinese civilization.

As shown in Figure 8.1, Chinese civilization can be analyzed based on three key components - Culture, Activities, and Organization. In contrast to Targowski's TEM model (i.e., Culture, Entity, and Infrastructure), a more general word organization is used to highlight the "weak" infrastructure in Chinese civilization. The culture component in our

TCM model is somewhat different from the one defined in TEM. In TEM, Culture is confined to the "invisible (interior) belief and values" of Chinese thinking, and Activities represent all "visible behaviors and accomplished events" in Chinese society. For Culture and Activities, a dashed circle is used to highlight the weakness of "Organization" as compared to the other two. With little study, it is easy to recognize that numerous "splendid footprints" have been left in Chinese history with respect to Culture and Activities. Some noticeable ones include Chinese philosophies, e.g., Confucianism and Daoism (i.e., the inward thinking), worldly known inventions, e.g., the compass and paper (i.e., the outward accomplishments), and architectural landmarks, e.g., pagoda, palace, and the Great Wall (i.e., a mixture of both inward and outward achievements) (Thorp & Vinograd, 2001). Nevertheless, China has experienced more than two dozen political struggles (i.e., to be exact, 24 dynasties plus one democratic revolution) over the past 5,000 years. The average length of each dynasty has been about 200 years, with the shortest being 15 years and the longest being 500+ years. Therefore, a dashed circle is used to highlight the instability of organization in Chinese civilization. But, the interesting fact is that Chinese civilization never dies. Rather, it was expanded through merging and assimilating foreign cultures into one conglomerate civilization (Gernet, 1999). This phenomenon is quite unique and still true for the evolving Chinese civilization as compared to several extinct civilizations such as Roman and Maya. While more research is needed, it is clear that the "political" organization is not a critical component in Chinese civilization and it has little effect on the sustainability of Chinese civilization (Jacques, 2010).

What makes Chinese civilization immune to political instability? Foremost, there are some unique characteristics in Chinese "culture" that create an "inherent stability" in Chinese civilization to balance against power (organization) changes and, furthermore, the changes become the driving force for Chinese civilization to assimilate other cultures. Indeed, there are some fundamental differences between the West and Chinese civilizations. These differences can be interpreted by a few factors that are indispensable to the survival of Chinese civilization and its resurgence in the 21st century. An elaboration of these factors follows.

- *Family-based Society.* Chinese culture is strongly family-based, and each family is an integral unit of the society. In contrast to the West, a number of human activities, from worship (of ancestors) to education (via home-based school) to discipline (by Home Laws 家法), are held in each family rather than in a public place. Moreover, Chinese focus on financial help more through family members than from the public agency. It is very common to see a Chinese family composed of members from several generations along with relatives from their siblings. This unique characteristic becomes the grass root of Chinese culture, an influential component in Chinese civilization. It also becomes the very reason that Chinese society is relatively stable even though there is no strong government and, in addition, it is able to survive even during financial hardships since most of the problems can be self-healed without exogenous help.
- *Self-motivated Altruistic Philosophy.* Nearly all Chinese have been educated with a strong focus of Confucianism, in which there is a fundamental teaching about the path of personal fulfillment. This can be identified by eight Chinese characters

(格致誠正修齊治平), which is a "personal philosophy" and materialized as a roadmap for each individual. The basic ideas of these eight characters are: focus your study on the environment (格物), seek your full knowledge (致知), purify your mind (誠意), straighten your heart (正心), improve yourself (修身), establish your family (齊家), govern your country (治國), and finally, universalize the whole world (平天下). This individual philosophy truly becomes the driving force for each Chinese to seek his/her best performance by working hard (self) to benefit the family (own offspring), the country (the people) and, eventually, the whole world. Due to this philosophy, poverty becomes a rare issue in Chinese society since most people carry the extra ability in helping others with a proud and voluntary heart. However, this philosophy does subtly internalize how the Chinese think and name their country "Middle Kingdom中國" (i.e., the Center of the World).

- *Education-first Value System.* Another discriminating force in Chinese culture is its value system that has been deeply-rooted in every Chinese mind. Unlike the Caste System in India (Pruthi, 2004), Chinese classify people into four groups: Intellectual (士), Farmer (農), Laborer (工), and Merchant (商), listed in an order of social status from high to low. Note that this value system motivates each Chinese individual to focus more on education (to become an intellectual, the highest) than on money-making (to become a merchant, the lowest). Also, the society gives more respect to farmers (i.e., self-employed natural producers) than to laborers (i.e., hiring hands by others), which fundamentally creates the foundation of stability as long as the society maintains its sufficiency via natural but essential productions (i.e., foods and other daily consumptions). Moreover, this value system is open to everyone and each individual has the opportunity to determine his/her social status, which is totally forbidden in the Indian Caste System.

- *Little-Self vs. Super Self Concept.* In Chinese history, the concept of "state" is very weak. Nearly the entire first half of Chinese history (i.e., more than 2,100 years), there was no political structure or organization in China. In 221 BC, China was united by Qin Shi Huang (秦始皇) and from that time point China entered a political system ruled by one emperor. However, the first "united nation," created by Emperor Qin, lasted only 15 years. While China became one country, there were more than twenty power changes (i.e., dynasties) during the subsequent 2500 years. As evidenced by the Chinese history, all these power struggles were led by civilians (not nobles) who were often illiterates such as monks, bandits, and famers (Keay, 2009). In history, Chinese intellectuals, the most prestigious group, seldom showed interest in pursuing the emperor's position, though they did seek opportunities to serve as high officials (e.g., Provincial Governors (郡守) or Prime Ministers (宰相)) for the emperor. This special phenomenon originated from Confucius' teachings of "Heaven (天), Earth (地), Emperor (君), Parent (親), Master (師)," later transformed into a feudalistic notion of "Little Self (小我) vs. Super Self (大我)." As known, Qin Shin Huang (秦始皇) compared himself to the "Son of Heaven" (Qu, 2006) and, naturally, Emperor Qin represents the Super Self (大我). Given this, an intellectual is but a Little Self (小我), who, as a follower of Confucianism, shall of course respect his Master (師), Parent (親), and, most of all, the ultimate greatest – Heaven (天). This "feudalistic ideology," rooted in each intellectual's mind, provided the legitimacy for Chinese emperors, including today's communist government, to enjoy a total dictatorship since it is quite a noble deed for each "Little Self" to sacrifice his benefits for the sake of the "Super Self" (犧牲小我成全大我). Clearly, from the viewpoint of democracy, it is a misfortune that Chinese people have given away their freedom and human rights over the past few thousands of years. Nevertheless, Chinese civilization did weather through numerous power changes.

While our elaboration may not be exhaustive, the above four factors do provide a solid answer to "Why has Chinese civilization lasted so long?" Simply put, Chinese civilization is hinged on a family-based structure, rather than on an external infrastructure such as well-organized top-down government. In particular, Chinese culture plays a pivotal role in Chinese civilization (see Figure 8.1). Families are the fundamental integral parts of Chinese society and most religious, financial, legal, and social activities occur within a family setting, which not only alleviates the function of an external government but also provides a strong self-healing power during unexpected financial crises or environmental chaos with a minimal level of social disorder. Moreover, Chinese culture values education and self-motivated betterment more than business wealth and self-interest. Since 500 BC, Chinese culture has been deeply influenced by Confucius' teachings, which were subtly exploited by Chinese political leaders (i.e., emperors) to create a new feudalism. Under this feudalistic Confucianism, Chinese were willingly giving away basic human rights (e.g., voting) and submitting to totalitarians with extra tolerance towards dictatorships as long as the environment provided essential and acceptable living conditions and resources. These resultant character changes in Chinese culture could be further exploited by the government to entertain its power or corrected by the West if democracy is effectively implemented in China. More discussion will be given in the following sections.

IMPLICATIONS OF THE RENAISSANCE OF CHINESE CIVILIZATION

The resurgence of Chinese civilization has resulted from China' fast economic growth over the past three decades which has made China the world's second largest economy in 2010, second only to the United States. If China maintains its current economic growth, then, as forecasted, China will pass the United States as early as 2030 (Bardoza, 2010). No doubt, China has been the major driver of the global economy for the past 30 years. China's continuous economic growth, on one hand, provides the Western capitalists ample opportunities to make unprecedented profit due to the low labor cost in China (Shenkar, 2005). On the other hand, many countries of the West, including Japan, have become more and more anxious about the rise of China and deeply worry that China will create threats to the Western World (Callahan, 2005). Many of such concerns raised by the West can be easily dispelled if there is a certain degree of understanding about Chinese civilization, especially its core component – Chinese culture. However, if the West simply worries about China's economic growth or does not properly react to China's rise, then unexpected disasters may also happen. The implications of Chinese civilization's resurgence can be summarized as follows:

1. *Civilization Impact:* China will again become the world center of civilization. China has lost its spotlight since the beginning of the 19th Century. It is the common dream and the first priority for both China and its people to return to the world platform. Chinese civilization reached its climax in Tang dynasty (AD 618-907), which was 1500 years ago; at that time, China was truly the center of world civilization. Since then, Chinese culture evolved through the teaching of Confucianism and many ethnic groups were assimilated by the largest ethnic group Han (漢). Today, the Han ethnic group accounts for 92% of the Chinese population (i.e., 1.16 billion) and 19% of the world's total population. Of course, even today China is not quite a perfect democratic nation; most Chinese living in China and overseas would like to see the continuous development of Chinese civilization such that it would put China back onto the stage of world platform – the common wish of all Chinese.
2. *Financial Impact:* China will become the world resource center. The saving rate of China is high from many perspectives – historical experience, international standards, and the predictions of economic models. Furthermore, the average saving rate has been rising over time, with much of the increase taking place in the 2000s, so that the aggregate marginal propensity to save exceeds 50%. What really sets China apart from the rest of the world is that the rising aggregate saving has reflected high savings rates in all three sectors – corporate, household and government (Ma & Yi, 2010). Historically, the Asian household saving rates are much higher than the West. In particular, due to the family-based Chinese culture, most Chinese choose to save money in a private mutual-saving system, which helps them gain higher interest without dealing with commercial banks or community credit unions. While there is a degree of risk that some members may not honor their obligation, by and large, Chinese retain their earnings with a high saving rate. This is a big contrast with the consumerism economy in the West. With high productivity and global strategies, China will continue to improve its economy and harbor its earnings through exports. As expected by the West, China will have no shyness to become the resource center for the whole world, though its GDP per capita may still remain far below that of the United States.
3. *Economic Impact:* The "Inland China" development will be the next project. Even though China has become the world's second largest economy, it is still a developing country. China's territory is about the same size as that of the U.S., but its population is not evenly distributed. Specifically,, 60% of the Chinese population (i.e., 800 million) lives in 22% of its land, and most live in a band of 600 miles wide along the coast. The other 40% of population (i.e., 500 million) spreads over 78% of Chinese territory, the so-called Inland China. The sharp increase in land value and labor costs in the coastal area has significantly reduced the competiveness and the growth of China's economy in the global economy. Therefore, the Inland China development (i.e., China's Great Western Development project) will be the next economic project for China (and the globe) to maintain economic growth in the coming two decades. It will of course provide jobs and business opportunities for the West to pursue corporate profits via talent sharing, low-cost manufacturing, and product consumption. As the world economy becomes more integrated as one market, the Inland China development will possibly sustain the global economy.

4. *Political impact:* A pan-China Federation may be established through dialogues. To some extent, Confucianism leads to "imperial thinking" (i.e., 格致誠正修齊治平) that has been deeply instilled into the mindset of every Chinese intellectual. This imperial thinking, different from imperialism, will motivate Chinese to develop a nation that will assure a peaceful society for the common good of all citizens (i.e., 大同世界). This nation, often seen as the utopia defined in Socratism (Erdmann & Hough, 1899), may not be realistic from the global viewpoint. However, as China gains more global leadership, it will be very likely that some countries with Chinese as their major residents (e.g., Singapore, Taiwan) as well as countries having a strong influence from Confucianism (e.g., Viet Nam, Korea) will attempt to join with China in forming a federated country. In fact, a federated nation was created several times in Chinese history. The Han dynasties – East and West (206 BC – 226 AD) and the Tang dynasty (618 – 906 AD) are a few of such good precedents.

The above implications may or may not be fully realized, and they all depend on one condition – the continuous stability of the Communist Leadership and its government. Even if there exists a great danger for the stability of the Communist Party in China, one thing for sure is that Chinese civilization will not perish; it will sustain taking into account the above implications. The potential challenges to Chinese civilization are detailed in the next section.

What Are Challenges to Chinese Civilization?

It is miraculous that China has maintained an average of 8-9% economic growth continuously for the past 30 years. This outstanding performance has sharply improved China's role in the global economy. Will this growing trend be continued for another two decades? The simple answer is "it depends" because there are a number of challenges that may cause significant impacts on the resurged Chinese civilization. As recently pointed out by the China's prime minister Wen Jiabao: "China must reform to maintain high levels of economic growth" (Lardy, 2012). What are to be reformed will be the key to identify these challenges to Chinese civilization. In brief, there are three major challenges: 1). How to maintain the stability of China's leadership? 2). How to keep high economic growths to justify the legitimacy of the current one party leadership (i.e., the dictatorship-like communist party)? 3). How to increase the openness of the political system (i.e., the so-called socialist democracy) in China? In fact, these three challenges are not independent of one and another. To understand the interactions among these three challenges, Figure 8.2 depicts their mutual relationships.

As seen in Figure 8.2, under the current socialist democracy in China, the legitimacy of the one-party (i.e., the communist party) leadership can be enhanced (i.e., a plus "+" sign) if China continues to generate high economic growth. In the meantime, due to the one-party leadership, the current government must have tight control over the different voices of other parties. Therefore, the stability of China's leadership will be worsened (i.e., a minus "-" sign) if the openness of the political system is improved. In other words, China's current one-party leadership (i.e., dictatorship) will be justified by high economic growth and will be threatened if the political system becomes more open and transparent.

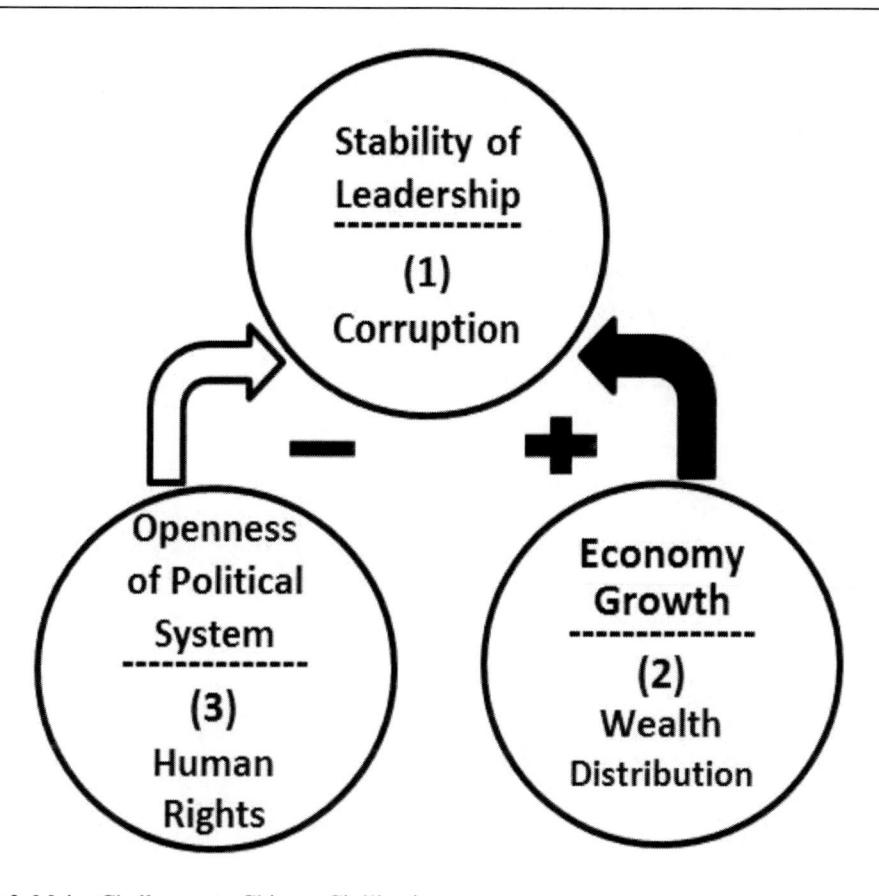

Figure 8.2. Major Challenges to Chinese Civilization.

Indeed, today's China is faced with these three steep challenges because there is a hidden concern behind each challenge. If each hidden concern is not effectively handled, then any of these three challenges may become out of control and subsequently generate a domino effect that will collapse China's leadership, its political system, and finally economic growth. This would cause the current progress of Chinese civilization to be hampered, though not destroyed. A brief highlight on the concern behind each challenge (see Figure 8.2) is given next.

- *Challenge 1:* How to maintain the stability of China's leadership? The key concern behind China's leadership today is corruption, which is prevalent from the bottom level (e.g., city mayor, county commissioner) to the top (e.g., provincial governors, party leaders) of the Chinese government. It is recognized as the number one crisis that can strike down the communist party and crumble its leadership in China. Given the current condition of corruption, many experts as well as most intellectuals believe that there is no hope in the Chinese communist party and its collapse is only a matter of time, which could happen anytime within ten years (Moses, 2012).
- *Challenge 2:* How to keep high economic growths to legitimize the current leadership? Maintaining high economic growths is still possible under the current Chinese leadership since the Inland China (i.e., the Great Western Development) Project will offer business opportunities to provide high economic growths. The real

concern behind high economic growth is uneven wealth distribution, which was pointed out that today China's success is built on 300 million people taking advantage of 1 billion cheap laborers. The unfair judicial system and the unfair distribution of wealth are making the challenges even greater (Lee, 2010). Similar to but even worse than the United States, 90% of China's wealth is in the hands of less than 1% of China's upper class, and 44% of the rich indicate that they want to migrate to overseas countries. Such a sharp, uneven distribution of wealth could easily cause the poor to protest that may turn into massive violence. In fact, China's leaders are aware of this concern and a reform plan has been undergone. The problem for solving the uneven wealth distribution is that it takes time and will require 10 years (Xinhua, 2012). Will it be soon enough to avoid the next civil revolution in China?

- *Challenge 3:* How to increase the openness of the current political system while maintaining the current leadership? This is probably the most difficult challenge as compared to the above two. If China maintains its one-party leadership, then it is almost certain that there will be no way to increase the openness of the current political system. However, due to the strong influence of Confucianism on Chinese culture, Chinese people are willing to give away "human rights" for a better economy and social stability. Thus, this challenge could be kicked aside by China if there is a way to keep high economic growth as well as a better wealth distribution. Even if this challenge is skillfully controlled, there is a hidden concern - Human Rights may turn into a hot issue that will force China to initiate political reform. If it happens, then it will be the beginning of the end of Chinese Communism.

The above three challenges to China may will create huge impacts on Chinese civilization and each of them could cause the downfall of the Chinese government if the hidden concerns (i.e., corruption, wealth distribution, and limited human rights) are not properly handled by the current government. To say the least, the downfall of China for sure would crash its economic growth, which of course is not what the West wants to see due to its detrimental impact on the global economy. However, the continuity of Chinese communists' leadership in China, with planned economic growth, may irrationally expand its military power at the expense of limited human rights which could endanger the safety and benefits of its neighboring countries. Worse yet, the rise of the Chinese communist party will become an unavoidable threat to the "democratic" West, which currently suffers from poor economy but has full human rights and individual freedom. Hence, our next question will be "How can the West respond to the resurgence of Chinese civilization such that China can continue to maintain its economic growth while also improving its human rights?" Finding an answer for this question requires the West to develop some strategic moves. Some suggestions are provided below based on the author's knowledge of and insight into the communist party in China.

THE WEST'S RESPONSE TO THE RENAISSANCE OF CHINESE CIVILIZATION

As pointed out earlier, Chinese civilization has survived more than 20 power struggles (i.e., dynasties) in Chinese history. One primary reason is the dominant component - Chinese culture in Chinese civilization as compared to the remaining two – Activities and Organization in the proposed civilization model (see Figure 1). As revealed in history, Chinese people are willing to trade human rights for national stability (i.e., tolerate dictatorship for improved social stability), which was influenced by Confucianism and its resultant "Little Self vs. Super Self" concept. To avoid the Chinese communist party's manipulation of the Chinese people via leveraging stability for stronger dictatorship, the West should respond to the rise of Chinese civilization with the following actions:

1. *Open Arms to Chinese Civilization by accepting what is good for the West.* China has 5000 years of history and Chinese civilization plays a critical role in world civilization. Historically, Chinese civilization has significantly benefited mankind, in particular people in Asia, through culture assimilation (i.e., soft power). Its culture and accomplishments in many aspects have outreached at least one third of the whole world population (i.e., people in China, Korea, Japan, and all countries in South Indo China). All these countries, except Japan, have never taken initiative to use hard power (i.e., military) to attack other countries. There are good reasons for the West to understand and learn unique components in Chinese civilization such as the family-based culture and self-motivated altruistic philosophy. Over the past fifty years, the West has made significant progress in science and technology to improve the materialistic aspect of human life. Nevertheless, less family value and reduced social morals have created an immense economic burden for the West and, subsequently, made the West an underdog in global competition. It is time for the West to reexamine its weakness in culture and social values, which may be remedied by what is good in Chinese civilization.
2. *Introduce human rights through an open education channel.* Though Chinese civilization has surged and outperformed the West in the past three decades, in fact, it is still quite temporary and feeble. One primary reason that Chinese civilization has risen is its huge supply of very inexpensive laborers, for which reason the West shifted its financial capitals and resources (e.g., technology, factories, and management expertise) to China in order to seek a quick fix for competition against other competitors (e.g., Japan, Korea). This in turn provided China with ample opportunities to catch up its economic development. Therefore, the Western entrepreneurs must be very careful since China does not share the same value system, ideology, and political infrastructure (i.e., democracy) with the West. Any economic opportunities offered by the West to China will solidify the communist party's tight control of human rights in name of improved national stability as well as legitimize the party's leadership by pushing China onto the world platform. As addressed in Figure 2, any improvement in human rights will increase the openness of the political system in China, which in fact is considered the most powerful way to challenge the current Chinese communist regime. Therefore, the West should max its power by

opening its education to more Chinese intellectuals, who in fact are the cream of the crop in China. These intellectuals, once educated, will either stay overseas and be used by the West for economic advancement or later return to China to transform the communist party. In either case, this action will produce a win-win for the West.

3. *Focus on self-improvement by making structural changes.* The West has made many progresses and have enjoyed its wonderful civilization since 1900. However, it is also true that the West has been easy on themselves (i.e., relaxed in materialism) for more than 30 years. Since early 1980s, many Asian countries (e.g., Japan, Korea, Taiwan, Singapore, and Hong Kong) have worked extremely hard in education and economic development. Their economic growths have outperformed the West and their wealth and talents soon became the catalyst to speed up the economic activities in China. By comparing what have been consumed (i.e., both natural and derived resources) by the West to those by China, there is no reason or excuse for the West to point finger at China about its economic activities or production gains in the global market. As mentioned before, the Asian countries have relatively high savings towards their GDP as compared to the West. Today, while in significant trade deficits, most countries in the West are still in the midst (or myth) of promoting consumerism (or consumption). The West should not be scared by the prosperity of Chinese civilization. Rather, a structural change in economy activity shall be made by the West with respect to two major aspects: 1). the consumers should change their life style – balancing the family (national) budget is the top priority. The rich's wealth (or national support) should be effectively used to help the poor. The best outcome is to minimize the overall deficit as close as possible to zero while engaging citizens in redefined economic activities. 2). the national economy should focus on activities that cannot be easily outsourced, for example, technology and innovation-based capital such as health care products (everyone needs it) or bio-medical engineering (with high entry barrier). This implies that education modifications are required for all young generations, and all economic units such as families and communities should take initiative in deriving economic plans that are in line with the state and national strategic plan. Finger-pointing is an easy way to shift our own faults to others who are working hard. The following remark by Mitt Romney, the Republican Presidential Nominee, is a typical example to highlight a wrong and naïve response from the West towards the rise of China (Rapoza, 2011).

"China is on almost every dimension cheating. We got to recognize that they're manipulating their currency and by doing so they're holding down the price of Chinese goods and making sure their products are artificially low-priced. It's predatory pricing. It's killing jobs in America."

The resurgence of Chinese civilization is not as surprising if the West understands the huge differences in labor costs and living standards between China and themselves. It is not really a threat to the West if proper responses are timely taken by the West to cope with their own weakness in the past thirty years or to prevent unwanted political moves by the Chinese communist party in global competition. The West should be willing to understand and learn the unique characteristics in Chinese civilization as a remedy to fix their own weaknesses. Also, the West should stand firm in its civilization virtue – human rights—and continue to provide an educational approach to Chinese intellectuals for the sake of improving the political system in China. Moreover, the West should make a structural change to the economic activities that will promote new product development and manufacturing that cannot be easily outsourced or duplicated. In doing so, consumerism is not the key solution to solve the economic problems encountered by the West.

CONCLUSION

Chinese civilization has lasted more than 5000 years. Why did it resurge? In this Chapter, a three-component model (TCM) is used to explain why Chinese civilization has survived after more than 20 dynasties (i.e., power changes). As compared to the West, Chinese civilization is dominated by the Culture component in the TCM model, not development (i.e., activities) and organization. The resurgence of Chinese civilization is truly expedited and influenced by the tacit values of Chinese culture such as a family-based society, an education-first value system, and the teachings of Confucianism (e.g., little-self versus super-self). Given these unique characteristics of Chinese civilization, the recent rapid economic growth in China will cultivate an environment that justifies the leadership of the Chinese Communist Party in China while providing limited human rights to its people. Subsequently, the further development of Chinese civilization may create huge impacts on the world civilization, financial activities, economic growth, and a possible formation of a pan-China federation in Asia. These implications may not happen because the current Chinese Communist Regime is faced with critical challenges (or concerns be exact) that include severe corruption (from private to public), uncertain economic growth, and restricted human rights. Any of these concerns could easily cause the downfall of the current Chinese Communist Regime, which may not be the best for the West to see due to the dangling impacts from China's downfall. Rather, the West should open their arms to Chinese civilization by learning/accepting what is good for the West, continue to stand firm and promote human rights in China, and, finally, make structural changes in the national economy that are meaningful towards global needs.

REFERENCES

Bardoza, D. (2010). China passes Japan as second-largest economy. *New York Times*, August 15.
Behrer, William H. (2010). China: a sleeping giant awakens. *The Real Truth*, March-April, 12-14.
Callahan, W. A. (2005). How to understand China: the dangers and opportunities of being a rising power. *Review of International Studies.*, *31*(04), 701-714.
Coffin, J., Stacey, R., Cole, J. & Symes, C. (2011). *Western civilizations: their history and their culture*, Volume 2 (17th Ed). U.S.A.: Houghton Mifflin.
Dullien, S, Kotte, D. J., Márquez, A. & Priewe, J. (2010). *The financial and economic crisis of 2008-2009 and developing countries*. New York and Geneva: United Nations Publications.

Erdmann, J. E. & Hough, W. S. (1899). *A history of philosophy*. Volume *3*, New York: The MacMillan CO.

Gernet, J. (1999). *A history of Chinese civilization*. (Second Edition). New York, New York: Cambridge University Press.

Huntington, S. P. (1997). *The clash of civilizations and the remaking of world order*. New York, New York: Simon & Schuster.

Jacques, Marin. (2010). Understanding the rise of China. Retrieved on August 11, 2012 at http://www.ted.com/talks/martin_jacques_understanding_the_rise_of_china.html.

Jacques, M. (2009). *When China rules the world: The end of the western world and the birth of a new global order*. New York: The Penguin Press.

Jones, A. (2007). Responding to the rise of China. *Security Challenges*, *3*(1) 7-17.

Keay, J. (2009). *China: A History*, New York, New York: Basic Books.

Lardy, N. (2012). China must reform to maintain high levels of economic growth. Feb 3, 2012. Retrieved on August 30, 2012 at http://www.publicserviceeurope.com/article/1459/china-must-reform-to-maintain-high-levels-of-economic-growth.

Lee, S. (2010). China's unequal wealth-distribution map causing social problems. China Post, June 28. Retrieved on Aug 30, 2012 at http://www.chinapost.com.tw/commentary/the-china-post/special-to-the-china-post/2010/06/28/262505/p1/China's-unequal.htm.

Lin, J. Y. (2009). Economic development and structural change, Lecture at Cairo University, Cairo, Egypt, November 5.

Ma, G. & Yi, W. (2010). China's high saving rate: myth and reality. *BIS Working Paper* (No. 312). Basel, Switzerland: Bank of International Settlements.

Michelbach, P. A. (2011). Democracy as vocation: political maturity in Luther and Hegel. *Journal of Democratic Theory*, *1*(4), 1-33.

Moses, R. L. (2012). The communist party's big problem? It's not Bo Xilai. *The Wall Street Journal*, Sept 6. Available at http://blogs.wsj.com/chinarealtime/2012/09/06/the-chinese-communist-partys-big-problem-its-not-bo-xilai/.

Poston, D. L. & Shu, J. (1987). The demographic and socioeconomic composition of China's ethnic minorities. *Population and Development Review*, *13*(4), 703-722.

Pruthi, R. K. (2004). *Indian caste system*. New Delhi, India: Discovery Publishing House.

Qu, L. (2006). The characteristics of the theory of history in ancient china. *Frontiers of History in China*, *1*(1), 1-18.

Rapoza, K. (2011). Romney says China is cheating. Forbes, November 21. Retrieved on August 30, 2012 at http://www.forbes.com/sites/kenrapoza/2011/11/21/romney-says-china-is-cheating/.

Rawski, T. G. (2011). The rise of China's economy. *Footnotes*, *16* (06). The Newsletter of FPRI's Wachman Center, Foreign Policy Research Institute.

Shenkar, O. (2005). *The Chinese century – The rising Chinese economy and its impact on the global economy, the balance of power, and your job*. Upper Saddle River, New Jersey: Pearson Education.

Stanczyk, M. T. (2008). Enter the dragon's lair: The new socialism and private property ownership in the People's Republic of China. *Journal of Civil Rights and Economic Development*, *22*(3), Article 7.

Targowski, A. (2009). *Information technology and societal development*. (Chapter 1). Hershey, Pennsylvania: IGI Global.

Thorp, R. L. & Vinograd, R. E. (2001). *Chinese art & culture*. New York, New York: Harry A. Abrams.

Xinhua, News. (2012). China to solve wealth distribution issues in 10 years, Retrieved on Aug 30, 2012. at http://www.chinadaily.com.cn/business/2012-5/28/content_15403600.htm *People's Daily Online.*

In: Chinese Civilization in the 21st Century
Editors: Andrew Targowski and Bernard Han
ISBN: 978-1-63321-960-1
© 2014 Nova Science Publishers, Inc.

Chapter 9

CHINESE CIVILIZATION VERSUS GLOBAL CIVILIZATION IN THE 21ST CENTURY

*Andrew Targowski**
Western Michigan University, US

ABSTRACT

The *purpose* of this investigation is to define the central issues of current and future relations between the Chinese and Global Civilization through an evaluation of the historic paths of both civilizations. The *methodology* is based on an interdisciplinary big-picture view of the Chinese and Global Civilization's **developments and interdependency**. Among the *findings* are: rising China once was a superpower of the world, just 650 years ago. Due to its 5,000 year old culture and ability to invent important civilizational tools (including the magnetic compass, paper, the printing press and gunpowder), China is becoming an independent developer of its own economic power, and it is very probable that it will benefit strongly from the development of the Global (Western) Civilization. *Practical implication:* Societies of Global Civilization should elaborate the path to their wiser development; otherwise they will transfer from developed to developing nations. *Social implication:* It is probable that the Chinese Civilization is more able to cope with globalization in liquid times than Global (Western) Civilization. *Originality:* This investigation, by providing an interdisciplinary and trans-civilizational approach, expands the scope of the traditional approach to this issue, which is mostly oriented around economics or political science.

INTRODUCTION

The main purpose of this investigation is to evaluate a question: whether the Chinese or Global Civilization will dominate the coming future of the world civilization? Nowadays, the spectacular economic development of China and the concurrent decline of Western Civilization provoke many predictions of the near-future world order. So far it seems that the West supports, unwisely but strongly, China's economic development through outsourcing

---
* Corresponding author: email andrew.targowski@wmich.edu.

Western manufacturing. However, the Chinese are not new in power struggles in the world. Just about 650 years ago China was the world super power. However, due to isolationism and rule by outsiders, China missed the Italian Renaissance, European Enlightenment and to certain degree the English Industrial Revolution. After World War II China broke with the feudal system and ruling by the outsiders and moved into domestic Communism *a la* China. This move lasted about 30 years and was replaced by Socialism with Chinese character in 1978. Also China learned a lesson from the fall of the Soviet Empire in 1991 and established a "democratic" authoritarian political system, in which the national government has a strong top-down way of controlling state affairs, and at the bottom lets people flourish in developing private businesses.

Due to this national policy China became the factory of the world and has penetrated business in almost every country of the world. Fortunately for the world, China promotes for its citizens the Chinese Dream, based on wealth, strength and pride. This means that China in comparison to Western Civilization, which promotes an ideology of democracy, does not have an ambition to promote an ideology. It is reminiscent of the policy of the former Ottoman Empire which treated its vassal countries quite well if they were paying taxes. Needless to say, this empire lasted 621 years (1301-1922).

Could Chinese Civilization lead the world this long? It is very doubtful, since the world does not have enough resources to support developed Chinese and Global Civilizations. However, in times of global crises triggered by liquid times, the Chinese are more able to survive since they have lived in such conditions for many centuries.

The methodology of this investigation is based on the interdisciplinary big-picture view of the world scene, driven by key events of Chinese and European history. A set of conclusions will be provided at the end of this paper, with practical and social implications for the eventual implementation of practices for both civilizations.

CHINA'S 5,000 YEAR LONG MARCH TO THE 21ST CENTURY

China is the most populous country in the world and is third in the world with respect to territory (after Russia and Canada). It also has an ancient history. With written records dating back 5,000 years, it is recognized as one of the four great ancient civilizations of the world, together with ancient Egypt, Babylon (Iraq), and India. Moreover, it is the only ancient civilization that has continued to this very day.

From 475 BC to the end of the 19th century, China went through a long feudal period. Before the 15th century, China was one of the most powerful countries in the world, occupying a leading position in the development of productivity and technology. Ancient China enjoyed a developed agriculture and advanced irrigation system, and an independent tradition of medicine and advanced botanical knowledge. China's four great inventions, namely, the compass, gunpowder, movable type printing and papermaking, not only changed the world but also accelerated the evolution of world history. In addition, China was rich in ceramics and silk textiles which were great inventions that exerted a great impact worldwide. China also kept the world's most detailed and earliest astronomical records. The first people to take note of such astronomical phenomena as comets, sunspots and new stars were all Chinese. It was also the Chinese who produced the most advanced astronomical observatory apparatus of the time. In metallurgy, China long held a leading position. When Europeans still could not turn out a single piece of cast iron in the 14th century, Chinese people had already produced cast iron on an industrial scale four centuries earlier.[1]

When commenting on the relationship between China's civilization and that of the rest of the world, the late Joseph Needham, historian of Chinese science and technology and professor at Cambridge University, once said that people must remember that China was way ahead of the West in almost every discipline of science and technology, from chart making to gunpowder, in early times and into the Middle Ages. Western civilization, he went on to say, did not begin to dominate until the era of Columbus, and China had left the Europeans far behind in science and technology before that time (Needham 1954).

Joseph Needham is famous for "Needham's Grand Question", also known as "The Needham Question," why China had been overtaken by the West in science and technology, despite its earlier successes. In the final volume of his monumental work on *Science and civilization in China* he suggests "A continuing general and scientific progress manifested itself in traditional Chinese society but this was violently overtaken by the exponential growth of modern science after the Renaissance in Europe. China was homeostatic, but never stagnant." (Needham 2004).

It is true that the Europeans were more science-oriented since the 15th century than Chinese, who lived in a closed society. But it was their choice to destroy their own fleet in 1443 and isolate themselves behind the Great Wall to protect China from foreign invasions. While the Great Wall had been built in earlier times, most of what is seen today was either built or repaired by the Ming Dynasty (1368-1644). In addition, the permanent threats of a new Mongol invasion drew military investment away from the expensive maintenance of the treasure fleets. By 1503 the navy had shrunk to one-tenth of its size in the early Ming. The final blow came in 1525 with the order to destroy all the larger classes of ships. China was now set on its centuries-long course of xenophobic isolation.

Historians can only speculate on how differently world history might have turned out had the Ming emperors pursued a vigorous colonial policy, as did the Portuguese and Spanish who triggered and developed colonialism in those times.

By the end of Qianlong Emperor's long reign (1735-1796), the Qing Empire was at its zenith. China ruled more than one-third of the world's population, and had the largest economy in the world. By area of extent, it was one of the largest empires ever in history.

In the 19th century, the empire was internally stagnated and externally threatened by Western imperialism. The defeat by the British Empire in the First Opium War (1839) led to the Treaty of Nanking (1842), under which Hong Kong was ceded and opium import was legitimized to make the Chinese more obedient to the new British rulers. Subsequent military defeats and unequal treaties with other imperial powers would continue even after the fall of the Qing Dynasty (1644-1911). The Opium War triggered by the Machiavellian British is considered the main source of Chinese misfortunes in modern times. However, according to Beardson (2013) the more humiliating factor is the fact that the Chinese people allowed themselves to be ruled by outsiders such as the Mongols and Manchus who ruled the country for two of its last three dynasties. The author perceives that the 1911 revolution was strongly influenced by Han Chinese who wanted to get rid of Manchus, a once nomadic people who founded the Qing Dynasty in 1644 and had been ruling this country since then.

---

[1] (*China.org.cn*. Retrieved 11/3/2013).

At the turn of the 20th century, a conservative anti-imperialist movement, the Boxer Rebellion, violently revolted against foreign dominance over vast areas in Northern China. In response, a relief expedition of the Eight-Nation Alliance invaded China to rescue besieged foreign missions. Consisting of British, Japanese, Russian, Italian, German, French, US, and Austrian troops, the alliance defeated the Boxers and demanded further concessions from the Qing government. The early 1900s saw increasing civil disorder, despite reform talk by Cixi and the Qing government. Slavery in China was abolished in 1910. The Xinhai Revolution in 1911 overthrew the Qing's imperial rule and led to the formation of the Republic of China (1912-1949).

Frustrated by the Qing court's resistance to reform and by China's weakness, young officials, military officers, and students began to advocate the overthrow of the Qing Dynasty and the creation of a republic. Two Chinese parties, Kuomintang (Nationalist Party or KMT) and the Communistic Party of China (CPC), entered into a civil war. The bitter struggle between the KMT and the CPC continued, openly or clandestinely, through the 14-year long Japanese occupation of various parts of the country (1931–1945). The two Chinese parties nominally formed a united front to oppose the Japanese in 1937, during the Sino-Japanese War (1937–1945), which became a part of World War II.

Following the defeat of Japan in 1945, the war between the KMT and the CPC resumed after failed attempts at reconciliation and a negotiated settlement. By 1949, the CPC had established control over most of the country. Since 1949, the CPC has ruled what is now called the People's Republic.

This very intensive and tragic history of such a great civilization and country convinces almost every Chinese student and adult that China was humiliated for many years by Westerners from the mid-19th century until the Communists took power in 1949. Further, history is full of phases and stages According to communists, there are stages and phases in history for the application of rules to overcome either economic or military crises in East Asia. Eventually, a power struggle followed Chairman Mao's death in 1976. The Gang of Four were arrested and blamed for the excesses of the Cultural Revolution, marking the end of a turbulent political era in China. Deng Xiaoping outmaneuvered Mao's anointed successor, chairman Hua Guofeng, and gradually emerged as the de facto leader over the next few years.

Deng Xiaoping was the Paramount Leader of China from 1978 to 1992, although he never became the head of the party or state, and his influence within the Party led the country to significant economic reforms. The Communist Party subsequently loosened governmental control over the citizens' personal lives and the communes were disbanded with many peasants receiving multiple land leases, which greatly increased incentives and agricultural production. This turn of events marked China's transition from a planned economy to a mixed economy with an increasingly open market environment, a system termed by some as "market socialism", and officially by the Communist Party of China as "Socialism with Chinese characteristics."[2]

---

[2] (http://en.wikipedia.org/wiki/History_of_China, Retrieved 11/3/2013).

During Mao's regime, a Chinese person had no hope for a better life, since the economic system was inefficient and ready to sacrifice any individual life for the success of Mao's doctrine. Since Deng Xiaoping said that "it is not a sin to be rich" the *Chinese Dream* has been born. Not only may Westerners have "the *American Dream*," the Chinese can also dream; and they dream big.

The long and rich history of China developed among its intellectuals' appetite for *gloire* as the driving force of this nation. This national strategy is well described in the book *Wealth and Power* (Schell and Delury 2013). This book's title comes from the Chinese term *fugiang*, *wealth and power*, which the authors defined as the directorial idea behind the people who led China since the beginning of the 19th century. The author argues that *wealth and power* is the remedy for years of humiliation of the Chinese by Westerners. A quick observation of any Chinese diaspora shows how the Chinese people are hardworking and economically successful and proud of their close families, either in Hong Kong, Paris, San Francisco, Sydney or Warsaw. This driving force-idea allows the Chinese to take good care of their lives under any political system where hard work brings results. This motivational idea is different than for example the national idea of the Russians or Polish, who first of all can easily die in wars or uprisings for the future success of their nations.

Schell and Delury discovered that the Chinese Economic Revolution by the end of the 20th century (particularly after the Fall of the Berlin Wall and accelerated off shore outsourcing of manufacturing by the Western Civilization) was not started for idealistic reasons, such as freedom or liberty, but for utilitarian purposes: restoring the national glory. The French ideals, *libertè*, *ègalitè*, and *fraternitè* have been lost in translation into Chinese and are: *wealth*, *strength*, and *pride*. According to the author, it was done through "serial economic, intellectual, cultural, and political organ transplants."

Eventually, the 4000 year Long March of the Chinese brought them to the times when they may have the Chinese Dream, which can be accomplished. This March's success can be illustrated by the growth of income of a Chinese citizen. During Mao's regime, a Chinese citizen was making 200 $/year, but since 1978, when Deng Xiaoping took control of China, that income rose 30 times and reached 6,000 $/year in 2013.[3]

Another example of the might of China is its supercomputer Tianhe-2 or Milky Way-2, which was developed by China's National University of Defense Technology and ranked the world's fastest on the 2012 list of the top 500 supercomputers. Tianhe-2, which took 280 researchers more than two years to complete, will be used at the National Supercomputer Center in Guangzhou for biomedicine and the development of new materials[4]. Needless to say many of its developers have been educated in the U.S. and returned to China to build its strength and pride.

The developmental timeline of Chinese Civilization versus Western Civilization is depicted in Figure 9.1.

---

[3] "Got on, bet the farm." The Economist, November 2, 20013, p. 11.
[4] China.org.cn. Retrieved 11/5/2013.

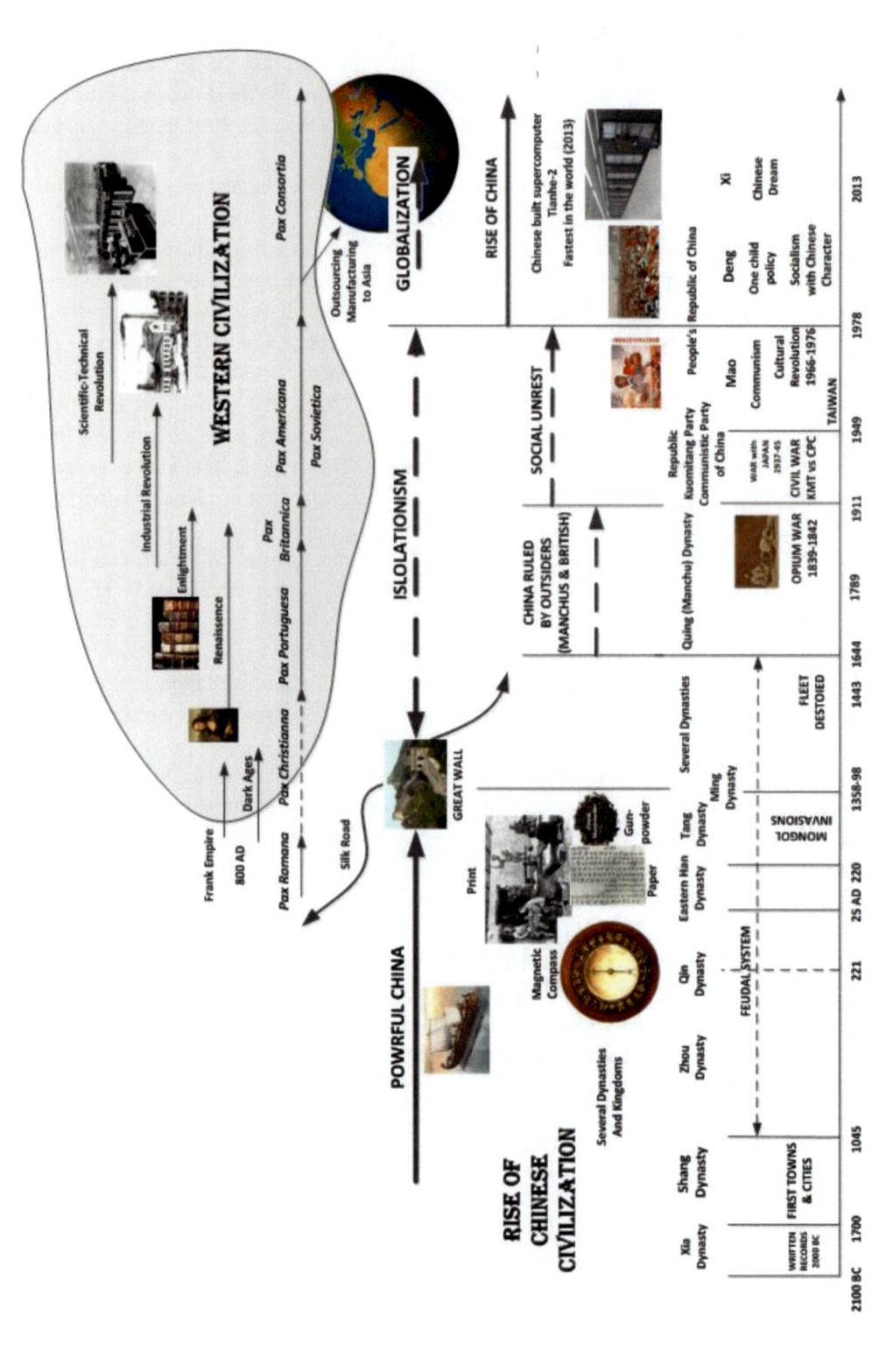

Figure 9.1. The developmental timeline of Chinese Civilization versus Western Civilization, (The Targowski Model).

CHINESE REMAKING THE WORLD IN THE 21ST CENTURY

In the 21st century, China is a major manufacturer for world products, called the World Factory. More and more, companies will see China as a market with increased purchasing potential. For consumer products, most of the purchasing capability will be along China's eastern coast. For businesses selling to manufacturers, customers will be more evenly spread. Virtually all of the leading companies in all sectors are Chinese companies. It is almost impossible for foreign brands to succeed on their own without Chinese partners; the only exceptions are a few luxury brands. As a first step, it is necessary to find out who these players are.

China is still affected by the legacy of the state-owned enterprises, which often are still major players in the economy. The finance and distribution sectors are still heavily influenced by government participation. Even in sectors where government influence is smaller, the government can still influence development through regulation. Sometimes, these regulations are introduced with very little public debate. This is a reality every business in China must be prepared to face. In China, the learning process never ends. Just when one thinks he/she is beginning to understand it, something happens to surprise him/her and to remind him/her of the complexities of China. For many, that is also a good part of the attraction of the country.[1]

China can for a long time be busy marketing to local consumers. However, the Chinese are ambitiously looking for not only wealth and strength but for glory (pride) too. Therefore, when China's largest automaker, Shanghai Automotive Industry Corporation (SAIC), opened its new U.S. headquarters in suburban Detroit in 2012, even General Motors—SAIC's joint venture partner in China—was surprised by something unexpected. It seems that no one on the Chinese side had bothered to tell them. And SAIC isn't the only Chinese firm with global ambitions: The Chinese outbound foreign direct investment (FDI) has more than quintupled over the last 10 years in the 21st century.[2]

The growing Chinese economy needs oil which is available in Africa. Therefore China has begun to invest in Africa. China's investment in Africa has increased a staggering 30-fold since 2005, with 2,000 Chinese firms now present in 50 African countries. According to China in Africa: *The Real Story* is as follows:[3]

- In 2012, the total volume of China-Africa trade reached US $198.49 billion, a year-on-year growth of 19.3%. Of this, US $85.319 billion consisted of China's exports to Africa, up 16.7%, and US $113.171 billion was contributed by China's imports from Africa, up 21.4%.
- From 2000 to 2012, the proportion of China-Africa trade volume as a part of China's total foreign trade volume increased from 2.23% to 5.13%. This shows that although China looms large for Africa, Africa is still a tiny part of China's overall trade.
- In 2012, the proportion of mechanical and electrical products as a part of China's total commodity exports to Africa reached 45.9%. A lot of these are vehicles, generators, telecoms and factory machinery.

---

[1] http://www.china-ready.com/ Retrieved 11/3/2013.
[2] http://www.chinaafricarealstory.com/ Retrieved 11/3/2013.
[3] http://www.chinaafricarealstory.com/ Retrieved 11/3/2013

- The cumulative Chinese FDI to Africa now amounts to US $21 billion (by official figures). Of this, manufacturing investment is at US $3.43 billion.
- The China Africa Development Fund has invested US $1.806 billion for 53 projects. So far, only one is in agriculture.
- China's agricultural exports to Africa are now at US $2.49 billion, having increased 57.6% since 2009. Yes, China exports food to Africa; Africa exports mainly industrial inputs like rubber, cotton, sisal, along with oil palm, sesame, cocoa, and peanuts to China.
- In 2012, Chinese enterprises completed construction contracts worth US $40.83 billion in Africa. This is a huge and under-appreciated sector of commercial interest for the Chinese.
- From 2010 to May 2012, China approved concessional loans worth a total of US $11.3 billion for 92 African projects. This includes preferential export buyer's credits, and foreign aid concessional loans. It is in fulfillment of the 2009 pledge of $10 billion over 3 years. All of these loan commitments would have come through China's Export Import Bank. This comes to about US$4.7 billion per year.

While these new Chinese multinationals have tried to tread quietly, many observers in Western Civilization have taken warning, and are beginning to get nervous. Indeed, some even talk of a new *economic cold war*, suggesting China's unique kind of state capitalism can decimate the traditional laissez-faire capitalism of Western Civilization.

CHINA IN GLOBAL COMPETITION OF MAKING GOODS-WORLD FACTORY

Hundreds of thousands of new Chinese companies have made this country the world's most competitive business environment. Indeed, China is now the world's largest and fastest-growing source of entrepreneurial start-ups. It is also an incubator for large businesses, both foreign and home grown.

Nearly 300,000 foreign-invested businesses have been established in China in the dawn of the 21st century, competing with the country's manufacturing base and reaching its consumer and business markets.

China is also an innovative center for outsiders. The best of the world's companies have come here to transform themselves, gaining experience and capabilities in China that can be applied to the rest of their business worldwide. Meanwhile, many of China's leading entrepreneurs, like Li Ning, see themselves as potential global competitors.

Companies such as computer maker Lenovo, white-goods firm Haier, and telecoms equipment manufacturers Huawei Technologies and ZTE are building platforms of sufficient scale to take their businesses worldwide. They will be joined, in turn, by hundreds and then thousands more.

During the past fifteen years (1998-2015), global companies have gone to China either to sell or manufacture goods. Over the next decade, international corporate leaders will go to China to integrate this vast market and sourcing hub with their global strategies and operations. Accomplishing this will require enormous leadership skills within China and outside the country, especially at headquarters level.

The economic growth has resulted in enormous waste, the environment has suffered, and demand has been a secondary consideration. China's emphasis will one day perhaps switch toward creating a more environment-sensitive economy, as well as a more productive and competitive one. One can expect that following Western rules, there will be a greater emphasis on demand as the main driver of growth versus investment, and on reducing the resources consumed per unit of output and the environmental impact, while raising technological and managerial standards.[4]

Conventional wisdom says that when it comes to West-China relations, commerce plays a stabilizing role, giving both sides a reason to work together. But in the next few years (2013+), commercial ties between the two countries will almost certainly become more competitive and could even disrupt the relationship.[5]

For many U.S. firms, the first battleground will be within China, where there is already significant competition between foreign and local companies for market share. A 2010 survey by the American Chamber of Commerce in China found that 38% of U.S. companies feel unwelcome in the Chinese market, up from 23% just two years earlier. And it's a sentiment that extends beyond technology companies, like Google, into the manufacturing sector. Numerous companies now complain about a host of issues, from intellectual property theft to nontariff barriers to aspects of China's regulatory regime. There is fear among U.S. firms that if China can quickly produce substitutable (but cheaper) products, foreign companies in China will be marginalized.[6]

But the next battleground will be the global marketplace for sophisticated technologies. In some sectors, such as high-speed rail, China is already a world leader, largely because it demanded technology as the price for domestic market access. China is a preferred partner in that sector for Argentina, for example.

One blogger stated that "The moment two elephants come on the same ground; they would fight for their dominion. Lion of the jungle is generally one. Interesting would be which countries will become the grass and how it will change their destinies."

The Chinese diaspora plays a strong role in supporting the global competition of China. Its diaspora has about 50 million people, who live in 30 plus countries. The Chinese people have a long history of migrating overseas. One of the migrations dates back to the Ming dynasty when Zheng He (1371–1435) became the envoy of Ming. He sent people - many of them Cantonese and Hokkien - to explore and trade in the South China Sea and in the Indian Ocean. Different waves of immigration led to subgroups among overseas Chinese such as the new and old immigrants in Southeast Asia, North America, Oceania, the Caribbean, Latin America, South Africa, and Russia. In the 19th century, the age of colonialism was at its height and the great Chinese diaspora began. Many colonies lacked a large pool of laborers and the Chinese were filling that pool as cheap and hardworking workers.

From the mid-19th century onward, emigration has been directed primarily to Western countries such as the United States, Canada, Australia, New Zealand, Brazil, and the nations of Western Europe, as well as to Peru where they are called tusán, Panama, and to a lesser extent to Mexico. Many of these emigrants who entered Western countries were themselves

---

[4] http://www.booz.com/global/home/what-we-think/the_china_strategy/competitive_china/Retrieved 11/3/ 2013.
[5] http://blogs.hbr.org/2011/04/watch-out-for-rising-us-china/Retrieved 11/3/2013.
[6] http://blogs.hbr.org/2011/04/watch-out-for-rising-us-china/Retrieved 11/3/2013.

overseas Chinese, particularly from the 1950s to the 1980s, a period during which the PRC placed severe restrictions on the movement of its citizens.

In recent years of the 20th and 21st centuries, the People's Republic of China has built increasingly stronger ties with African nations. As of August 2007, there were an estimated 750,000 Chinese nationals working or living for extended periods in different African countries.[7] An estimated 200,000 ethnic Chinese live in South Africa.[8]

After the Deng Xiaoping reforms, the attitude of the PRC toward overseas Chinese changed dramatically. Rather than being seen with suspicion, they were seen as people who could aid PRC development via their skills and capital. During the 1980s, the PRC actively attempted to court the support of overseas Chinese by among other things, returning properties that had been confiscated after the 1949 revolution. More recently PRC policy has attempted to maintain the support of recently emigrated Chinese, who consist largely of Chinese seeking graduate education in the West. Many overseas Chinese are now investing in the People's Republic of China providing financial resources, social and cultural networks, contacts and opportunities.[9]

Overseas Chinese are estimated to control 1.5 to 2 trillion USD in liquid assets and have considerable amounts of wealth to stimulate economic power in China (Fukuda 1998). Overseas Chinese often send remittances back home to family members to help better them financially and socioeconomically. China ranks second after India of top remittance receiving countries in 2010 with over 51 billion USD sent.[10] The overseas Chinese business community of Southeast Asia, known as the bamboo network, has a prominent role in the region's private sectors (Weidenbaum 1996). A good example of the Chinese diaspora's business role is a formed "Network beyond Empire" (The bamboo Network) of Chinese business and nationalism in the Hong-Kong-Singapore Corridor. It was formed in 1914-1941 but is growing and getting more influential in the 21st century (Huei-Ying Kuo 2012).

The Chinese for a long time have been practicing study abroad. Both Deng Xiao Ping and Zhou En Lai (past Chinese leaders) studied in France. Nowadays, China has the largest number of overseas students in the world, with a record 1.27 million studying abroad at the end of 2010, according to the latest statistics from the Ministry of Education.[11] Currently, more than 3 million Chinese students, scholars and their families are scattered abroad, temporarily living outside their homelands – of all ages, from every part of China.[12]

It is clear that most of China's future leaders will emerge from the thousands of scholars who have studied or worked overseas. But the rest of Chinese students and professionals who study and work abroad have China on their minds. They feel that they can accomplish many things for their country, which for centuries was either isolated or colonized and suffered bad times.

---

[7] Chinese flocking in numbers to a new frontier: Africa.com. Retrieved 11/5/2013.
[8] SA-Born Chinese and the Colours of Exclusion, allAfrica.com. Retrieved 11/5/2013.
[9] The Cultural Imperative - Richard D. Lewis - Google Books. Books.google.ca. Retrieved 10/5/2013.
[10] Migration and Remittances: Top Countries. http://siteresources.worldbank.org/INTPROSPECTS/Resources/334934-1199807908806/Top10.pdf/Retrieved 11/5/2013.
[11] http://www.omf.org/omf/us/get_involved_1/welcoming_ministry_diaspora/ chinese_diaspora_ministry/ Retrieve11/ 5/2013.
[12] Op.cit.

CHINESE DREAMS-- WEALTH, STRENGTH, AND PRIDE

The *Chinese Dream* is a new term within Chinese socialist thought and describes a set of ideals in the People's Republic of China.[13] It is used by journalists, government officials, and activists to describe the role of the individual in Chinese society.[14]

In 2013 the Communist Party (CPC) General Secretary Xi Jinping began promoting the phrase as a slogan, leading to its widespread use in the Chinese media.[15] Xi has described the dream as "national rejuvenation, improvement of people's livelihoods, prosperity, construction of a better society and military strengthening."[16] He has stated that young people should "dare to dream, work assiduously to fulfill the dreams and contribute to the revitalization of the nation."[17] According to the party's theoretical journal Qiushi, the Chinese Dream is about Chinese prosperity, collective effort, socialism and national glory.[18] A translation of a New York Times article written by the American journalist Thomas Friedman, "China Needs Its Own Dream", has been credited with popularizing the concept in China.[19]

A Chinese author Helen H. Wang (2010) was the first one to connect the Chinese Dream with the American Dream. In her book The Chinese Dream, Wang wrote: "The Chinese Dream, taking its title from the American Dream, alluding to an easily identifiable concept..." Wang attempts to demonstrate that the Chinese people have similar dreams as those of the American people. "This new [Chinese] middle class...." Wang wrote, "Which barely existed a decade ago, will reach the size of more than two Americas in a decade or two. They number in the hundreds of millions, with the same hopes and dreams that you and I have: to have a better life, to give our children an even better life...." "The growth of China's middle class rivals the growth of China's overall economy as a phenomenon with huge implications for the entire world. Whether China will become a more liberal and democratic society, ... whether it will develop a spiritual power to match its material influence — these and other questions are Helen Wang's topic in this fascinating book. It rings true to what I have seen in China and suggests new possibilities."[20]

Generally speaking the Chinese Dream gives the Chinese people the ideas which should motivate their lives and make them more productive and happier

Shortly speaking the Chinese Dream is the essence of Socialism with Chinese characteristics and includes the following motivational ideas:

- Sustainable development - a prosperous lifestyle reconciled with a sustainable lifestyle.

---

[13] Central Party School/Central Committee of the Communist Party of China. "The Chinese Dream infuses Socialism with Chinese characteristics with New Energy". Qiushi. chinacopyrightandmedia. wordpress.com. Retrieved 9 June 2013.
[14] Chasing the Chinese dream," The Economist May 4, 2013, pp 24-26.
[15] Xi Jinping and the Chinese Dream," The Economist May 4, 2013, p 11.
[16] Osnos, Evan (March 26, 2013). "Can China deliver the China dream(s)?". New Yorker.
[17] Yang Yi, "Youth urged to contribute to realization of 'Chinese dream'", Xinhuanet English.news.cn 2013-05-04.
[18] Shi, Yuzhi (20 May 2013). Seven reasons why the Chinese Dream is different from the American Dream]. Qiushi (in Chinese). Central Party School/Central Committee of the Communist Party of China. Retrieved 19 June 2013.
[19] "The role of Thomas Friedman". The Economist. May 6, 2013.
[20] James Fallows, National Correspondent of The Atlantic, the author of Postcards from Tomorrow Square: Reports from China – wrote about Wang's book in his opinion in Amazon.com.

- National renewal - a call for China's rising international influence.
- Individual dreams – individual achievement through the common goods bestowed by civil society.
- Economic and political reform - urbanization, the reduction of government bureaucracy, and weakening the power of special interests.

In October 2013, Britain's Chancellor of the Exchequer, George Osborne, described the Chinese Dream as a political reform that includes "rebalancing from investment to consumption."[21] After reviewing the detailed concept of the Chinese Dream, one can disagree with Schell and Delury (2013) that it is *wealth, strength*, and *pride*, since it is rather *prosperity, strength, and pride*.

CHINESE CIVILIZATION VERSUS GLOBAL CIVILIZATION

In the dawn of the 21st century one can notice that Western Civilization has transformed into Global Civilization. Since as Toynbee (1934) argued every civilization is characterized by a religion, one can also argue that Christianity, characterizing Western Civilization, has been replaced nowadays by a religion of the Global Civilization (Targowski 2014). Hence, a question arises: what is the religion of Global Civilization? It is business, which emerges on a global basis as a secular religion of Global Civilization.

Business is a secular religion and it is nothing new, since secularization has mounted since the seventeenth century, and today one's status as a business person does not require further *religious* identification, since business itself has become a "religion." Not only is greed good, as Gordon Gekko so persuasively insists in Oliver Stone's famous "Wall Street" episode, but, beyond that, it is virtuous, and in fact it is a religion of its own that is free and clear of its earlier involvement with Protestantism as described by Max Weber. It now throws a wider net than the northern European Protestant sect could ever have imagined.

Business religion, as almost every religion, has its own saints. *Among them one can mention such ones as:* Adam Smith, Henry Ford, Andrew Mellon, John Rockefeller, Sam Walton, Bill Gates, Warren Buffet, and others. They are supported by *Business Apostles* such as Frederic Taylor (scientific management), Peter Drucker ("business is everywhere"), Bill Clinton ("New Economy"), Lawrence Summers ("too big to fail"), Timothy Geithner ("less regulations the better"), Thomas Friedman ("almost every American should outsource"), Jagdish Bhagwati ("globalization is good"), C.K. Prahald ("core competency is good, everything else outsource"), Gregory Mankiv ("making hamburgers at MacDonald is manufacturing"), Steve Forbes ("sky is the limit"), and too many others to count.

This kind of secular business religion triggered the rise of Global Civilization in the dawn of the 21st century. However, Chinese Civilization, which has its own strong Buddhist religion, is the main beneficiary of the rising Global Civilization. The mindless pursuit for profit by Global Civilization supports the growth of that civilization. It can only be done by strong involvement of Chinese Civilization, which so far is the supplier of cheap labor. Table 9.1 compares main characteristics of both civilizations.

---

[21] "Chancellor's speech to students at Peking University". gov.uk. Retrieved 16 September 2013.

Table 9.1. The Comparison of Global and Chinese Civilizations

Criteria	Global civilization	Chinese civilization
State	Nation-states	Civilization-state spread through country and diaspora around the globe
Government	Pseudo-Democracy Rulers guided by lobbyists	Authoritarian Hierarchy Rulers guided by CPC
Religion	Secular, *a la* business	Buddhism and other
Culture	A few years old	4000 years old
Main values	Individualism, Wealth Neglect of Seniors Wisdom from own mistakes	Wealth, Strength, Pride Common Good Wisdom from seniors
Hardship threshold	Low	High
Focus	Short and Instant	Long and Patient
Strongest knowledge	Scientific and Universal	Conventional and Scientific
Infrastructure	Complex	Simple and Complex
Interest	Extraverted	Introverted
Level of energy needed to support life activities	High	Low to Medium
Character	Arrogant	Submissive
Survival ability	Moderate	High

This comparison indicates that Chinese Civilization has better characteristics than Global Civilization to survive in and gain from global competition. The deciding criteria are:

- Chinese Civilization's authoritarian government is more able than the pseudo-democracy of the Global Civilization in liquid times (permanent crisis of all sorts). In the coming years the colonial globalization will deeply deplete strategic resources and life will be driven by coupons, controlled by the top-down government. It will lead to civic unrest in Global Civilization but in Chinese Civilization it will be accepted *modus operandi*.
- The main values of Global Civilization come from values formed during the 18th-20th centuries of Western Civilization's rise after the industrial revolution. However, in the 21st century it leads towards the negligence of the common good and the decline of states and civilization's infrastructure.
- The Chinese introverted character is more suited for coping with adversarial problems of international affairs than the extraverted character of citizens of Global Civilization.

In general, the Chinese leaders are wiser than Western-Global leaders whose pursuit for huge profits makes them blind to rising social problems in countries where they live and should pay taxes.

Conclusion

One can draw the following conclusion:

1. Chinese Civilization is not a new power in the world. This country already was the world super power about 650 years ago. Due to its isolationist politics and ruling by outsiders, it suffered in these mentioned years. But its spirit, knowledge and skills are sophisticated, and enhanced by Global Civilization today.
2. Nowadays, China must choose a wise strategy of development. If it accepts full westernization of business, industry, and agriculture, sooner or later it will follow the declining process of Western Civilization. Particularly, the westernized policy of agriculture may lead to the rapid development of cities, filled with migrating peasants. Eventually it may lead to the decline of cities, as a good example is dying Detroit today, once the heart of American industrialism.
3. The rise of Chinese Civilization is relatively easy, since Global Civilization helps this process enormously. In other words, Global Civilization is declining, because its internal politics and culture is in profound and permanent crisis.
4. The coming Death Triangle of Civilization (relations between Population, Ecology and depletion of Strategic Resources Bombs) and the declining culture of Global (Western) Civilization will test which civilization will survive? It is very probable that the Chinese have more wisdom and skills to live in tough times than Westerners.

References

Beardson, T. (2013). *Stumbling giant: the threats to Chinese future*. New haven, CT: Yale University Press.

Cardenal, J. P. & Araujo, H. (2013). Transl. C. Mansfield. *China's silent army: the pioneers, traders, fixers and workers who are remaking the world in Beijing's image*. New York: Crown.

Fukuda, Kazuo John. (1998). Japan and China: The meeting of Asia's economic giants. New York: Routledge.

Huei-Ying Kuo. (2012). Network beyond empires: Chinese business and nationalism in the Hong-Kong-Singapore corridor, 1914-1941. *The ISCSC Newsletter*, vol. *51*, no. 1, p. 25

Needham, J. (1954). *Science and civilization in China*. Cambridge, UK: Cambridge University Press.

Needham, J. (2004). *Science and civilization in China*. Cambridge, UK: Cambridge University Press. Part 7.

Schell, O. & Delury, J. (2013). *Wealth and power: China's long march to the twenty-first century*. New York: Random House.

Targowski, A. (2014). *Global civilization in the 21st century*. New York: NOVA Science Publishers.

Toynbee, A. J. (1934). *A Study of history*. Oxford, UK: Oxford University Press.

Wang, H. H. with Foreword by Lord Wei. (2010, 2012). *The Chinese dream: the rise of the world's largest middle class and what it means to you*. Bestseller Press (Amazon Digital Service).

Weidenbaum, M. L. (1996). *The bamboo network: how expatriate Chinese entrepreneurs are creating a new economic superpower in Asia*. Martin Kessler Books, Free Press. 4–5.

In: Chinese Civilization in the 21st Century
Editors: Andrew Targowski and Bernard Han

ISBN: 978-1-63321-960-1
© 2014 Nova Science Publishers, Inc.

Chapter 10

WHERE IS CHINA HEADING?

Andrew Targowski[*]

Western Michigan University, US
President Emeritus of the International Society
For the Comparative Study of Civilizations(2007-2013)

ABSTRACT

The *purpose* of this investigation is to define the future for China. The *methodology* is based on an interdisciplinary big-picture view of the Chinese Civilization's legacy, the present status of China among leaders of globalization at the dawn of the 21st century, the present *new ability* of the Chinese Civilization to compete with other civilizations, the challenges facing China at the dawn of the 21st century, the future of the Chinese Civilization in the globalizing world of the 21st century, and what other civilizations can learn from Chinese Civilization. Among the *findings* are: the legacy of a 5,000 year long culture is a strong factor why China is rising today. Also the will of strong people and political leadership contribute to the current success of China. Among other factors are educated thinking by a good part of the population and a growing educated elite with university degrees. *Practical implication:* Shortage of fresh and clean water, overwhelming pollution and an ancient alphabet can weaken China's ability to be a state where people would like to live and compete globally. Some suggestions are offered regarding what other civilization should learn from Chinese Civilization. *Social implication:* The future of China is in accepting the goal to develop and operate Sustainable China for Ever, which requires complying with the defined Seven Principles. *Originality:* This investigation, by providing the interdisciplinary and civilizational approach, expands the scope of the traditional approach to this issue, which is mostly economic or political science-oriented.

The following conclusions about *modus operendi* of the Chinese Civilization in the 21st century one can provide:

---

[*] E-mail: Andrew.targowski@wmich.edu.

A. The legacy of the Chinese Civilization past 5,000 yearsd

Longevity – the 5,000 year long Chinese Civilization is the longest still active civilization in the world. Its history and legacy makes the Chinese people mature, responsible, and wise in their "second coming" in the 21st century. It is evident more if one compares it with other active civilizations today, such as African, Hindu, Buddhist, Eastern, Western, Islamic, and Japanese. Their longevity is several times shorter than the Chinese Civilization's.

Administration – China had 24 dynasties and elaborate administration systems which contributed to the Chinese accepted subordination to political power. Mandarins were administrators, who created a self-perpetuating ruling class chosen by high performance in rigorous exams in the Chinese classics. Mandarin was the standardized language they spoke no matter what Chinese dialect might have been their tongue by birth. Their management of knowledge, wisdom and skills were supported by Confucianism[1] which is an ethical and philosophical system developed from the teachings of the Chinese philosopher Confucius[2] (Figure 10.1). The core of Confucianism is humanism, or what the philosopher Herbert Fingarette (1976) calls "the secular as sacred".

Figure 10.1. Confucius (551-472 BC) was a Chinese teacher, philosopher, and politician whose conventional wisdom has been passing to next generation of Chinese, making them wiser. Mao Zedong (1893-1976) was a Chinese Communist revolutionary and the founding father of the People's Republic of China, whose Little Red Book (LRB) covered 23 topics and 200 selected quotations to guide the Chinese in all walks of life. During the Cultural Revolution (1966-1971), studying the book was not only required in schools but was also a standard practice in the workplace as well. Today Confucius is still greatly admired and LRB is a piece of nostalgia. (Photo: Wikipedia).

---

[1] In Classic Civilization (later transformed into Western Civilization) about 100 years after Confucius lived three giant philosophers Socrates (469- 339 BC), Plato (427-347 BC), and Aristotle (384-322 BC) provided universal rules of conventional thinking and acting. The Sophists (Vthcentury BC, like Protagoras et al.) taught how to speak publically and act rationally, which may look like "European Confucianism.".

[2] In Western Civilization Niccolò Machiavelli (1469-1527) can be well compared to Confucius. He lived 2000 years after the Chinese sage and was a founder of modern political science and specifically political ethics. "Machiavellianism" is a widely used negative term to characterize unscrupulous politicians of the sort Machiavelli described in The Prince. The book itself gained enormous notoriety and wide readership because the author seemed to be endorsing behavior often deemed as evil and immoral.

Figure 10.2. A mandarin, one of the class of people who were the administrators of the Chinese government for a thousand years or so, until the Chinese Revolution overthrew the emperor in the early part of the 20th century. On the right, an office of administration. (Photo: able2know.org).

Confucianism focuses on the practical, especially the importance of the family, and not on a belief in gods or the afterlife. Confucianism, broadly speaking, does not exalt faithfulness to divine will or higher law. This stance rests on the belief that human beings are teachable, improvable, and perfectible through personal and communal endeavors, especially self-cultivation and self-creation. Confucian thought focuses on the cultivation of virtue and maintenance of ethics. Historically, cultures and countries strongly influenced by Confucianism include mainland China, Taiwan, Hong Kong, Macau, Korea, Japan, and Vietnam, as well as various territories settled predominantly by Chinese people, such as Singapore. In the 20th century, Confucianism's influence has been greatly reduced in places such as Mainland China. Nowadays, people often see Confucian ethics as a complementary guideline for other ideologies and beliefs, including democracy, Marxism, capitalism, Christianity, Islam and Buddhism. It is not surprising that the highest quality institutions in the world are in Singapore and Hong Kong, and China's institutions have comparable quality to France and America's in the 21st century. Administration practice during several millennia has had a strong impact on today's ways of governing. The first "bureaucrats" in China were mandarins as it is shown in Figure 10.2. For around 1,300 years, from 600 to 1905, mandarins were selected by merit through the extremely rigorous imperial examination. However, most high ranking positions were filled by relatives of the sovereign and the nobility.

Population – China has the largest population of the world. This is the result of many additive factors. China has the third largest territory in the world (after Russia and Canada), and it is similar to the U.S.'s territory with good arable land and climate. Therefore since the beginning of history, and for the majority of human settlement, China has had the largest population in the world. It is a resource rich area with a lot of water to grow crops in. Rice is a stable staple crop to grow, and cities were established there very early on. Having a larger family meant there was more help on the farms so you had an easier time surviving despite being poor. In developing countries it is sometimes beneficial to have more children (farmers in America do this as well) who are like a retirement system, later taking care of parents. China's population today (1.3 billion) is much greater than it was in 1900 (~415 million), Europe as a whole, in 1900, had a population on par with China. In 2013, China has almost 2 times as many people as Europe. Why? Chairman Mao-Zedong (1893-1976) encouraged the Chinese to have large families — he said: "Each mouth to feed comes with two hands to work." He also gave economic benefits for 3rd, 4th, and 5th children. He viewed a large population as a goal, to build up and fill out the country, to ensure it is unable to be taken by outside forces, and many other reasons. Mao repeatedly said that China should be "rich in workers, farmers and soldiers" and strongly encouraged having many children. The population sky-rocketed (Figure 10.3) over just a single generation until Deng Xiaoping (1904-1997) in 1978 put on the brakes and later, when the Chinese Communist Party (CCP) realized its mistake, the 1-Child Policy was set up.

Wars – the Chinese conducted wars according to Sun Tzu (544-496 BC) who was a Chinese military general, strategist and philosopher. His book on *Art of War* presents a philosophy of war for managing conflicts and winning battles. It is accepted as a masterpiece on strategy and is frequently cited and referred to by generals and theorists since it was first published, translated, and distributed internationally. The text outlines theories of battle, but also advocates diplomacy and cultivating relationships with other nations as essential to the health of a state. His famous principle is "to win a war without a battle." This principle is embedded in the Chinese middle of the road attitude, applied beyond military settings. It emphasizes balanced problem solving with wisdom as the preferred solution. In Western Civilization a similar war strategist came2300 years after, General Carl von Clausewitz (1780-1831),who stressed the "moral" and political aspect of war, which is "the continuation of politics with other means." Unfortunately his moral aspect of the war was neglected by his compatriots in European wars in the 20th century.

Figure 10.3. Is the large population the strength or weakness of Chinese Civilization? (Photo: jordanink.wordpress.com).

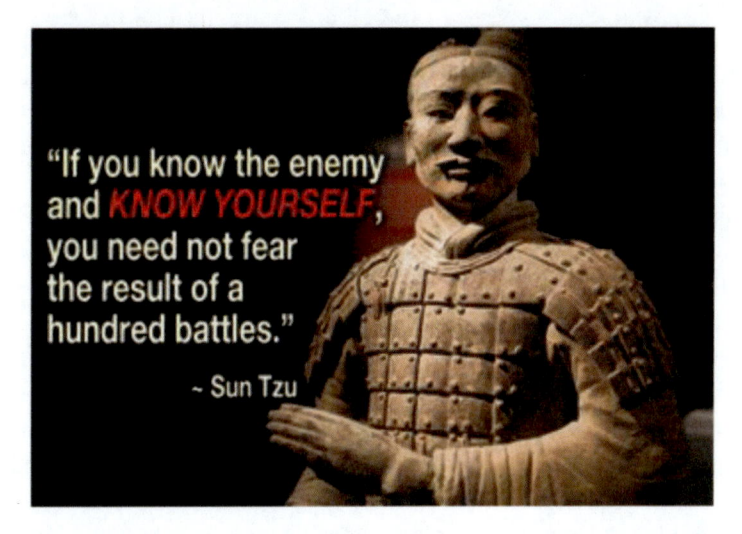

Figure 10.4. Sun Tzu Chinese military general whose wisdom has been proudly applied in the last 2500 years by the Chinese. (Photo: personalexcellence.co).

Isolation – the disastrous Emperor's decision to destroy the Chinese fleet in 1433 led to a century long of isolation and retardation in process of modernizing its civilization. In those times China has about 85 million people and Portugal about 1 million; the former was the most technologically advanced country in the world and had more ships (about 350) than the latter, exploring East Africa and lands around the Indian Ocean. The former was exploring west coast of Africa. But what Portugal had that China didn't was the will to explore. That was why, in the end, when the two nations met at last, it was on the Chinese coast (Macao) and not on the Portuguesa coast. But the previous Chinese voyages weren't a total loss, either. They facilitated Chinese penetration into Southeast Asia, both culturally and in the way of emigration, and did encourage trade. Within next 600 years this region became the Sinosphere, which today is under China's strong influence.

Figure 10.4. A Chinese opera is the distinctive example of Chinese culture which is shared among the Chinese, who are proud of it. (Photo: Wikipedia).

Religion – Chinese religion is rational, since Buddhism is in fact a secular religion and associated with Confucianism and Taoism which are secular sets of rules of the art of living. The Chinese are spiritual by being in reality rather than some who practice sacred religions by looking beyond reality. The long lasting Communism in China in the 20th and 21st centuries impacted the religious beliefs of citizens; hence only 25 percent of the population is practicing religions. It reminds one of the situation in Western Europe, where below 10 percent of French and Germans go to churches. As a practical rule indicates, better off people practice less religion.

Culture – Chinese culture is one of the world's oldest cultures which is continuously practiced by about 20 percent of the world population. The area in which the culture is dominant covers a large geographical region in eastern Asia (Sinosphere) with customs and traditions varying greatly between provinces, cities, and even towns. Important components of Chinese culture include literature, music (Figure 10.4), visual arts, martial arts, cuisine, religion etc.

Family – Family is a complex system which is characterized by the Chinese kinship and clan. In the Chinese kinship system maternal and paternal lineages are distinguished. For example, a mother's brother and a father's brother have different terms. The relative age of a sibling's relation is considered important. For example, a father's younger brother has a different terminology than his older brother. The gender of the relative is distinguished, as in English. Chinese kinship is agnatic, emphasizing patrilineality. A Chinese clan is a patrilineal and patrilocal group of related Chinese people with a common surname sharing a common ancestor. In southern China, clan members could form a village known as an ancestral village. In Hong Kong, clan settlement is exemplified by walled villages. An ancestral village usually features a hall and shrine honoring ancestral clan members. A clan pedigree can be found recording male members of the clan. A married woman is considered part of her husband's clan. These two family systems make a family a strong element of the Chinese society. After 1433 China went into isolation from the world, being to certain degree exploited by their own or foreign rulers. As a result, the Chinese went into poverty, with the exception of some narrow elite. To survive they maintained and still maintain strong relations among family members, stronger ones than with the state, which was seen as the oppressor. For the Chinese, a strong family is the best art of living to survive harsh condition of life and sustain its *modus operandi* for future (Figure 10.5).

Technology – ancient Chinese scientists, mathematicians and doctors made significant advances in science, technology, mathematics, and astronomy. Traditional Chinese medicine, acupuncture and herbal medicine were also developed through empirical observation and scientific experimentation. Among the earliest inventions were the abacus, the "shadow clock," and items such as Kong Ming lanterns. The Four Great Inventions, the compass, gunpowder, papermaking, and printing, were among the most important technological advances, only known in Europe by the end of the Middle Ages, 1000 years later. The Chinese junks (ships) (Figure 10.6) were better than Portuguese caravels in the 15 century, which discovered America and went around Africa to China. The Jesuit China missions of the 16th and 17th centuries introduced Western science and astronomy in China. In the 19th and 20th century the introduction of Western technology was a major factor in the modernization of China. One question that has been the subject of debate among historians has been why China did not develop a scientific revolution and why Chinese technology fell behind that of Europe. Many hypotheses have been proposed ranging from the cultural to the political and economic. For example, John K. Faibank (1992) argued that the Chinese political system was hostile to scientific progress. As for Joseph Needham (1986), he wrote that cultural factors prevented traditional Chinese achievements from developing into what could be called "science." It was the religious and philosophical framework of the Chinese intellectuals which made them unable to believe in the ideas of laws of nature. Mark Elvin (1972) argues that the Chinese population was large enough, workers cheap enough and agrarian productivity high enough to not require mechanization: thousands of Chinese workers were perfectly able to quickly perform any needed task.

Economy – When the Western Civilization accelerated its development in the 20th century, after the Industrial Revolution (19th century) and two World Wars (1914-2018 and 1939-1945), particularly the United States, whose population (5% of the world) used 30% of world resources – the undeveloped Chinese Civilization's strategic resources had been consumed by the economically successful America and Western Europe.

Figure 10.5. A Chinese family in the 19th century was an insurance policy for surviving harsh life conditions (Photo: Wikipedia).

Figure 10. 6. A Chinese junk from the 13th century and modern junk in Hong Kong in the 21st century. (Photo: Wikipedia).

B. The present status of China among leaders of globalization at the dawn of the 21st century

Emerging will – When Western Civilization and other civilizations which are declining or stagnant, the Chinese Civilization (Sinosphere) with countries such as China (including Hong Kong), Taiwan, and Singapore are rising civilizationally and economically. China belongs to the BRIC countries (Brazil, Russia, India and China) which demonstrate good economic growth and overall societal dynamism. Table 10.1. supports this statement. China today is the second largest economy in the world. It has a longer life expectancy than Russia and is closing the gap with the U.S. China's GDP/capita in (PPP-Purchasing Power Parity) is 1.9% smaller than Russia's and 5.7% smaller than America's since China has a large population. However, China as a country takes advantage of its citizens' low income and creates large financial surpluses in the national budget, which allows modernizing the country in terms of common infrastructural projects such as highways, railroads, cities, and so forth. This principle is supported by a very low debts/capita acquired by the Chinese government. For example, China's private and public debts are 23.5 times smaller than America's, 26 times smaller than Germany's and 1.6 than Russia's. Furthermore, China is a net exporter like Japan, Germany, and Russia while the U.S. is a net importer. All these strategic factors show that China as a state is well governed, perhaps better than the U.S. and Russia. These latter countries are the strongest competitors of China, the U.S. in terms of economy-ideology and Russia in terms of ideology-economy in the post-Soviet times.

Table 10.1. The basic characteristics of selected economically leading countries in the world in the 21st century

CRITERIA	CHINA	USA	JAPAN	GERMANY	RUSSIA
Population [1]	1,306,313,800 (2006)	317,800,000 (2014)	127,417,200 (2006)	82,431,400 (2006)	143,420,300 (2006)
Pop. Density Sq. Miles [1]	352	80	873	598	22
Overall Life expectancy [2]	74.2 years	79.8 years	84.5 years	81 years	70 years
GDP in US $ [3]	8,221,015(2012)	16,244,575 (2012)	5,960,269 (2012)	3,429,519 (2012)	2,029,813 (2012)
GDP/capita in US $/PPP[3]	7,083/9,055 (2014/2012)	52,839/51,704 (2013/2012)	39,321/35,855 (2013/2012)	43,952/38,666 (2013/2012)	14,973/17,518 (2013/2012)
Private and Public Debts in US $ [4]	3 Billion (06.31.2013)	17.3 Billion (02.02. 2014)	3 Billion (12. 21,2012)	5.7 Billion (06. 30, 2011)	0.6 Billion (12. 31, 2012)
Private and Public Debts/Capita in US $ [4]	2,220	52,170	24,000	57,755	3,634
Export/ Import of Goods and Services as % of GDP [5]	27/25	14/17	44/17	52/46	29/22

Sources: [1]. CIA World Facts Book (2006). [2] World Health Organization (2013). [3] International Monetary Fund (2012). [4] Wikipedia. [5] The World Bank-2012. PPP-Purchasing Power Parity.

Table 10.2. The strategic factors characteristic of selected economically leading countries in the world in the 21st century

FACTORS	CHINA	USA	JAPAN	GERMANY	RUSSIA
Size of Labor Force in Million [1]	795 (2010)	156 (2013)	66 (20110	44 (2012)	76 (2013)
Percentage of Labor in Manufacturing	10% (2010) [2]	9% (2012) [3]	16.6% (2012) [4]	20% (2012) [1]	20% (2012) [8]
Percentage of Labor in Service	35.7% (2011) [6]	80% (2012) [4]	70% (2010) [7]	70% (2010) [1]	63% (2012) [5]

Source: [1] Wikipedia. [2] The Economist April 21, 2012.[3]National Association of Manufacturers (2014). [4] U.S. Department of Labor: Bureau of Labor Statistics. [5] Thompson (2012), [6] http://www.tradingeconomics.com/china/employment-in-services, Retrieved 03-21-2014. [7] Economy of Japan (Wikipedia), [8] Author's estimation.

World Factory – with the world population of 7.2 billion in 2014 the most important issue is what to do with such a large labor force, which reached 3.3 billion in 2012 (The World Factbook).[3] In the 20th century the developed nations became "developed" since the middle class increased due to advancements in manufacturing. In general terms manufacturing is the strongest factor in stabilizing a national economy. When in the 21st century developed nations were outsourcing manufacturing mostly to China, they destabilized their economies and stabilized China's economy. It is illustrated in Table 10.2 – for example in China 79.5 million people work in manufacturing, while in the U.S. only 14 million work today, in comparison to the1980s when 25% of the American labor force worked in manufacturing. It means that about 16% of the labor force or 22 million (averaging the size of labor force in the last 25 years) people dropped from the middle class, causing long lasting melancholy in the American economy. Since 80% of people employed in the service economy are poorly paid, they do not have enough of the discretionary income to support the healthy growth of the economy. Contrary to this situation in Western Civilization, China and its satellites gained 79.5 plus million members of new rising middle class. These people provide *new will* and social energy for the development of Chinese Civilization in the globalizing world.

C. The present *new ability* of the Chinese Civilization to compete with other civilizations.

Educated thinking – China had outstanding thinkers through millennia; however, in the Second Millennium AD, Western Civilization overpassed Chinese Civilization in generating ideas and innovations coming from good education, since the latter for the last 300 years of that Millennium was stagnant. In the 21st century this gap is decreasing. It is very difficult to compare with other countries the size of China's educational infrastructure due to its huge population. Certain data in Table 10.3 need commentary. It is true that the number of home computers is low in China in comparison to other countries, but the Internet's penetration by

---

[3] The World Fact Book is also known as the CIA World Factbook., which is used by public officials and administration in the U.S.

the population is at a relatively good level, thanks to public access places. The low number of Chinese members on Facebook only indicates that the Chinese understand that this social network is in fact a marketing network. The number of colleges and universities is almost 6 times larger than Germany's, 2.5 larger than Japan's, 2 times larger than Russia's and only the U.S.' has 1.4 more education institutions of that kind. Student-wise, China with 15 million follows only the U.S. with 21 million, but the number of college & university students per 10,000 habitants needs to be higher in China. On the other hand, China graduates almost 5 times more engineers than the U.S., than Japan, than Russia and 13 times than Germany. The only question is whether the quality of this kind of education is on par with the mentioned countries. Nerveless, China as the World Factory with 79.5 million employed in manufacturing needs many engineers, while outsourcing Western Civilization does not need so many engineers, since there are not enough factories left to employ them. The trend bringing manufacturing back to America is based on "dark" factories, where working robots and automation do not need any lights.

Table 10.3. The factors of intellectual ability characteristic of selected economically leading countries in the world in the 21st century

FACTORS	CHINA	USA	JAPAN	GERMANY	RUSSIA
Number of PC computers per 100 people [1]	6 (2007)	81 (2006)	40 (2004)	65 (2006)	13 (2006)
Number of Internet users	538,000,000	245,203,319	101,228,736	67,483,860	67,982,547
Facebook members 2012 [3]	(633,000)	(166,029,240)	(17,196,080)	(17,196,080)	(7,963,400)
Internet penetration of population, 2012 [1]	40%	81%	79%	83%	53%
Enrolment & intertiary (theory based) education (2-3 years) 2011 [8]	22%	82%	58%	46%	75%
Number of colleges & universities (4-6 years) [2]	1,956 (2013)	2,774 (2010)	778 (2010)	333 (2010	1000 (2007-2008)
Number of students of higher education in million [2]	16	21	2.8	2	8
Number of students/10,000 habitants	115	710	628	243	558
Number of engineers graduated per year [4][5][6][7]	517,225 (2005)	112,000 (2003)	100,000 (1994)	40,000 (2011)	132,000 (2009)

Source: [1] World Bank,[2] Wikipedia, National Center for Education Statistics, European University Institute, China: http://www.stats.gov.cn/tjsj/ndsj/2013/indexch.htm". [3] Internet World Stats.[4] Blue et al. (2005).[5] Blue (2011). [6] Japan, Retrieved 03-23-2014 http://www.nsf.gov/statistics/nsf97324/chp4.htm. [7] Loyalka (2012).[8] Pocket World in Figures, the Economist 2011.

Rising infrastructure–infrastructure is one of three main components of civilization (besides society and culture). In the last 600 years when China was isolated and stagnant– its infrastructure was undeveloped. Since the World Factory was has raised income, China has spectacularly developed its infrastructure (Table 10.3). In the last 35 years this country built 92,000 km of highways which are 1.3 times longer than the U.S. which have been built since the 1950s. China overpassed Russian's length of highways 119-times and the latter is competing with China in the same political framework. The density of highways in Germany and Japan is higher, but these countries are land dwarfs. The same can be said about the development of Chinese railroads which use locally made high-speed trains (Figure 10.7).

The new highways and railroads should limit traffic jams. For example, the worst traffic jam in history was a 100km queue on the Beijing-Tibet highway in August, 2010, where drivers were help up for over 20 days. The cause of the chaos was hundreds of heavy trucks transporting coal from Inner Mongolia to power stations in the capital Beijing, with the lack of suitable rail links being blamed for the problems that lasted for nearly three weeks.

Table 10.3. The factors of infrastructural ability characteristic of selected economically leading countries in the world in the 21st century

FACTORS	CHINA	USA	JAPAN	GERMANY	RUSSIA
Land area Sq. Miles [1]	3,705,405	3,717,811	145,882	137,846	6,592,768
Length of Highwayskm [1]	96,200 (2012)	76,334 (2012)	7,803 (2011)	12,800 (2010)	806 (2009)
Area (mile^2) per km Railroad [2]	38	49	19	11	8,180
Length of Railroads in km [2]	98,000 (2012)	224,792 (2011)	23,474 (2007)	41,981 (2011)	87,157 (2011)
Area (km^2) per km track [2]	105	43	16	9	133
Population per km track [2]	14,722	1,379	5,451	2,210	1,117
Number of cars and trucks sold in 2012 [3]	17.4 (2012)	14.5 (2012)	5.2 (2012)	3.3 (2012)	2.9 (2012)
Percentage of Population living in cities 2011 [4]	47%	82%	67%	74%	73%
Improved-water access, % of population [4]	89	99	100	100	96

Source: [1] List of countries by road network size, Wikipedia). [2] List of countries by rail transport network size, Wikipedia). [3] Coyle (2013). [4] Pocket World in Figures, the Economist 2011.

Figure 10.7. Transportation in China at the dawn of 21st century is at the world-class level. (Photo: Wikipedia).

Figure 10.8. The downtowns of Shanghai or Beijing look like New York or Chicago. (Photo: Public domain).

Moving on up – This means that societal progress is exemplified by living in cities rather than in villages in the rural areas. China is quickly developing cities to move more people out of the country side and be on par with developed countries. With 47% of people living in cities, China can fill the gap with Western Civilization very quickly. In 1980-2014 the population of urban China has grown by more than 500 million people, from 100 to 611 million in 2013. This means that China "has" 2 Americas or 87% of Europeans living in its cities. The architecture of these cities is up to date even by modern standards. (Figure 10.8).

This fast growth of Chinese cities created real estate bubbles and disappointments. On March 16th, 2013 the government unveiled a new people-centered plan for urbanization. Its purpose is to minimize the spread of "urban disease" with worsening congestion, pollution, and a risk of social tension. It calls for a "new style" of urbanization, focusing on making cities fairer for migrants. Thus far many migrants have been considered "second class" citizens, threatening the stability of the state. The plan calls for the gradual elimination of the *hukou* system from the 1950s, which limits the registration of households allowed living in a city. By 2020 another 100 million migrants will be allowed to be accepted by the *hukou* system. This means, according to this government document, about 200 million migrants will be illegal habitants of Chinese cities. The government sets the modest target of urbanization at the level of 60%. It looks like China is trying to catch up with the pace of urbanization in some leading nations. The question is--is it the right strategy nowadays to follow leaders whose cities after deindustrialization do not know what to do with unemployed industrial workers and professionals.

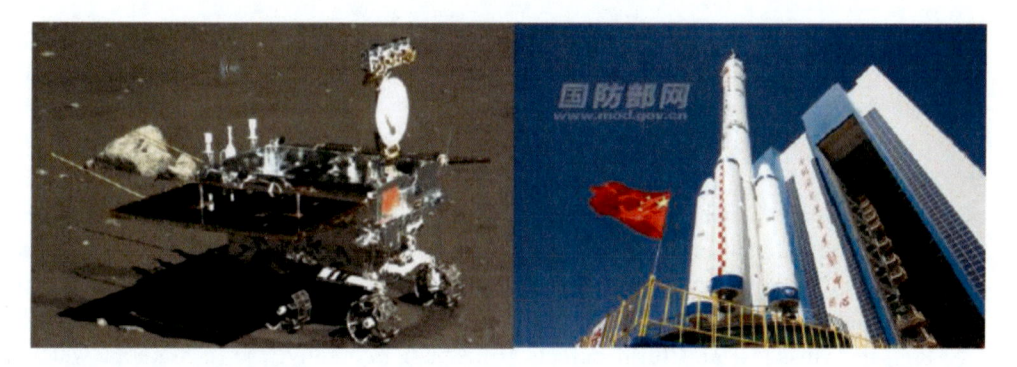

Figure 10.9. China as the second nation in history to have sent a vehicle to the Moon on December 14, 2013.(Photo: www.edfeathers.com and arstechnica.com).

From colonized to colonizer - the U.S. has led in major technological advances in the 19th and 20thcenturies, inventing, enhancing or perfecting many small steps and giant leaps. So why shouldn't America continue to lead in space exploration -- including establishing a permanent human presence beyond our Earth? Perhaps China is thinking about going into space and colonizing some planets first, having enough candidates to travel there? Since recently, China landed the unmanned *Yutu* rover on the Moon (Figure 10.9), although the country appears to have lost contact with the vehicle and the outcome is hazy. Even if *Yutu* never moves again, it and the Chang's 3 lander will keep taking data. And Chinese officials have already talked about Chang's 4, a mission similar to Chang's 3 that will launch to a different part of the Moon next year. One must applaud any country that wants to explore space and further our understanding of our solar system. China has come a long way since the Mao Zedong era of glorifying power of manual agriculture. It has embraced market socialism -- though it still needs to embrace a sustainable economy to lead the world.

D. The challenges facing China at the dawn of the 21st century

Big challenges – the Earth is not forgiving people for our aggressiveness in coping with nature (Figure 10.10). China's ecological foot print in global hectares (gha/person) – is nowadays 2.21/capita but its bio-capacity in gha/person is 0.98, which means that the Chinese have twice as much bio-capacity as allowed and create the negative balance of -1.22 gha[4]. Furthermore, rapidly industrializing China uses too much water, without which life is impossible.

   a. *Water* - as China's population and economy have grown, so has its thirst for water. Today China is the world's biggest water user, accounting for 13 percent of the world's freshwater consumption ("In Deep," Economist, 18 August 2001, p. 31) which comes from 7 percent of world's total water volume. The first issue is in the disparity in water supply between the north and south. The second issue is China's pollution. Even in water-rich areas of China, pollution is decreasing the supply of clean, usable water. According to estimates, a full 70 percent of China's rivers and lakes are currently contaminated, half of China's cities have groundwater that is

---

[4] wikipedia.org/wiki/List_of_countries_by_ecological_footprint, Retrieved 03-25-2014.

significantly polluted, and one-third of China's landmass is affected by acid rain (Zijun Li (2006). Today, most of the Yellow River is unfit even for swimming. According to Sekiguchi (2006) - in terms of health, China's water crisis has had serious consequences. About 300 million people in China—a quarter of its population (or a number equivalent to the entire U.S. population)—drink contaminated water every day. Almost two-thirds of these people—190 million - fall ill. Children are suffering, too, with more than 30,000 dying each year from diarrhea caused by contaminated water. In addition, China's water has been blamed for the recent high rates of various health abnormalities like cancer, stunted growth, low IQs, miscarriages, and birth defects (Elizabeth Economy 2005). Without water in northern China, people can't survive, and the economic development that has been going on cannot continue.

b. *Pollution*–According to research data evaluated by Kahn and Yardley (2007) the industrial pollution is causing the following devastating effects:

   i. According to the Chinese Ministry of Health, industrial pollution has made cancer China's leading cause of death.
   ii. Every year, ambient air pollution alone killed hundreds of thousands of citizens.
   iii. 500 million people in China are without safe and clean drinking water.
   iv. Only 1% of the country's 560 million city dwellers breathe air considered safe by the European Union, because all of its major cities are constantly covered in a "toxic gray shroud". Before and during the 2008 Summer Olympics, Beijing was "frantically searching for a magic formula, a meteorological *deus ex machina*, to clear its skies for the 2008 Olympics."
   v. Lead poisoning or other types of local pollution continue to kill many Chinese children.
   vi. A large section of the ocean is without marine life because of massive algal blooms caused by the high nutrients in the water.
   vii. The pollution has spread internationally: sulfur dioxide and nitrogen oxides fall as acid rain on Seoul, South Korea, and Tokyo; and according to the Journal of Geophysical Research, the pollution even reaches Los Angeles in the USA.
   viii. The Chinese Academy of Environmental Planning in 2003 had an internal and unpublished report which estimated that 300,000 people die each year from ambient air pollution, mostly of heart disease and lung cancer.
   ix. Chinese environmental experts in 2005 issued another report, estimating that annual premature deaths attributable to outdoor air pollution were likely to reach 380,000 in 2010 and 550,000 in 2020.
   x. A 2007 World Bank report conducted with China's national environmental agency found that "...outdoor air pollution was already causing 350,000 to 400,000 premature deaths a year. Indoor pollution contributed to the deaths of an additional 300,000 people, while 60,000 died from diarrhea, bladder and stomach cancer and other diseases that can be caused by water-borne pollution." World Bank officials said "China's environmental agency

insisted that the health statistics be removed from the published version of the report, citing the possible impact on 'social stability'".

Economic cost of all sorts of pollutions (waste, deforestation, electronic waste, industrial, water, air, organic, other) cost about 3-10% of the GDP (Vennemo et al. 2009). While spectacular economic growth may continue in years to come, the benefits of this growth may be contrasted by the harm from the pollution unless environmental protection is decisively increased and executed by local and national rules.

c. *Communicating with the globalizing world* - Chinese is spoken by about 1.3 billion people mainly in the People's Republic of China, the Republic of China (a.k.a. Taiwan), Singapore and other parts of Southeast Asia. There are also communities of Chinese speakers in many other parts of the world. However, this language is so difficult for foreigners that it is learned only by those who really have to or by the language enthusiasts. Chinese is written with characters (汉字 [**漢字**] hànzì) which represent both sound and meaning. Words in Chinese can be made up of one of more syllables and each syllable is represented by a single character. There are relatively few different types of syllable in spoken Chinese - about 1,700 in Mandarin, compared to languages like English with over 8,000 - yet there are tens of thousands of characters. As a result there are multiple characters for each syllable, each of which has a different meaning. This type of writing system is known as semanto-phonetic, logo-graphic or logo-syllabic. For non-Asian people Chinese is very difficult to learn well. If China wants to be a well establish leader of globalization then should modernize its alphabet and vocabulary. It was done successfully by other countries' languages such as Japanese, Korean, Hebrew, Turkish, and others. But it won't be easy to change 5,000 years long Chinese habits. On the other hand Chinese children could learn how to read and write sooner than as today they gain these skills when they are about 10 years old.

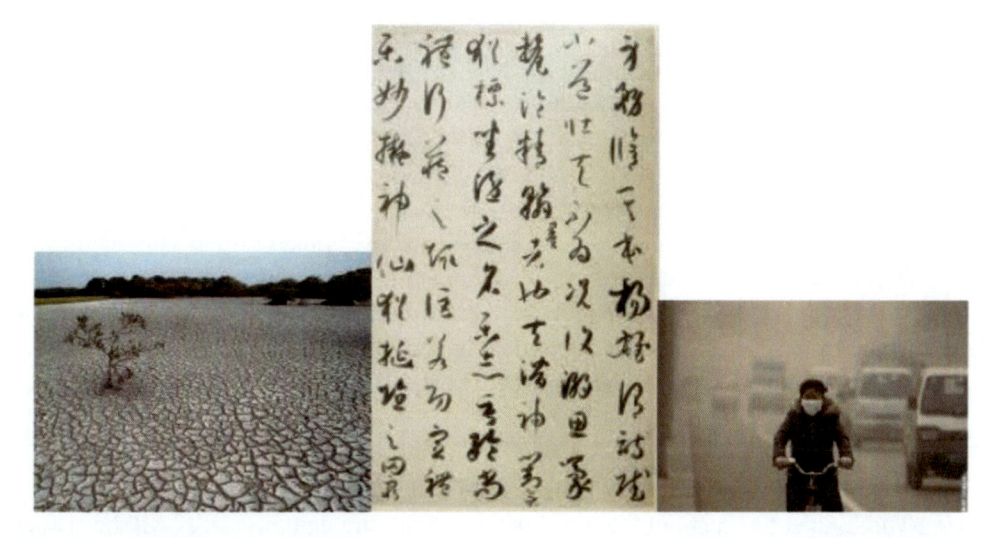

Figure 10.10. Three big challenges of China in the 21st century; water shortage, communication with the world and pollution (Photo: Wikipedia).

E. The future of the Chinese Civilization in the globalizing world in the 21st century.

Strategic barriers – the main obstacles in developing Chinese Civilization include: economic success (as self-poisoning rational thinking about the reality), shortage of fresh and clean water, pollution and large population. Minimizing these barriers should be the first step in developing the future of China and its civilization.

The state of the world - the World Civilization in the 21st century is in the declining phase caused by overpopulation, gradual depletion of strategic resources, aggressive technology replacing human labor, over-efficient economy supporting super-consumerism, and a corrupted and disengaged from reality political class. Shortly and frankly speaking, Turbo-Capitalism and Democratic-Socialism promote constant, growth of the economy, if possible, as the right socio-political solution. As the result, Western Civilization has been transforming into Global Civilization which promotes super-consumerism and expanding business as a new secular religion. It only accelerates the growth of Global Economy which likes a growing population since it is seen as a growing customer base and good for business.

Improving or inventing a new political system– China should not follow recommendations proposed by the advisers coming from Western Civilization, who would like to improve China *a la* America. Their recommendations usually mimic *Americanism* as the best solution for China as does David Lampton (2014). But the current world is not like used to be, when *Americanism* worked quite well in the 20th century. Today *Americanism* is not doing well even for America. China has the chance to invent its own political system, adequate for the current state of world civilization's affairs. Perhaps it can be a system which eventually will be accepted by other countries. One can call this new political system *sustainable market socialism and people power with Chinese character*, leading to *Sustainable China for Ever* (SCE) Its Seven Principles are as follow (Figure 10.11):

I. The natural environment must be in perfect condition to sustain current and future generations to live successfully in the future millennia.
II. People are more important than material resources. Citizens are not subjects and can dream about a better life.
III. Strategic resources like water, clean air, energy, and food should be used in efficient ways which should limit super-consumerism.
IV. Market socialism can work as long as the strategic resources like fresh and clean water and air as well as alternative energy, healthy food production, and sufficient goods and services supply will allow for it.
V. People power can work as long as polls of the citizens' opinions support policies taking care of the common good of society.
VI. National and local governments observe a maximum of two terms of duties and are elected from several candidates recruited by legitimate political parties.
VII. Justice in social and daily life is the core value of Chinese society and cannot be compromised under any circumstances.

This new model of the Chinese political system is planned for when the world population reaches 10 billion people in about the year 2050+ and the strategic resources will be at such a low level that countries will wage wars for resources. At this time, these resources will be distributed by coupons and wars will be conducted to minimize the enemy's human resources so that there will be less people looking for fresh water, food and energy. Therefore the contemporary Chinese political system will be better off if it aims at this model today rather than changing to liberal democracy and turbo-capitalism *a la* Western Civilization. Since the latter system already has put the world civilization in a lasting crisis after the 2008 financial crisis. Assuming pessimistically that the 2008 financial crisis will not go away due to unethical behavior of global financiers and corporations, will they incidentally change their minds and want to be socially responsible? Also, it is doubtful that the U.S. and European countries using the Euro will stop borrowing money to minimize budget deficits. It is certain that these countries will borrow even more just to pay premiums and climbing interest, and they will never be able to pay off all debts. These members of the world elite who are in charge of the contemporary world will maximize benefits of their positions to the last moment, not seeing that the "Titanic" is sinking.

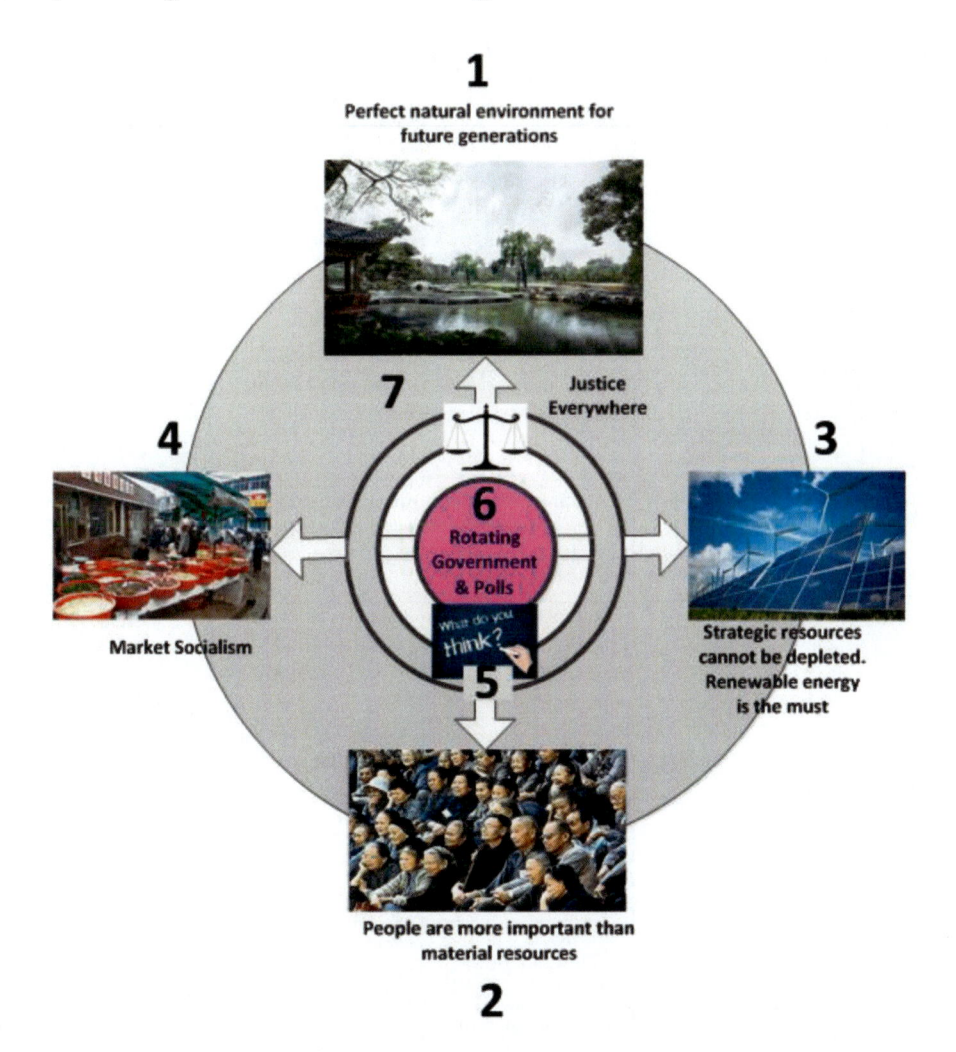

Figure 10.11. The Model of Sustainable Market Socialism and People Power with Chinese Character (Sustainable China for Ever—SCE) for the 21st century. The numbers indicate the national priorities of the Seven Principles.

The Chinese should pack these people not in a "Slow boat to China" but in a "Fast boat from China."Off course this system is not ideal, but a nonpolitical system is today ideal. Its weakness is in its ability to practice corruption and cronyism. On the other hand the political system based on turbo-capitalism without human face and lobbyists-driven democracy has the same ability for shortcomings which are almost incurable nowadays. The choice, then, is between these two political systems. Eventually one approaches the famous question—is better to live better but shorter or longer but worse?

The roadmap of implementing *sustainable market socialism and people power with Chinese character,* meaning *Sustainable China for Ever (SCE)* – China has amuch positive experience in shifting its revolutionary goals and strategies as is indicated in Table 10.4. Hence, it should not be so difficult to shift again in the coming years to the described model of sustainable China for ever (SCE).

Table 10.5. The Main Chinese Political Movements in the last 20th and 21st centuries

POLITICAL MOVEMENTS	PERIOD	GOAL	STRATEGY	LEADER
Long March	1934-1936	Controlling China	Communistic military action against Kuomintang	Mao Zedong versus Chiang-Kai-Shek
War with Japan	1937- 1941-1945	Occupation versus liberation	Defense	Chiang-Kai-Shek and Mao Zedong
Civil War	1946-1949	National Government versus Communists	Military action against Kuomintang	Mao Zedong versus Chiang-Kai-Shek
Communist Revolution or War of Liberation	1949	Communism replacing Capitalism	Establishing People's Republic of China	Mao Zedung
100 Flowers Bloom	1956-1957	Promoting progress in art science, and technology	Speaking up opinion about the regime and taking "snakes out of their caves"	Mao Zedung
Great Leap Forward	1958-1961	Fast transformation of China from an agrarian to a communist society	Collectivization of private ownership	Mao Zedung
Cultural Revolution	1966-1976	Re-educating bourgeois	Educated people were sent to villages, students were teaching professors	Gang of Four (Jian Qing, Zhang Chunqiao, Yao Wenyuan, Wang Hongwen)
Four Modernizations	1978-1989	Reforms and opening up	Capitalism at the bottom of Society	Deng Xiaoping
Rising Power	1989-2002	Restoring economic stability and growth	Check and balance One country two systems	Jiang Zemin, Hu Jintao
Chinese Dream	2012--	Revitalization of the nation	Asking public opinion though wide spread of polls	Xi Jinping
Sustainable China for Ever (SCE)	2015--	Lasting China at sustainable level of life styles	Seven Principles	Xi Jinping

Figure 10.12. Middle and upper classes are the challenge for China's sustainability in the 21st century and beyond (Photo: Wikipedia).

The SCE implemental strategy should first of all emphasize the intellectual awareness that the Western strategy of gaining wealth at the cost of fast depletion of strategic resources leads to civilizational suicide. Therefore a wise China cannot follow this strategy. Perhaps 800 million villagers understand it but the rising middle and upper class in the cities will be disappointed and will sabotage it (Figure 10.12).

Every principle of the SCE should be explained in plain Chinese how it will be applied in the *revitalized nation* which will look for the healthy balance between the common and individual's good, taking into account the 5,000 yearlong legacy of Chinese Civilization, 65 yearlong legacy of the Chinese character of politics and the world civilization progress which like globalization is impacting China, which is the rising and accepted leader of this process. The principles of market socialism and public opinion gathered from polls are already well established. The principle that nature is more important than people is new for the Chinese, but the principle that people are more important than material resources isnot new for the Chinese, since the idea of the Chinese Dream falls in this category. Justice everywhere and uncompromised—it is a widely recognized problem in China and steadily confronted by those in authority. President Xi Jinping has said that his anti-corruption campaign, announced January 2013, would go after "flies and tigers," meaning that it would target corruption at all levels. According to the Corruption Perception Index 2013, China with 40 points was in80th place, while Singapore with 87 points occupied 5th place and Taiwan with 61 points was in 36th place. Singapore's very high place in the world ranking indicates that the Chinese can be almost corruption free if society is well managed.

The Chinese Dream as *Prosperity, Strength, and Pride* should interpret *prosperity* as a long-lasting China and with sustainable life styles; *strength* means a strong and healthy environment, and *pride* means that the Chinese are wise in self-managing their country better than others.

F. What other civilization can learn from Chinese Civilization?

Contemporary civilizations such as African, Buddhist, Hindu, Islamic, Eastern, Western, and Japanese should learn from Chinese Civilization how to:

a. Protect family and spread respect for seniors.
b. Learn from others to avoid common mistakes.
c. Apply traditional culture to integrate and sustain the well-being of society.
d. Behave according to the "middle of the road" principle.
e. Win a war without a battle.
f. Constantly revitalized their nations according to their characters andnew contexts and circumstances. For example in the last 65 years (since 1949), China shifted its political system's paradigm 9 times.
g. Learn from mistakes and improve the next ways of living.
h. Keep the right balance between the common and individual's good.
i. Be hard working and wise and do not complain much.
j. Others.

CONCLUSION

1. China cannot expect to reach prosperity at the high level of Western Civilization in the 21st century because there are not enough strategic resources on the small planet Earth for a population of 10 billon around 2050. If China reaches such a level, it will be the end of world civilization as we know today.
2. Chinese strategic development cannot be confined to China only but has to take into account the context of the whole world. Off course the whole world must be aware of it and together with China should plan how to shift its goals and strategies to accept that "not the sky" but the ground is the limit and to sustain mankind. Hence, *wise civilization* development and operations must be the goal of the current and future generation.
3. China, if wise, should soon enter the phase of its politics into the Sustainable Chine Forever Model and apply its Seven Principles.

REFERENCES

Banister, J. (2005). Manufacturing Employment in China, Monthly Labor Review, pp.11-27.
Blau, J. (2011). Germany faces a shortage of engineers. *The EEEI Spectrum*. Retrieved 03-23-2014http://spectrum.ieee.org/at-work/tech-careers/germany-faces-a-shortage-of-engineers.
Blue, Ch. et al. (2005). *The engineering workforce: current state, issues, and recommendations*. Washington, DC: National Science Foundation.
Coyle, E. (2013). 8 countries that buy the most cars. *Wall Street Cheat Sheet*. Retrieved 03-23-2014 http://wallstcheatsheet.com.
Elizabeth Economy (2005). The Lessons of Harbin. *Time. com*, 27 November 2005.
Elvin, M. (1972). The high-level equilibrium trap: the causes of the decline of invention in the traditional Chinese textile industries in W. E. Willmott, *Economic organization in Chinese society*. Stanford, CA: Stanford University Press.

Faibank, J. K. (1992). *China: a new history.* (with Merle Goldman) Enl. ed. Cambridge, MA: Belknap Press of Harvard University Press.

Fingarette, H. (1976). *Confucius: the secular as sacred.* Prospect Heights, Ill: Waveland Press, Inc.

Kahn, J. and J. Yardley. (August 26, 2007). As China roars, pollution reaches deadly extremes. *The New York Times.* Retrieved 2012-05-12.

Lampton, D.M. (2014). How China is ruled, why is getting harder for Beijing to govern. *Foreign Affairs*, January/February, 93(1):74-84.

Loyalka, P. et al. (2012). Getting the quality right: engineering education in the BRIC countries. Pal Alto, CA: Stanford University Paper. Retrieved 03-23-2014 https://cepa.stanford.edu/sites/default/files/Getting%20Quality%20Right%20-%20Engineering%20Education%20in%20the%20BRIC%20countries%20pkl.pdf.

Needham, J. (1986). *Science and civilization in China: Volume 3, mathematics and the sciences of the heavens and the earth.* Taipei (Taiwan): Caves Books, Ltd.

Sekiguchi, R. (2006). Water issues in China. *SPICE STANFORD.* September 2006.

Shammas, M. (2011). Number of US engineers in decline relative to China and India. *The Chronicle of Higher Education*, September 20.

Thompson, M.A. (2012-09-28). *Employment trends:* Russia.GOINGGLOBAL.com/articles/1114.

Vennemo, H., H. Lindhjem, and H.M. Seip. (2009). Environmental pollution in China: status and trends". *Review of Environmental Economics and Policy*, 3(2):209.

Zijun Li. (2006). China Issues New Regulation on Water Management, Sets Fees for Usage. *Worldwatch Institute*, [7 September].

INDEX

#

20th century, 10, 36, 38, 45, 46, 48, 49, 54, 74, 76, 96, 101, 105, 123, 138, 147, 151, 178, 179, 193, 194, 196, 197, 199, 206

A

abolition, 49
abuse, 112
access, 72, 97, 101, 105, 106, 122, 128, 137, 147, 200
accessibility, 52
accounting, 21, 124, 203
acculturation, 66
acid, 204
acupuncture, 196
AD, vii, viii, ix, 7, 29, 30, 31, 32, 33, 34, 141, 165, 166, 199
adaptability, 59
adjustment, 96
administrators, 19, 192, 193
adults, 119, 129
advancement(s), 32, 141, 170, 199
adverse conditions, 156
advocacy, 47
aesthetic(s), 68, 76
Afghanistan, 10, 151
Africa, 7, 9, 10, 13, 37, 91, 141, 147, 181, 182, 183, 184, 195, 196
African Civilization, viii, 9, 11
age, ix, 14, 18, 21, 24, 30, 33, 46, 50, 54, 112, 119, 129, 154, 183, 196
agencies, 122, 134
aggregation, 94
aggression, 26, 82
aggressiveness, 203
agricultural exports, 182

agricultural sector, 130
Agricultural Wave, 93
agriculture, 17, 18, 23, 28, 30, 42, 71, 72, 73, 92, 93, 103, 104, 105, 106, 108, 109, 111, 112, 119, 124, 126, 127, 128, 130, 133, 141, 176, 182, 188, 203
airports, xiv, 99
alfalfa, 31
alternative energy, 206
ambassadors, 81
ambient air, 204
America, 7, 21, 76, 107, 116, 138, 139, 145, 147, 156, 170, 183, 193, 194, 196, 197, 198, 200, 203, 206
American Dream, ix, x, xiii, 117, 118, 179, 185
American Revolution, 138
ammonia, 110, 133
ancestors, 22, 23, 46, 58, 77, 162
ancient forms, 24
ancient villages, 93
ancient world, 31
anger, xvii
animal farm, 112, 115, 126, 127, 133
animal husbandry, 23, 112, 119, 126, 127
annotation, 76
antibiotic, 112, 134
antibiotic resistance, 134
antitrust, xvi
Ape Man, 4
apex, 50
appetite, 140, 179
appointees, 56
Arab world, 61
Argentina, 183
Aristotle, 192
arrests, 56
Asia, vii, xii, xviii, xix, 13, 30, 31, 32, 34, 37, 41, 42, 59, 61, 62, 80, 90, 91, 139, 142, 143, 145, 146, 155, 156, 157, 160, 161, 169, 171, 178, 183, 184, 188, 189, 195, 196, 205

Asian countries, 170
Asian Doctrine, xviii
Asimov, 142, 156
assault, 49
assets, xiv, 49, 128
assimilation, 169
atmosphere, 133
attitudes, 49, 75, 131
Australia, 37, 147, 183
Austria, 37
authenticity, 75
authorities, 26, 58, 59, 112, 115, 127, 131
authority, 25, 50, 145, 209
automation, 154, 157, 200
autonomy, 49, 57, 59
Autumn Period, 24, 25
awareness, 10, 71, 73, 85, 131, 209

B

bacteria, 133, 134
ban, 134
bandwidth, 97
banking, xiv, 18, 107
banks, xvii
barriers, 130, 206
base, 79, 94, 117, 130, 133, 139, 182, 206
basic services, 97
beams, 79
beef, 112, 126, 147
behaviors, 51, 66, 78, 162
Beijing, xii, 18, 23, 33, 38, 50, 56, 58, 59, 61, 73, 76, 79, 82, 91, 92, 95, 97, 102, 103, 120, 126, 188, 201, 202, 204, 211
Belarus, 10
Belgium, 98
belief systems, 45
benefits, 48, 73, 75, 78, 139, 145, 149, 160, 164, 168, 194, 205, 207
beverages, 115
Bhagwati, 186
Bhutan, 10
Bible, 55, 60
billionaires, xii, xiv, xv, xvi, xvii
black market, 60
blame, 71
blindness, 130
blogger, 183
blogs, 132, 134, 172, 183
blood, 58
BMI, 129
Boat, 77
Bolshevik Revolution, 139

bonds, 117, 123, 142
bones, 21, 23
Boxers, 178
Brazil, 183, 198
breast cancer, 112
BRIC, 198, 211
Britain, xvi, 34, 35, 38, 138, 186
British, ix, 34, 35, 36, 41, 139, 141, 177, 178
British Empire, 34, 139, 177
Brzezinski, 155, 156
Buddhism, vii, 30, 46, 47, 53, 57, 59, 61, 62, 66, 187, 193, 196
Buddhist, viii, 9, 10, 12, 32, 47, 48, 52, 53, 54, 60, 62, 186, 192, 209
budget deficit, 207
Bulgaria, 10
bun, 20
Bureau of Labor Statistics, 118, 199
bureaucracy, xvi, 30, 31, 32, 186
Burma, xviii
burn, 48
Bush, George W., 80
business environment, 182
business management, 103
businesses, xvii, 37, 75, 110, 176, 181, 182
buyer, 182

C

CAFO, 133
Cairo, 172
caliber, 123
calorie, 128
Cambodia, vii, 10
Canada, 176, 183, 193
canals, 28
cancer, 112, 132, 134, 204
candidates, 48, 203, 206
capitalism, xiv, xv, xvii, 139, 145, 148, 149, 153, 157, 182, 193, 207, 208
Capitalism, xii, 139, 146, 206, 208
carbon, 121, 133
carbon dioxide, 121, 133
Caribbean, 183
Carter, Jimmy, 39
case study, 103
cash, 110, 116
cash crops, 110
casinos, xiv
casting, 26
catalyst, 170
catastrophes, 160
Catholic Church, 55

Catholics, 54, 56, 57
cattle, 20, 23, 110, 112
Caucasians, 129
CDC, 115
cell phones, 52, 61
censorship, 29
Census, 107, 118, 132, 134
Central Asia, 30, 31, 32, 34, 58, 61
cephalosporin, 134
cephalosporin antibiotics, 134
certification, 55
challenges, 7, 9, 10, 12, 13, 41, 70, 78, 159, 160, 166, 167, 168, 171, 191, 203, 205
Chamber of Commerce, 183
chaos, 71, 89, 164, 201
charities, 81
charm, 94, 96
chemical(s), xiv, 110, 112, 115, 124, 126, 127
Chiang-Kai-Shek, 208
Chicago, 62, 202
chicken, 133
children, 20, 127, 144, 185, 193, 204, 205
Chinatowns, 146
Chinese business community, 184
Chinese character, xiii, xiv, xvii, 119, 146, 162, 176, 178, 185, 206, 208, 209
Chinese civilization, 12, 13, 17, 19, 20, 32, 45, 48, 58, 61, 79, 81, 82, 85, 86, 87, 91, 96, 102, 103, 106, 119, 138, 144, 150, 153, 156, 159, 160, 161, 162, 164, 165, 166, 167, 168, 169, 170, 171, 172, 187
Chinese culture, vii, 4, 24, 25, 37, 46, 66, 69, 70, 71, 77, 79, 80, 81, 82, 87, 95, 96, 132, 134, 143, 144, 146, 160, 161, 162, 163, 164, 165, 168, 169, 171, 195, 196
Chinese diaspora, 37, 52, 146, 179, 183, 184
Chinese Dream, x, xiii, 105, 131, 176, 179, 185, 186, 208, 209
Chinese dynasty, 34
Chinese economy, 10, 36, 96, 99, 122, 139, 145, 160, 172, 181
Chinese family, 162, 197
Chinese firms, 181
Chinese Giant, xi
Chinese government, 15, 35, 36, 53, 61, 72, 74, 96, 101, 123, 127, 128, 130, 144, 167, 168, 193, 198
Chinese junk, 196, 197
Chinese medicine, 196
Chinese Nightmare, xiii, 105, 131
Chinese opera, 195
Chinese people, x, xii, xix, 3, 5, 33, 39, 60, 67, 68, 69, 70, 71, 72, 75, 76, 78, 79, 82, 87, 128, 144, 164, 168, 169, 177, 179, 183, 185, 192, 193, 196

Chinese Political Movements, 208
Chinese robot, 142
Chinese urbanization, 94, 123
Chinese writing, 21
Chou En Lai, 13
Christianity, 45, 54, 55, 56, 57, 60, 62, 87, 186, 193
Christians, 54, 55, 56, 60, 62, 63
CIA, 106, 198, 199
circulation, 32, 33
cities, 7, 13, 14, 15, 20, 23, 31, 73, 76, 77, 78, 92, 93, 94, 98, 112, 117, 120, 122, 123, 133, 147, 188, 193, 196, 198, 201, 202, 203, 204, 209
citizens, 50, 51, 73, 75, 156, 166, 170, 176, 187
citizenship, 138
City, 25, 69, 112, 140
civil disorder, 178
civil society, 151, 186
civil war, 30, 38, 178
Civil War, 208
Civilization Index, v, 3, 5, 10, 11, 12
civil-service, viii
classes, 24, 53, 177, 209
classification, 15
clean air, 206
cleaning, 110, 122
climate, 106, 132, 133, 134, 193
climate change, 106
clothing, 76, 94, 144
CO_2, 133
coal, 34, 121, 122, 147, 149, 201
coastal region, 18, 48
cocoa, 182
cognitive development, 127
cold war, 182
Cold War, 39, 139
college students, 60
colleges, 156, 200
colonization, ix, 87
commerce, 30, 144, 183
commercial, xvii, 32, 81, 93, 109, 127, 165, 182, 183
commercial bank, 165
commercial ties, 183
commodity, xiv, xv, 13, 181
common sense, 74
communication, 6, 7, 10, 19, 36, 52, 59, 74, 75, 78, 88, 131, 140, 154, 205
communism, xv, 46, 50, 51, 62, 139, 144, 145, 152, 153, 168, 176, 196, 208
Communist Party, 14, 38, 39, 50, 92, 152, 166, 171, 178, 185, 194
Communist Regime, 160, 171
Communistic Party of China, 178

communities, 18, 36, 37, 52, 53, 57, 102, 107, 117, 123, 170, 205
community, xii, 18, 46, 53, 54, 56, 57, 61, 73, 96, 165
compass, 3, 5, 18, 33, 87, 91, 141, 162, 175, 176, 196
competition, xvi, 26, 151, 155, 169, 183
competitive advantage, 94
competitors, 169, 182, 198
complement, 96
complexity, 23, 153
composition, 71, 75, 172
compounds, 110
computer, x, xi, 74, 75, 96, 103, 104, 141, 182
computer education, 96
computing, 102
conception, 71, 74
conference, 9, 103
conflict, 25, 36, 38, 55, 61, 63, 71, 110, 146, 155
confrontation, 10, 150, 155
Confucianism, vii, 24, 26, 28, 31, 46, 48, 49, 53, 66, 70, 82, 162, 164, 165, 166, 168, 169, 171, 192, 193, 196
Confucius, viii, 17, 24, 41, 47, 49, 53, 62, 63, 67, 71, 95, 142, 163, 164, 192, 211
Confucius Institute, 53, 95, 142
Congress, 127, 134
Congressional Budget Office, 116, 118
consciousness, 66
conservation, 103, 116
consolidation, 109
construction, viii, xiv, 6, 7, 13, 51, 53, 76, 78, 90, 92, 94, 98, 99, 101, 102, 103, 104, 182, 185
consumer protection, xvii
consumers, xvii, 142, 143, 170, 181
consumption, xvii, 75, 76, 94, 115, 121, 124, 127, 128, 129, 140, 144, 147, 148, 166, 170, 186, 203
containers, 19
contaminated water, 204
cooling, 133
cooperation, 73, 96, 112, 134, 138, 156
copper, 23, 147
corruption, xvii, 32, 34, 146, 167, 168, 171, 208, 209
cosmetics, 95
cost, 109, 116, 122, 126, 139, 153, 164, 166, 205, 209
cotton, 113, 124, 182
CPC, 71, 178, 185, 187
created in China, 95
creativity, 151, 152
crises, 164, 176, 178
Crisis, 151
criticism, 29, 50, 70, 151

crony-capitalism, xiv, xv
cronyism, 208
crop(s), 19, 110, 112, 113, 114, 115, 116, 124, 125, 127, 130, 170, 193
crop production, 112
crude oil, 147
crust, 149
crystallization, 91
CT, xix, 63, 188
cultivation, 20, 50, 60, 70, 95, 119, 132, 134, 193
cultural heritage, 72, 78, 81, 123
cultural influence, 49
Cultural Revolution, 39, 45, 50, 51, 52, 55, 56, 71, 178, 192, 208
cultural tradition, 34, 117
cultural transformation, 66
Culture, v, vii, 4, 18, 20, 26, 38, 42, 43, 65, 66, 69, 70, 71, 74, 79, 82, 143, 152, 161, 162, 171, 187, 196
currency, 33, 35, 37, 170
curriculum, 31, 97
customers, 147, 181
cycles, 6

D

damages, 49, 117, 122
dance, 123
danger, 78, 131, 134, 144, 166
Daoism, 24, 26, 46, 47, 48, 53, 57, 60, 62, 63, 162
Darwinism, 156
database, 97
DDT, 127
Death Triangle of Civilization, 148, 149, 150, 152, 156, 188
deaths, 39, 127, 204
debts, 35, 142, 198, 207
defects, 204
deficit, 142, 170
deforestation, 153, 205
Delta, 38, 128
democracy, xii, xiv, 38, 49, 71, 74, 75, 138, 144, 145, 146, 153, 159, 164, 166, 167, 169, 176, 187, 193, 207, 208
democratic pattern, 75
demography, 58
Deng Xiaoping, 13, 40, 51, 71, 72, 96, 145, 178, 179, 184, 194, 208
Denmark, 131
Department of Agriculture, 109, 128
Department of Commerce, 118
Department of Labor, 118
depth, 142, 161

derivatives, 75
designers, 75, 76
destruction, viii, 49, 71, 93, 105, 123
developed countries, 70, 94, 95, 96, 98, 101, 202
developed nations, 93, 199
developing countries, 96, 143, 171, 193
developing nations, 175
developmental process, 12
diabetes, 129, 131, 132, 134
dialogues, 166
diarrhea, 204
diet, 77, 126, 127, 128, 131
dietary habits, 105
diplomacy, 31, 56, 74, 194
direct cost(s), 126
disaster, xiii
diseases, 134, 204
disorder, 164
dissatisfaction, 36, 139
distribution, 107, 108, 131, 148, 168, 172, 181
divergence, 151
DNA, 93
doctors, 196
dogs, 20
domestic demand, 14
dominance, 13, 25, 96, 178
donations, 52
drawing, 119
dream, ix, xiii, 81, 147, 165, 179, 185, 189, 206
drinking water, 112, 204
drought, 33, 39
drugs, 134
drying, 149
dynamism, 198

E

earnings, 117, 165
Earth, ix, 148, 149, 151, 163, 203, 210
East, vii, xvii, xviii, xix, 7, 10, 11, 30, 31, 35, 41, 42, 45, 55, 57, 59, 70, 91, 99, 144, 147, 155, 166, 178, 195
East Asia, vii, xviii, xix, 41, 42, 45, 57, 59, 178
Eastern Civilization, viii, 9
eating habit, 78
echoing, 93
Ecological Bomb, 149
economic activity, xiii, 101
economic cooperation, 155
economic crisis, 131, 139, 142, 171
economic development, 69, 72, 75, 95, 101, 105, 106, 138, 139, 169, 170, 175, 204

economic growth, 51, 147, 159, 160, 164, 166, 167, 168, 170, 171, 172, 183, 198, 205
economic power, 41, 137, 140, 147, 149, 175, 184
economic problem, 171
economic reform(s), 13, 40, 72, 105, 178
economic systems, 145
economic transformation, 120
economics, x, 138, 144, 175
ecosystem, 7, 153
education, 39, 40, 51, 70, 71, 77, 78, 85, 86, 87, 92, 96, 101, 102, 103, 105, 131, 144, 159, 162, 163, 164, 169, 170, 171, 184, 199, 200, 211
education system, 71, 78, 86
Efficiency, 109
egalitarianism, 151
Egypt, 172, 176
Egyptian Civilization, vii, 9
Eight Elders, xii
elaboration, 162, 164
election, 143
electives, 96
electricity, 120
elephants, 183
e-mail, 78
emigration, 183, 195
empathy, 66
Emperor Yan, 5
employment, 23, 108, 117, 118, 121, 142, 199
enculturation, 67
enemies, 32, 145
energy, 41, 81, 120, 121, 122, 126, 130, 133, 139, 147, 149, 152, 154, 187, 199, 206, 207
energy consumption, 120, 121, 139
energy prices, 126
enforcement, 7
engineering, 3, 32, 33, 95, 103, 141, 170, 210, 211
England, 160
English Revolution, xii, 138
entrepreneurs, 13, 56, 60, 169, 182, 189
environment, 41, 51, 68, 79, 97, 110, 120, 127, 148, 154, 155, 160, 163, 164, 171, 178, 182, 183, 206, 209
environmental impact, 183
environmental issues, 106
environmental protection, 17, 205
EPA, 111, 133
epidemic, 105, 115, 116, 129, 132, 134
equilibrium, 96, 210
equipment, 182
erosion, 112
ESI, 133
estrogen, 112
ethanol, 115, 149

ethical standards, 86
ethics, 192, 193
Ethiopia, 147
ethnic background, 161
ethnic culture, 57
ethnic groups, 45, 57, 59, 165
ethnic religions, 45, 57, 61
ethnicity, 154
EU, xvii
Europe, viii, ix, xii, 35, 58, 75, 139, 142, 149, 151, 155, 161, 177, 183, 194, 196, 197
European Union, xvii, 130, 134, 146, 204
evaporation, 108
evidence, 18, 19, 21, 23, 112
evil, 32, 50, 55, 192
evolution, 6, 17, 26, 47, 88, 93, 111, 176
examinations, viii, 32, 86
excavations, 18, 19, 21
exclusion, 47
execution, 130
exile, 39, 59, 61
expanded trade, 36
expenditures, 109, 117, 129
expertise, 61, 169
exploitation, 36
exporter, 198
exports, 35, 165, 181, 182
exposure, 61, 112, 122
expulsion, 38
external costs, 112
externalities, 110, 117
extraction, 147
extracts, 147

F

Facebook, 200
factories, 13, 73, 110, 169, 200
faith, 46, 48, 50, 53, 54, 57, 58, 60, 62, 63, 70
families, 31, 37, 75, 170, 179, 184, 194
family, 7, 13, 22, 24, 31, 36, 49, 53, 67, 70, 71, 74, 75, 107, 117, 119, 123, 126, 131, 144, 149, 159, 162, 163, 164, 165, 169, 170, 171, 184, 193, 196, 197, 210
family life, 75
family members, 22, 36, 123, 162, 184, 196
family system, 196
family values, 67, 107, 144
famine, 33
farm size, 109
farmers, 13, 29, 32, 35, 66, 93, 112, 115, 116, 124, 130, 134, 163, 193

farming, 18, 107, 109, 110, 112, 116, 124, 125, 126, 131, 132, 133, 134
farmland, 37
farms, 13, 54, 107, 108, 109, 110, 115, 116, 117, 124, 126, 130, 131, 132, 133, 193
fast food, 78
fat, 128
FDA, 112, 134
FDA approval, 112
FDI, 181, 182
fear, 127, 183
federal government, 142
federal law, 134
feelings, 76, 151
fertilizer(s), 109, 110, 112, 124, 125, 126, 131, 133
feudalism, 164
fiber, 49
films, 75
financial, xiv, 15, 35, 36, 52, 56, 59, 76, 138, 155, 159, 162, 164, 169, 171, 184, 198, 207
financial capital, 169
financial resources, 184
financial support, 36, 52, 56
firearms, 33
fires, 88
first generation, 14
fish, 124, 148
fishing, 18, 120
flexibility, 52, 59
flight, 99, 141
flights, 99
food, 7, 28, 78, 96, 105, 106, 109, 112, 124, 126, 127, 128, 130, 131, 133, 134, 148, 182, 206, 207
food production, 7, 106, 109, 127, 130, 131, 206
food products, 109, 131
food security, 126, 127
force, 14, 37, 50, 53, 55, 61, 73, 118, 134, 146, 162, 163, 168, 179, 199
forecasting, 140
foreign aid, 182
foreign companies, 95, 183
foreign direct investment, 181
foreign exchange, 142
foreign investment, 13, 96
foreign policy, 74
foreign supermarket, 94
formation, 7, 26, 34, 37, 94, 100, 119, 171, 178
formula, 204
foundations, 9, 105
France, xvi, 36, 37, 38, 98, 131, 138, 139, 143, 156, 184, 193
free market economy, 116
free trade, 143

freedom, 59, 71, 144, 152, 153, 159, 164, 168, 179
French Revolution, xii, 138
fresh water, xiii, 149, 207
freshwater, 106, 130, 131, 133, 203
fruits, 124
fuel consumption, 154
funding, 93, 126
funds, 37
fusion, 96
future of China, 191, 206

G

G7, 143
Gang of Four, 178, 208
GDP, 14, 118, 139, 140, 143, 165, 170, 198, 205
GDP per capita, 14, 140, 165
General Motors, 181
genetic engineering, 110
genetics, 15
genocide, 160
geography, 157
Germany, 11, 37, 38, 63, 98, 138, 143, 145, 157, 160, 198, 200, 201, 210
GHG, 133
Global Civilization, vi, vii, xii, xiii, 3, 5, 10, 12, 60, 137, 139, 142, 146, 153, 155, 175, 176, 186, 187, 188, 206
global competition, 169, 170, 183, 187
global economy, 137, 138, 139, 143, 147, 148, 149, 164, 165, 166, 168, 172
Global Economy, x, 206
global leaders, 166
global recession, 160
global village, 59, 81
global warming, 133
globalization, 3, 65, 74, 79, 82, 96, 142, 144, 145, 154, 175, 186, 187, 191, 198, 205, 209
Globalization Wave, 139
Glob-Chin Civilization, 142
God, 45, 46, 55, 58, 61
goods and services, 206
google, 184
governance, 17, 41
governments, vii, 38, 49, 139, 142, 143
grades, 97
graduate education, 184
grants, 47, 126
graph, 161
grass, 133, 162, 183
grassroots, 81
Great Britain, 138, 145
Great Leap Forward, 39, 42, 208

Great Wall, viii, ix, x, 3, 4, 28, 33, 140, 162, 177
Greece, 31
greed, 186
greenhouse, 132, 133
greenhouse gas (GHG), 133
greening, 130
gross domestic product, 117
groundwater, 203
growth, xvii, 10, 13, 14, 45, 53, 56, 59, 86, 99, 105, 109, 110, 118, 120, 125, 126, 129, 134, 147, 148, 149, 156, 159, 160, 164, 165, 166, 167, 168, 171, 172, 177, 179, 181, 183, 185, 186, 199, 202, 204, 205, 206, 208
growth hormone, 110
growth rate, 14
Guangdong, 120
Guangzhou, 120, 179
guidance, 56
guidelines, 122
gunpowder, 3, 5, 18, 32, 33, 87, 141, 175, 176, 177, 196

H

hair, 20, 95
Han Chinese, 21, 33, 57, 58, 60, 177
HAN Dynasty, 29, 30, 31, 41, 86, 88, 90, 91
happiness, 76
hard currency, 35
hardness, 19
harmful effects, 112
harmonious society, 53, 62
harmony, 68, 70
harvesting, 28
Hawaii, 42
hazards, 134
healing, 164
health, 7, 60, 78, 110, 117, 122, 127, 128, 129, 131, 170, 194, 204, 205
health care, 7, 122, 170
health problems, 127
health services, 129
heart disease, 130, 204
hegemony, 34, 147
height, 55, 73, 183
hemisphere, 10, 96
hemp, 20
Henry Ford, 186
herbal medicine, 196
herbicide, 112, 114
high school, 97
high technology, 75
higher education, 200

highway system, 100
highways, 29, 102, 198, 201
Hindu Civilization, 9
hiring, 163
Hong Kong, xi, xv, xvi, xviii, 5, 36, 40, 52, 71, 120, 160, 170, 177, 179, 193, 196, 197, 198
Hongxi Emperor, 141
hormones, 110, 112
horses, 26, 29, 88, 102
host, 183
hostilities, 37, 38
hotel, 69
House, xviii, 63, 82, 172, 188
Hu Jintao, 208
Hua Guofeng, 178
Huang Di, 5
hub, viii, 56, 182
hukou system, 202
human, vii, x, xii, xvii, 7, 20, 27, 33, 46, 48, 55, 56, 59, 62, 66, 69, 70, 78, 79, 88, 89, 105, 106, 110, 115, 122, 124, 127, 128, 133, 134, 142, 145, 154, 155, 159, 160, 162, 164, 168, 169, 170, 171, 193, 203, 206, 208
human activity, 106
human behavior, 27, 66
human body, 124
human existence, 106
human health, 122, 127, 128
human nature, 70, 78
human resources, 206
human right, 56, 59, 145, 159, 160, 164, 168, 169, 170, 171
human rights, 56, 59, 145, 159, 160, 164, 168, 169, 170, 171
humanism, 70, 192
Hungary, 37
hunting, 7, 18, 23
husband, 196
hydrogen, 110
hydrogen sulfide, 110

I

ideal(s), xii, 50, 53, 61, 70, 179, 185, 208
identification, 186
identity, 40, 60, 119, 120
ideology, xii, 71, 72, 77, 164, 169, 176, 198
illusion, 161
image(s), 81, 132, 134, 188
IMF, 143
imitation, 78
immigrants, 37, 117, 151, 183
immigration, 183

immortality, 47
imperial examination system, 87, 102
imperialism, 55, 166, 177
implants, 127
imports, 35, 126, 127, 181
improvements, 32, 122, 144
income, 78, 119, 142, 150, 179, 198, 199, 201
income inequality, 119
incubator, 182
independence, xviii, 9, 117, 141
India, 35, 47, 141, 145, 147, 148, 155, 163, 172, 176, 184, 198, 211
Indian Ocean, 33, 91, 183, 195
Indians, 147
individual rights, 145
individuals, 51, 60, 66, 67, 116, 142, 146
Indonesia, 12
Industrial Revolution, xii, xvi, 34, 89, 138, 149, 160, 176, 187, 197
Industrial Wave, 93
industrialization, xiii, 70, 72, 93, 102, 105, 107, 120, 130, 142, 148
industries, xvi, 210
industry, xvii, 39, 40, 71, 72, 73, 75, 76, 78, 92, 99, 103, 117, 121, 126, 130, 133, 188
inequality, xii, 139, 148, 151
inflation, 34
information infrastructure, 92, 101, 102, 154
information superhighway, 88
information technology, 96, 101, 102
Information Wave, 93, 94, 139
infrastructure, 3, 6, 9, 14, 85, 86, 87, 92, 101, 102, 103, 104, 140, 154, 159, 161, 164, 169, 187, 199, 201
initiation, 87
injure, 142
insecticide, 127
instinct, 156
institutions, xv, xvi, 33, 71, 193, 200
insurance policy, 197
integration, 23, 70, 82, 98, 146
intellectual property, 95, 183
intellectual property rights, 95
interdependence, 102
international affairs, 63, 74, 96, 187
international division of labor, 103
International Monetary Fund, 139, 198
international relations, 45
international standards, 81, 165
Internet, 52, 61, 72, 74, 75, 88, 97, 101, 140, 144, 145, 154, 199, 200
interpersonal relations, 78
interpersonal relationships, 78

intervention, 36
invasions, 177
inventions, 5, 17, 32, 33, 41, 87, 104, 162, 176, 196
inventors, 87
investment(s), 13, 14, 52, 139, 177, 181, 182, 183, 186
Iraq, 151, 176
iron, 26, 147, 177
irrigation, 28, 131, 176
Islam, 57, 58, 193
Islamic Civilization, vii, viii, 9, 10
isolation, ix, 101, 141, 177, 195, 196
isolationism, 176
issues, xix, 9, 17, 56, 65, 85, 134, 137, 138, 154, 173, 175, 183, 210, 211
Italy, xiii, 37, 98

J

Japan, vii, 13, 14, 36, 37, 38, 98, 143, 145, 151, 152, 155, 160, 164, 169, 170, 171, 178, 188, 193, 198, 199, 200, 201, 208
Japanese, viii, ix, xviii, xix, 9, 10, 12, 13, 14, 31, 36, 38, 139, 140, 144, 148, 155, 178, 192, 205, 209
Japanese Civilization, 9, 10, 14
Java, 91
Jews, 58, 144
Jiang Zemin, 208
journalists, 185
junior high school, 97
jurisdiction, 52

K

Kazakhstan, 147
Kenya, 33
kidney, 130
kidney failure, 130
kill, 204
kindergarten, 78
kinship, 196
KMT, 178
knowledge, viii, xvi, xix, 6, 10, 15, 17, 48, 59, 71, 85, 87, 95, 101, 103, 104, 123, 128, 141, 143, 144, 149, 151, 152, 154, 155, 156, 163, 168, 176, 187, 188, 192
knowledge economy, 101
Korea, vii, 12, 36, 39, 98, 160, 166, 169, 170, 193, 204
Kung Fu, 95
Kuomintang, 38, 39, 178, 208

L

labor force, 14, 23, 107, 124, 130, 137, 138, 143, 150, 199
lakes, 203
Lamaism, 57, 59, 61
landscape, 48, 53, 56, 57, 95
landscape painting, 95
language barrier, 52
language development, 119
languages, 57, 205
Lao Tzu, 47, 62
Laos, 10
laptop, 95
Latin America, 9, 183
laws, xvi, 26, 27, 29, 32, 37, 41, 50, 75, 95, 154, 155, 197
lead, xiii, 23, 78, 102, 110, 122, 137, 140, 141, 147, 148, 150, 154, 156, 176, 187, 188, 203
leadership, 7, 39, 55, 61, 145, 155, 159, 166, 167, 168, 169, 171, 183, 191
learners, xi, 53
learning, xvi, 30, 66, 119, 171, 181
learning process, 181
legacy, 9, 14, 66, 69, 82, 102, 181, 191, 192, 209
Legalism, 24, 26, 27
leisure, 66, 73
Leninism-Stalinism, 152
Li Ning, 182
liberalism, 46
liberation, 59, 208
liberty, 59, 179
life cycle, 6
life expectancy, 122, 198
life experiences, 76
life quality, 144
lifetime, 112
light, 62, 88, 94, 106, 148
Limits to Growth, 148
Lion, 183
liquid assets, 184
Little Red Book, 50, 192
liver, 127
liver damage, 127
livestock, 134
living conditions, 72, 164
loans, 142, 143, 182
local community, 93, 149
local government, 142, 206
logistics, 91
loneliness, 70
Long March, ix, xii, 176, 179, 208
longevity, 68, 86, 192

Longshan culture, vii, 4, 20, 21
love, 55, 75, 76, 77
lower prices, 94
loyalty, 50
lung cancer, 204
Luo, 48, 53, 58, 59, 63, 103

M

Macao, 120, 195
Machiavellianism, 192
machinery, 181
magnet, 87
magnetic declination, 87
magnetic field, 149
magnetization, 87
magnitude, 110
Mainland China, 193
majority, 10, 13, 28, 37, 57, 66, 116, 120, 142, 193
malaise, 119
Malaysia, 12
malnutrition, 148
man, xix, 17, 18, 26, 48, 61, 99, 149
managed-marketed economy, 145
management, 46, 59, 73, 88, 90, 98, 132, 134, 155, 169, 186, 192
Manchurians, ix, 161
Manchus, 33, 34, 41, 177
Mandarin, 119, 192, 205
Mandarins, 192
manipulation, 7, 52, 169
manufactured goods, 94
manufacturing, xi, 14, 94, 95, 118, 138, 139, 140, 142, 143, 154, 166, 171, 176, 179, 182, 183, 186, 199, 200
manure, 110, 133
Mao, 39, 40, 42, 49, 50, 51, 54, 55, 57, 59, 178, 179, 192, 194, 203, 208
Mao-Zedong, 194
marches, 160
marginal costs, 109
market access, 183
market economy, 51, 72
market share, 94, 183
market socialism, xiii, xvii, 178, 203, 206, 208, 209
marketing, 140, 142, 181, 200
marketplace, 14, 142, 183
marriage, 71
Mars, 141
martial art, 47, 123, 196
Marx, 87
mass, 26, 32, 154
mass media, 154

material resources, 206, 209
materialism, 170
materials, 179
mathematics, 141, 196, 211
matrix, 151
matter, 21, 122, 160, 167, 192
Max Weber, 186
MB, 97
measurement(s), 29, 119
meat, 20, 112, 126, 127, 128, 133, 147
media, 6, 59, 74, 95, 127, 153, 154, 185
medical, 112, 117, 129, 134, 170
medicine, 28, 32, 35, 176
Mediterranean, 30
meet, 88, 101
merchandise, 32, 35, 73, 75
Mesopotamia, vii
Mesopotamian Civilization, 7
messages, 52
metabolism, 112
metallurgy, 18, 23, 177
metamorphosis, 47
meter, 119
methodology, 3, 17, 65, 85, 105, 137, 138, 159, 175, 176, 191
Mexican Revolution (1910), 139
Mexico, xv, 183
middle class, 138, 142, 185, 189, 199
Middle East, 7, 10
migrants, 61, 202
migration, 13, 123, 126
military, ix, 9, 24, 26, 28, 29, 34, 36, 37, 73, 82, 87, 88, 140, 155, 168, 169, 177, 178, 185, 194, 195, 208
Milky Way, xi, 179
Milky Way-2, xi, 179
Ming Dynasty, 33, 42, 86, 88, 90, 91, 177, 183
Ministry of Education, 97, 184
minorities, 57, 58, 61, 161, 172
miscarriages, 204
mission(s), 52, 54, 133, 178, 196, 203
misuse, xvii
mixed economy, 155, 178
mobile device, 72, 81
mobile phone, 78, 95, 139
mobile telecommunication, xv
models, 131, 165
modern science, 177
modern society, 70, 95
modern world, 18, 138
modernity, 78, 79, 82
modernization, xiii, 14, 15, 49, 60, 61, 65, 66, 71, 74, 82, 85, 196

modifications, 161, 170
modus operandi, xvi, 5, 10, 187, 196
Moldavia, 10
Mongol Dynasty, 33
Mongol invasion, 177
Mongolia, 10, 33, 57, 78, 201
Mongolian(s), ix, 33, 57
Mongols, 32, 33, 59, 161, 177
monks, 52, 163
Moon, x, 99, 141, 203
moral code, 69, 70
morality, 70, 145
Mordak, 154
mosaic, 6
Moses, 167, 172
motivation, 14, 95
multimedia, 88
multinational companies, 94
multiracial culture, 96
museums, 93
music, 65, 68, 71, 74, 75, 78, 79, 123, 196
Muslims, 57, 58, 61, 62
mythology, 119

N

National Academy of Sciences, 134
National Association of Manufacturers, 199
National Center for Education Statistics, 200
national culture, 78
national income, 130
national policy, 176
national security, 102, 127, 131
national strategy, 179
nationalism, xix, 36, 184, 188
nationality, 94
natural disaster(s), 33
natural gas, 32, 147
natural resources, vii, xiv, xv, 101
navigation technology, 90, 91
Nazism, 139
negative consequences, 129
Nepal, 10
Netherlands, 98
networking, 102
new media, 74
New York, iii, xix, 15, 18, 19, 31, 34, 41, 42, 62, 63, 64, 103, 131, 132, 134, 140, 152, 156, 157, 171, 172, 173, 185, 188, 202, 211
New Zealand, 183
next generation, 96, 192
NGOs, 70
Nile, 149

nitrogen, 112, 124, 204
nitrous oxide, 125, 133
Nobel Prize, 152
nobility, 23, 151, 193
nontariff barriers, 183
North America, 147, 154, 183
North Korea, 39
nostalgia, 192
nutrients, 53, 204

O

Obama, President, 143
obedience, 25, 26, 50, 60
obesity, 115, 116, 117
obesity epidemics, 115
obstacles, 206
obstruction, 36
Occupy Wall Street, 143
Oceania, 183
oceans, 149
OECD, 156
officials, vii, xvii, 49, 52, 60, 71, 88, 145, 163, 178, 185, 203, 204
oil, xiii, xiv, 10, 122, 128, 147, 148, 149, 155, 181, 182
oilseed, 124
opening up, 99, 102, 208
openness, 40, 66, 159, 166, 167, 168, 169
operations, 10, 37, 40, 126, 141, 153, 183, 210
Opium War, 34, 36, 37, 39, 54, 177
opportunities, vii, xi, 13, 96, 163, 164, 166, 168, 169, 171, 184
ores, 23
organ, 179
organization, 9, 24, 54, 56, 60, 86, 91, 161, 162, 163, 171, 210
organize, 7, 47, 60
Ottoman Empire, 176
outsourcing, xi, 14, 102, 138, 139, 140, 143, 144, 155, 175, 179, 199, 200
overpopulation, 206
oversight, 23
overweight, 116, 129
ownership, 37, 172
oxygen, 133
ozone, 122

P

Pacific, 41, 80, 91, 96
painters, 76

Panama, 183
paper money, 18, 33, 141
papermaking,, 5, 33, 87, 176, 196
paradigm shift, xii
parents, 50, 144, 194
parity, 139
participants, 12
pastures, 133
patents, 128
pathogens, 110
PCBs, 127
peace, 9, 32, 34, 39, 40, 53, 61, 74, 91
pedigree, 196
Peking Man, 4, 18
penicillin, 134
permission, xvii
Persian Gulf, 33, 91
personal benefit, 38
personal life, 144, 145
personality, 66, 69, 70, 71
Peru, 147, 183
pesticide, 111, 112, 132, 134
pharmaceutical(s), 110, 112
Philadelphia, 132
Philippines, xviii
philosophy, 24, 26, 31, 47, 48, 49, 53, 66, 68, 71, 78, 163, 169, 172, 194
phosphorus, 112
physical exercise, 60
physics, 78, 141
Picasso, 76
pigs, 20, 119, 126, 134
planets, 149, 203
plants, 91, 149
platform, 75, 97, 160, 165, 169
Plato, 192
playing, 67, 78, 96
pneumonia, 134
Poland, 105
polarization, 39
police, 93
policy, 13, 14, 39, 56, 71, 99, 122, 126, 127, 145, 153, 176, 177, 184, 188
political instability, 162
political leaders, 131, 164, 191
political parties, 206
political power, 28, 37, 38, 161, 192
political system, 66, 67, 74, 82, 119, 137, 144, 152, 153, 155, 163, 166, 167, 168, 169, 171, 176, 179, 197, 206, 208, 210
politics, x, 59, 61, 71, 75, 86, 87, 119, 138, 146, 156, 188, 194, 209, 210
pollutants, 110, 133

pollution, xvii, 105, 106, 110, 112, 117, 122, 125, 126, 127, 130, 134, 191, 202, 203, 204, 205, 206, 211
pop culture, 65, 71, 74, 75, 76, 77, 78, 79, 81, 82
population, viii, ix, x, 9, 19, 20, 28, 30, 34, 37, 45, 51, 57, 58, 61, 89, 90, 93, 96, 101, 106, 107, 109, 116, 118, 119, 120, 122, 124, 129, 130, 131, 137, 140, 147, 148, 149, 156, 165, 169, 177, 191, 193, 194, 196, 197, 198, 199, 200, 201, 202, 203, 206, 210
Population Bomb, 149
population growth, 34, 89, 120, 122, 130, 148
population size, 106
portability, 75
portraits, 50
Portugal, 9, 138, 157, 195
poverty, 103, 119, 139, 163, 196
PRC, 38, 39, 40, 82, 95, 184
precedents, 166
precipitation, 94
predatory pricing, 170
premature death, 122, 204
preparation, 102
preservation, 29, 68, 77, 123, 130
president, vii, xvii, 39, 105, 137, 143, 191, 209
President Obama, 143
prestige, 37, 74
primary school, 78, 97
principles, 24, 78, 90, 139, 209
printing, viii, 3, 5, 32, 33, 87, 123, 141, 175, 176, 196
private ownership, 51, 208
private sector, 184
probe, 45
problem solving, 194
producers, 126, 127, 163
production costs, 127
professionals, 14, 40, 47, 48, 50, 53, 59, 184, 202
profit, 94, 110, 112, 128, 143, 150, 164, 186
profitability, 126
prognosis, 140
project, 28, 79, 92, 127, 134, 165
propaganda, 50
propagation, 50, 52, 54, 58, 61
prophylactic, 10
prosperity, 30, 32, 34, 85, 96, 170, 185, 186, 209, 210
protection, 53, 72, 73, 93, 94, 102, 103, 128
protectionism, 143
Protestants, 54, 56, 57
public debt, 119, 198
public domain, viii
public health, 60, 110, 117, 127, 131

public interest, 70
public life, 88
public officials, 199
public opinion, 208, 209
public policy, 126, 128
publishing, 72

Q

Qin Dynasty, 24, 26, 27, 28, 29, 30, 31
Qing Dynasty, 28, 33, 34, 36, 37, 41, 66, 177, 178
quality of life, 76, 117
query, 21
quotas, 40

R

race, 145, 147, 148, 154
radio, 75, 88
Ramadan, 57
readership, 192
reading, 87
real estate, xiv, 202
reality, 21, 55, 59, 76, 138, 140, 145, 147, 155, 156, 160, 172, 181, 196, 206
reasoning, 103
recession, 142, 144
recognition, 85
recommendations, 134, 160, 206, 210
reconciliation, 178
reconstruction, 93
recovery, 51, 103
recreational, 35
redevelopment, 12
reform(s), xvii, 13, 29, 36, 37, 40, 49, 50, 51, 54, 59, 71, 74, 94, 99, 102, 103, 120, 124, 141, 159, 166, 168, 172, 178, 184, 186
regulations, 60, 181, 186
relatives, 25, 46, 162, 193
relief, 178
religion, xii, 3, 6, 9, 14, 24, 45, 46, 47, 48, 49, 50, 51, 53, 55, 57, 58, 59, 60, 61, 63, 64, 65, 186, 196, 206
religiosity, 46, 50, 53
religious beliefs, 50, 196
religious revival, 51, 52, 61
religious traditions, 45
remittances, 184
renaissance, 45, 46, 55, 61
Renaissance, 53, 164, 169, 176, 177
rent, xiv

Republic of China, 21, 34, 37, 38, 39, 49, 73, 95, 172, 178, 184, 185, 192, 205, 208
reputation, 59
requirements, 79, 92
researchers, 116, 132, 134, 143, 179
resentment, 36, 37
reserves, 147, 149
resistance, 112, 134, 178
resolution, xii
resources, ix, xiii, xvii, 10, 11, 26, 31, 95, 97, 105, 106, 112, 127, 129, 130, 137, 138, 140, 147, 148, 149, 152, 155, 156, 164, 169, 170, 176, 183, 187, 197, 206, 209, 210
response, xiv, 7, 10, 19, 29, 36, 115, 160, 170, 178
restoration, 52
restrictions, 184
retail, xv, 107
retardation, 195
retirement, 194
retrospection, 50
rights, xvii, 32, 36, 60, 168, 169, 171
rings, 185
risk, xii, xiii, 112, 123, 126, 154, 165, 202
risks, 110, 134
Roman Civilization, 9
Roman Empire, 151
root(s), 3, 49, 70, 131, 144, 162
routes, 31, 33, 99
routines, 53
rubber, 182
rules, 10, 26, 35, 59, 66, 87, 122, 152, 155, 156, 172, 178, 183, 192, 196, 205
runoff, 112
rural areas, 13, 53, 55, 120, 202
rural development, 105
rural people, 73
rural population, 93, 120
Russia, xii, xv, 10, 37, 38, 80, 98, 138, 152, 176, 183, 193, 198, 200, 211

S

sabotage, 209
safety, 102, 119, 127, 143, 168
Salmonella, 110
saturation, 12
savings, 76, 165, 170
savings rate, 165
scaling, 126
scatter, 123
SCE, 206, 207, 208, 209
school, 24, 26, 49, 76, 87, 96, 97, 142, 156, 162, 192

science, ix, x, 33, 38, 49, 61, 66, 72, 78, 85, 86, 87, 95, 97, 127, 130, 132, 134, 138, 141, 151, 169, 175, 177, 191, 192, 196, 208
scientific knowledge, viii, 128
scientific progress, 177, 197
Scientific-Technological Revolution, 139
scope, 10, 65, 85, 91, 102, 103, 138, 142, 154, 175, 191
seafood, 148
Second World, 76
secondary data, 85
secondary schools, 96, 97
secularism, 46
security, 41, 102, 126
sediment, 112
seed, 58, 93, 127
self-confidence, 141
self-employed, 163
self-improvement, 170
self-interest, 164
self-sufficiency, 124
separatism, 58, 59
services, xiv, 7, 55, 72, 76, 107, 120, 199
settlements, 17, 18, 19
Seven Principles, 191, 206, 207, 208, 210
sewage, 117
Shang Dynasty, 21, 22, 23, 24, 119
Shanghai, 22, 54, 63, 76, 81, 99, 102, 120, 181, 202
shape, 19, 26, 46, 66, 101, 150
sheep, 20
Shenzhen, 13, 76, 120
Shenzhou 5, 141
shortage, 138, 205, 206, 210
showing, 81, 134
shrubs, 133
shyness, 165
Siberia, 34
sibling(s), 162, 196
side effects, 105
signals, 10
signs, 19, 89, 112
silk, 28, 30, 31, 35, 62, 87, 176
Silk Road, xii, 30, 33, 57, 90, 91
silkworm, 20
silver, 35, 36, 37
Singapore, vii, xi, xv, xvi, xvii, xviii, xix, 12, 160, 166, 170, 184, 188, 193, 195, 196, 198, 205, 209
skeleton, 100
Slavery in China, 178
slaves, 151
small communities, 36, 50
smoothing, 19
snakes, 208

social activities, 164
social behavior, 46, 144
social class, 48
social construct, 92
social costs, 153
social development, 15, 66, 89, 102
social environment, 51
social life, 14, 74, 149
social network, 75, 200
social order, 147
social organization, 24
social problems, 172, 187
social reality, 68
social relations, 45, 46, 48, 106
social relationships, 46, 48
social revolution, xii, 137, 155
social status, 144, 163
social structure, 66, 67
socialism, xiii, xiv, xvii, 153, 172, 178, 185, 203, 206, 208, 209
Socialism, 139, 146, 152, 176, 178, 185, 206, 207
Socialism with Chinese Character, 152
socialization, 67
Socrates, 192
sodium, 128
soil erosion, 112
soil pollution, 112, 117, 125
solar system, 149, 203
solidarity, 154
solution, 11, 35, 115, 130, 142, 143, 171, 194, 206
Somalia, 33
Song Dynasty, 32, 48
South Africa, 37, 183, 184
South America, 7, 147
South Asia, 91
South China Sea, xvii, xviii, 183
South Korea, 12, 39, 57, 204
Southeast Asia, 33, 37, 183, 184, 195, 205
sovereignty, xix, 39
Soviet Empire, xii, 176
Soviet Union, xix, 71, 73, 139, 152
sowing, 24
soy bean, 127
soybeans, 114, 127, 147
space station, 141
space-time, 13
Spain, 98, 138
Spanish Revolution, 139
specialists, 29, 142
specialization, 109
species, 114, 154
speech, 55, 145, 186
spending, 14

spirituality, 45, 47, 59, 153
Spring, 24, 25, 62, 71, 77, 91, 145
Sri Lanka, 10
stability, 30, 33, 34, 41, 144, 146, 159, 162, 163, 166, 167, 168, 169, 202, 205, 208
standardization, 29
starch, 115
stars, 79, 81, 112, 176
starvation, 37
state-owned enterprises, 181
statistics, 53, 97, 107, 184, 200, 205
steel, 79, 139
stereotypes, 74
sterile, 128
stomach, 204
Strategic Resources Depletion Bomb, 149
stress, 132, 133
stroke, 130
strong force, 65, 87
structural changes, 170, 171
structure, 7, 10, 14, 48, 66, 67, 69, 123, 163, 164
style, ix, xvii, 23, 34, 37, 47, 59, 71, 73, 75, 76, 79, 81, 90, 94, 106, 126, 170, 202
subgroups, 183
subsidies, 93, 116, 130, 131
subsidy, 116, 131
subsistence, 57, 66, 107
Sudan, 147
Sui Dynasty, 31, 87, 90, 91
suicide, xiii, 128, 209
sulfur, 204
sulfur dioxide, 204
Sun, 24, 37, 42, 50, 132, 146, 194, 195
Sun Tzu, 24, 146, 194, 195
sunspots, 176
super-consumerism, xii, 60, 206
supernatural, 46, 50, 61
superstition, 46, 49, 60
supervision, 52, 59
supplier, 186
supply chain, 103
support services, 38
survival, 86, 105, 106, 110, 117, 156, 162
sustainability, 130, 153, 159, 161, 162, 209
sustainable development, 102
sustainable economic growth, 157
sustainable growth, 148
sustainable market socialism, 206, 208
Sweden, 98
Switzerland, 98, 172
synthesis, 55, 65, 70

T

tactics, 27, 38
Taiwan, vii, xi, xv, 12, 38, 39, 40, 48, 52, 56, 71, 146, 155, 160, 166, 170, 193, 198, 205, 209, 211
talent, 166
Tang dynasty, 91, 165, 166
Tang Dynasty, 32, 54, 82, 90
tanks, 133
target, 9, 49, 55, 202, 209
Targowski, v, vi, vii, xix, 3, 6, 9, 11, 15, 60, 63, 137, 149, 152, 153, 154, 156, 157, 160, 161, 172, 175, 180, 186, 188, 191
tax credits, 143
taxes, 29, 32, 131, 176, 187
taxpayers, 115
teachers, 25, 142
techniques, 19, 47, 131
technological advancement, 29
technological advances, 196, 203
technological progress, 95
technologies, viii, 32, 33, 88, 102, 110, 127
technology, ix, x, xi, xvii, 6, 9, 15, 24, 26, 29, 33, 41, 52, 61, 71, 72, 73, 75, 76, 77, 78, 81, 86, 88, 89, 90, 91, 94, 95, 97, 98, 101, 102, 103, 127, 128, 130, 141, 151, 154, 156, 169, 170, 172, 176, 177, 183, 196, 206, 208
telecommunications, 101
telephone(s), 52, 101
TEM, 160, 161, 162
tension, 202
territory, xviii, 25, 29, 30, 48, 57, 59, 102, 140, 165, 176, 193
terrorism, 10, 58
terrorist attack, 61
terrorists, 145, 151
testing, 48, 71, 116
textbook(s), 97, 117
textiles, 94, 176
Thailand, 10
theatre, 81
theft, 183
thoughts, 70, 75
threats, 10, 33, 149, 152, 160, 164, 177, 188
throws, 186
Tian, 41, 68, 70
Tianhe-1A, 141
Tibet, 10, 33, 34, 57, 59, 201
Tibetans, 59
tin, 23
top-down, xiv, xvi, 164, 176, 187
total product, 115
tourism, x, 78, 93

toxic effect, 127
Toynbee, 15, 45, 186, 188
toys, 94
trade, 17, 29, 31, 32, 33, 34, 35, 36, 62, 141, 143, 169, 170, 181, 183, 195
trade deficit, 170
trade war, 34
trading partners, 106
Tradition, 42
Traditional Chinese culture, 69, 70
traditions, 19, 24, 45, 123, 124, 196
trafficking, 36
training, xi, 26, 57
transformation(s), xii, 15, 24, 41, 56, 57, 59, 65, 70, 71, 81, 94, 102, 107, 109, 110, 137, 146, 208
translation, 179, 185
transmission, 67, 88, 103, 104
transport, 89, 99, 201
transportation, 7, 23, 29, 39, 85, 88, 89, 90, 91, 98, 102, 103, 122, 133, 154
transportation infrastructure, 85, 102, 154
treaties, 36, 70, 177
treatment, 129, 133
Treaty of Nanking, 36, 177
trial, 75
tribesmen, 5
triggers, 10
Turkey, 98, 147

U

U.S. Department of Labor, 199
UK, 42, 62, 63, 98, 188
Ukraine, xii, xv, 10, 146
UN, 39
UNESCO, 21, 29
uniform, 26
unions, 165
United Kingdom, 37
United Nations, xii, 39, 133, 171
United States, ix, xviii, 13, 21, 36, 37, 39, 40, 94, 99, 101, 106, 107, 109, 112, 115, 122, 126, 127, 128, 132, 133, 138, 145, 146, 151, 164, 165, 168, 183, 197
universe, 68
universities, 40, 87, 200
upper class, 48, 168, 209
uranium, 149
urban, 6, 13, 14, 21, 31, 49, 56, 60, 85, 90, 93, 94, 102, 103, 106, 107, 117, 120, 126, 130, 154, 202
urban areas, 13, 49, 60
urban population, 120

urbanization, 14, 70, 72, 73, 94, 105, 119, 120, 122, 123, 128, 130, 147, 186, 202
USA, vii, 3, 41, 42, 45, 80, 118, 124, 138, 143, 148, 160, 191, 198, 199, 200, 201, 204
USDA, 110, 128, 133
USSR, 39, 145
utilitarianism, 77

V

vacuum, 50, 51
varieties, 112, 114, 115, 127
Vatican, 56
vegetables, 124, 128
vehicles, 122, 181
ventilation, 133
vertical integration, 126
vessels, 23
videos, 75
Vietnam, vii, 31, 193
Viking, 131, 133
violence, 50, 51, 52, 168
Virtual Civilization, 139
vision, 153
vocabulary, 205
volatility, 126
vote, xii
voters, 149
voting, 164

W

wages, 15
walking, 89, 102
Wall Street, 143, 172, 186, 210
war, ix, xviii, xix, 9, 11, 31, 33, 36, 38, 48, 50, 82, 146, 147, 178, 194, 210
warfare, 26, 36, 37, 39
warlords, 38
Washington, 112, 133, 157, 210
waste, 110, 133, 155, 183, 205
waste management, 110
watches, 75
water, xiii, 31, 88, 89, 90, 92, 105, 106, 110, 112, 116, 117, 119, 120, 125, 126, 127, 130, 131, 132, 133, 149, 191, 193, 201, 203, 204, 205, 206, 207
water resources, 106, 130
water shortages, 126
waterways, 112
WB, 143
weakness, 71, 162, 169, 170, 178, 194, 208

wealth, 6, 7, 71, 79, 81, 103, 137, 139, 144, 145, 159, 164, 168, 170, 172, 173, 176, 179, 181, 184, 186, 209
wealth distribution, 159, 168, 173
weapons, 5, 23, 26, 38, 87
wear, 19
web, 21, 132, 134
welfare, 37, 119
well-being, 11, 148, 153, 154, 156, 210
West, xii, xvii, 9, 12, 30, 31, 49, 60, 61, 66, 70, 79, 82, 120, 137, 138, 139, 140, 141, 142, 143, 144, 145, 146, 150, 151, 152, 153, 155, 156, 159, 160, 162, 164, 165, 166, 168, 169, 170, 171, 175, 177, 183, 184
Western countries, 145, 183
Western Europe, 183, 196, 197
wild animals, 5
Wise Civilization, 153
withdrawal, 39
witnesses, 115
wood, 68, 123
work ethic, 155
workers, 14, 38, 108, 138, 140, 143, 183, 188, 194, 197, 202
workforce, 155, 210
working class, 66
working conditions, 140
workplace, 192
World Bank, xi, 125, 133, 157, 198, 200, 204
World Factory, x, xi, 181, 182, 199, 200, 201
World Health Organization, 122, 130, 134, 149, 198
world order, 15, 138, 155, 159, 160, 172, 175
World War I, ix, xvi, xix, 139, 176, 178

World War II, ix, xvi, xix, 139, 176, 178
worldwide, 91, 101, 109, 124, 176, 182
worry, 160, 164
writing, 15, 21, 23, 29, 205
WTO, 143
WWW, 97

X

Xi Jinping, xvii, 185, 208, 209
Xia Dynasty, 5, 21, 42, 66
Xinhai Revolution, 34, 37, 178
Xuande Emperor, 141

Y

Yale University, 41, 63, 188
Yangshao culture, 4, 19, 20
Yellow Emperor, 5
Yellow River, vii, 4, 5, 18, 19, 20, 21, 40, 204
yield, 18, 87, 115, 124, 125
Yin Dynasty, 22
young people, 74, 77, 78, 185
young women, 112
Yuan Dynasty, 32, 33, 54

Z

Zheng He, 91, 92, 141, 183
Zhou Dynasty, 21, 23, 24, 25, 89